STRATEGIC INITIATIVES IN EVANGELICAL THEOLOGY

The seminal works in this series (SIET) have strategic relevance for both evangelical scholarship and the evangelical church. They aim to foster interaction within the broader evangelical community and ignite discussion in the wider academic community and around emerging, current, groundbreaking or controversial subjects. The series provides a unique publishing venue for both more senior and younger promising scholars.

While the volumes demonstrate a depth of appreciation for evangelical theology and the current challenges and issues facing it, the series seeks to engage the full range of academic disciplines from theology and biblical studies to history, literature, philosophy, the natural and social sciences, and the arts.

SIET Editorial Advisory Board

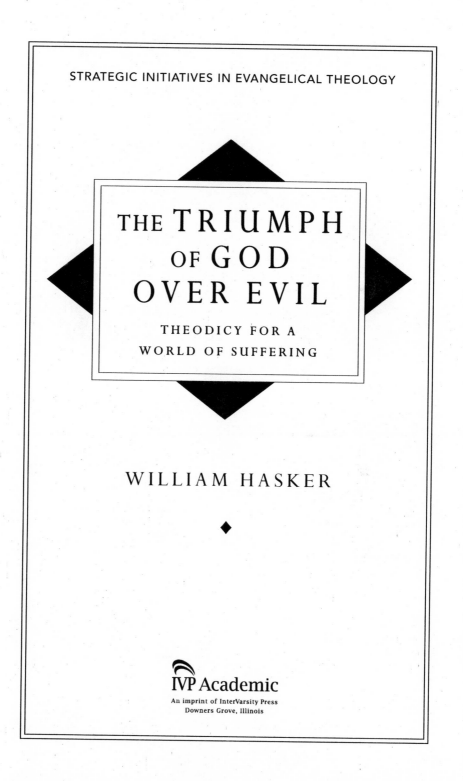

STRATEGIC INITIATIVES IN EVANGELICAL THEOLOGY

THE TRIUMPH
OF GOD
OVER EVIL

THEODICY FOR A
WORLD OF SUFFERING

WILLIAM HASKER

IVP Academic

An imprint of InterVarsity Press
Downers Grove, Illinois

InterVarsity Press
P.O. Box 1400, Downers Grove, IL 60515-1426
World Wide Web: www.ivpress.com
E-mail: email@ivpress.com

InterVarsity Press® is the book-publishing division of InterVarsity Christian Fellowship/USA®, a movement of students and faculty active on campus at hundreds of universities, colleges and schools of nursing in the United States of America, and a member movement of the International Fellowship of Evangelical Students. For information about local and regional activities, write Public Relations Dept., InterVarsity Christian Fellowship/USA, 6400 Schroeder Rd., P.O. Box 7895, Madison, WI 53707-7895, or visit the IVCF website at <www.intervarsity.org>.

Design: Cindy Kiple
Image: Expulsion of Adam and Eve by Jacopo Pontormo at Uffizi, Florence, Italy. Scala/Art Resource, NY

ISBN 978-0-8308-2804-3

Printed in the United States of America ∞

Library of Congress Cataloging-in-Publication Data

Hasker, William, 1935-
  The triumph of God over evil: theodicy for a world of suffering/
William Hasker.
    p. cm.
  Includes bibliographical references and index.
  ISBN 978-0-8308-2804-3 (pbk: alk. paper)
    1. Theodicy. 2. Good and evil. I. Title.
BT160.H39 2008
231'.8—dc22
                                                                    2007049471

P	21	20	19	18	17	16	15	14	13	12	11	10	9	8	7	6	5	4	3	2
Y	28	27	26	25	24	23	22	21	20	19	18	17	16	15	14	13	12				

For Nancy, friend and wife

Contents

Preface

This is a book I never intended to write. My previous writings on the problem of evil have focused on specific and often rather technical aspects of the topic.[1] I believe that taken together these essays address most of the major issues that need to be considered in a philosophical treatment of the subject. However, there are a couple of drawbacks to this piecemeal approach. One is that, even if all the major phases of the subject have been covered, it may not be readily evident to the reader how the various pieces fit together into an overall picture. "Some assembly required"—those dreaded words on the box of a Christmas toy can also apply to a collection of philosophical bits and pieces waiting to be fitted together. The other drawback, however, is more fundamental. It should be apparent to Christians, at any rate, that a full response to the problem of evil requires nothing less than a general account of the place of evil and suffering in the overall scheme of things—and this in turn calls for drawing on the resources of Christian theology more deeply than is customary in philosophical writings. I have been aware of this for a long time but have been content to leave this task to others. In fact, however, it is not too easy to find books that combine a philosophical approach to the problem of evil with a broad theological response to the issue. And the failure to do this leaves the purely philosophical works at something of a disadvantage, however excellent their detailed arguments. Often we get the impression that the theistic and Christian response to the problem is purely defensive, and this in turn

---

[1]See William Hasker, *Providence, Evil, and the Openness of God* (London: Routledge, 2004).

easily leads to the impression of special pleading. To put it more briefly: a Christian response to the problem of evil should not be focused too exclusively on evil. This book attempts to remedy this in two ways. First, by an explicit consideration of the topic of creation: Can we understand, in however thin and abstract a fashion, what sorts of considerations might motivate God's choice of a world to create? But also, and more importantly, How can we understand the triumph of God over evil? For the story of the Bible is just that: a story, partly completed and partly anticipatory, of God's ultimate victory over evil of every kind. So my final chapter is devoted to this victory, and thus to the relegation of evil to its true place in the scheme of things.

The first chapter sets the stage for what follows by explaining the nature of the problem of evil and the various strategies—defenses and theodicies—that may be deployed in countering arguments from evil. I have been warned that in some theological circles the word *theodicy* has a bad odor. I have no wish to give offense, but the concept is an important one and no preferable replacement term is available. *Defense* could perhaps be used, but I believe a useful distinction can and should be made between defenses and theodicies. So rather than replace the word, I invite my readers to consider with me what the word, as I shall use it, stands for. Are they averse to a theodicy that "justifies too much"—that concludes, in Alexander Pope's famous words, that "whatever is, is right"? If so, I share the aversion; the theodicies presented here will have no such implication. Are they suspicious of claims to "know the mind of God"—to have penetrated into the divine counsels, and to say with confidence just why God has done certain things and left others undone? I share that suspicion, and the theodicies offered here give only *possible* reasons for God to have permitted this or that instance of evil, always leaving open that God's actual reasons may be other, and better, than anything we have been able to think of. So it is my hope that readers whose initial reaction to the theodicy project is negative will keep an open mind about this for the time being.

But to return to my summary of the book's contents: the second chapter considers and rejects the possibility that the Holocaust and other egregious examples of terrible evil overwhelm any possible theistic response to the problem of evil. The third chapter reviews the arguments that God and evil are logically incompatible—that it is simply contradictory to claim that a God of unlimited power, wisdom and goodness can coexist with evil. The fourth chapter addresses the topic of creation: what, if anything, can we say about God's choice of a world to create? (Leibniz's contention that this world has been chosen because it is the "best of all possible worlds" comes in for sustained examination.) The fifth chapter, the longest in the book, develops a theodicy of natural evil; some inadequate attempts are rejected, and I argue that there are good reasons why a maximally excellent Creator might very well have chosen to bring into being a world like the one in which we exist. The sixth chapter presents a free-will theodicy for moral evil, bringing into focus not only the inherent value of the power of choice but the other important values that would be unattainable in a world lacking free creatures. The seventh chapter addresses the complaint that a good God should be doing much more than is in fact being done to prevent the apparently pointless evils that are so common in the world we live in. The eighth and final chapter puts all the rest in context by speaking of the triumph of God over evil—a triumph already partly realized in the history of Israel and of Jesus Christ, and to be consummated in the life of the world to come.

This treatment of the problem of evil employs Christian theology more explicitly than is usually done, so the question inevitably arises: Which theology? The part of theology that is most crucial for our purposes is the doctrine of divine providence, which considers how it is that God governs the world he has created. But there are many different ways in which Christians have understood divine providence, as evidenced in Terrance Tiessen's excellent book *Providence and Prayer* (InterVarsity Press, 2000), which details some eleven different views. Far too many pages would be consumed were we to consider all of these options here. But beyond that, not all of the views are really distinct at a fundamental level. (Tiessen's own "Middle Knowledge Calvinist Model," for example, differs only in emphasis from more standard Calvinistic approaches.) Among those who share the theistic belief in unlimited divine power, the key variables are the nature of human freedom and the nature of divine knowledge, especially God's knowledge of the future. For reasons set out in chapter four, I believe that for theists whose view of God is essentially orthodox the distinct options reduce to three: theological determinism (often termed Calvinism or, in some Catholic circles, Thomism); the theory of divine middle knowledge, or Molinism; and the "openness of God," or open theism. There are two other views, the view of God as timelessly eternal, and the doctrine of "simple foreknowledge," that do not actually yield doctrines of divine providence distinct from that of open theism, though they are often thought to do so. Process theism, with its greatly curtailed understanding of divine power, will be considered only briefly in these pages.

It will come as no surprise that of the three main options my preference is decidedly for open theism over divine determinism and Molinism. I have tried to be fair in characterizing the other views and in discerning their implications for divine providence and the problem of evil. Proponents of those views will no doubt find that in places I have described their views differently than they themselves would have done. My claim, however, is that the characterizations I will give represent legitimate implications of those views as held by their proponents. When I express my dismay at some of these implications, I sincerely hope this will not be taken as implying disrespect for the devout believers who hold the views in question. In any case, not all of what is said about the problem of evil is dependent on the specific tenets of open theism. Much of the argument of chapters two, four and five should be available to Christian theists—indeed, to theists generally—apart from more specific theological views. Chapters three and six clearly presuppose a libertarian view of free will and an opposition to determinism of any stripe, but the arguments in these chapters do not discriminate between different versions of free-will theology. It is only in the final two chapters that the distinctive merits (as I see them) of open theism become crucial; even here, however, it is my hope that the spirit of the discussion remains broadly Christian rather than narrowly partisan.

This is a very personal book, yet most of the ideas in it come from others. I have tried to acknowledge as many of these debts as possible in the references contained in the text and notes. However, it is more than likely that in one place or another I have appropriated the work of others without giving proper credit. To those thus victimized I offer my sincere apology, together with this word of consolation: If I have mistaken as part of our common intellectual property ideas that properly belong to you, this says that your creations are doing well in the marketplace, even if in the process the manufacturer's label has been stripped off! I will mention here three sources from which help arrived recently enough that it stands out against the general background. My thanks to Professor (and Rabbi) Robert Oakes, who answered some questions about contemporary Jewish thought and also called to my attention the remarkable kabbalist doctrine of divine *Tzimzum*, which is featured in one section of chapter five. While the book was in progress I was privileged to read the manuscript of Michael Murray's book *Nature Red in Tooth and Claw: Theism and the Problem of Animal Suffering* (Oxford University Press, 2008). While I do not agree with Murray that Darwinian evolution creates a special problem with respect to the suffering of animals, I find myself happily in agreement with many of the suggestions for theodicy found in his book. And finally I should mention N. T. Wright's book *Evil and the Justice of God* (InterVarsity Press, 2006), from which I borrow extensively in the final chapter of the present work. I should point out, however, that Wright does not really deal with the philosophical problem of evil, and in fact his book is sprinkled with a number of jabs at philosophy and philosophers! It's clear that my only proper response to this is to turn the other cheek; I am certain that my own book contains no disparaging references to either bishops or New Testament scholars!

My thanks to David Basinger, Stephen Davis, Alan Padgett, John Sanders and an anonymous reader for InterVarsity Press, all of whom read all or part of the manuscript and offered valuable suggestions. Thanks also to editor Gary Deddo, both for his own comments on the manuscript and for help in many other ways in bringing this project to completion.

What Is the State of Play?

Imagine that you are creating a fabric of human destiny with the object of making men happy in the end, giving them peace and rest at last, but that it was essential and inevitable to torture to death only one tiny creature— that little child beating its breast with its fist, for instance—and to found that edifice on its unavenged tears, would you consent to be the architect under those conditions?

FYODOR DOSTOEVSKY, *THE BROTHERS KARAMAZOV*

What is the state of play in discussions of the problem of evil? For at least a century and a half the existence and prevalence of evil in the world has been generally recognized as the single most formidable obstacle to theistic belief. Furthermore, this is one of very few philosophical topics that can be counted on to gain and hold the attention of almost any audience, from seasoned professionals to philosophically untutored laypersons. During the past few decades the topic has seen more intensive investigation than any other in the philosophy of religion. In view of all this we may ask, what is the present state of this protracted argument?

Obviously, no single answer to this question will satisfy everyone. The most any one philosopher can do is to sum up the results from his or her own perspective, putting forth the arguments and drawing the conclusions that seem to be most reasonable. To say this is not to surrender to any kind of relativism; it merely reflects the fact that the disagreements have been and continue to be intractable. I can only hope, then, that the solutions that seem reasonable and helpful to me will be of use also to at least some others, both philosophers and (if they have the courage to persevere) interested general readers.

ARGUMENTS FROM EVIL, DEFENSES AND THEODICIES

Broadly stated, the philosophical problem of evil is the problem of accounting for the evil in the world in the light of the theistic conception of God, where God is said to be perfect in knowledge, power and goodness. No one can deny that much that we see in the world is surprising and indeed shocking when we consider that the world is said to be governed and controlled by such a being. Can the claims about God and the facts of evil be brought together into a consistent and coherent pattern? If so, how? These questions take shape in the form of *arguments from evil*—arguments that claim to show, on the basis of the world's evil, that this evil is either logically inconsistent with the existence of God or, failing that, provides compelling reason to disbelieve in the existence of such a being.

But to whom are the arguments from evil addressed? In a sense, of course, the answer is, to everyone. Anyone with the capacity to understand the arguments may attempt to assess them and to draw some conclusion concerning what the arguments show concerning the existence or nonexistence of God. However, the conclusions that will be reached are likely to depend crucially on additional assumptions which will vary according to the overall worldview of the person making the assessment. It seems clear, furthermore, that the most important question that needs to be asked about these arguments concerns their cogency *as judged in the light of assumptions that are congruent with the religious worldview that is being called into question.* If an atheist assesses an argument from evil and concludes that the evil that exists is incompatible with the existence of a God, it may seem that nothing of great import has taken place. The atheist, after all, did not believe in any such God to begin with, and if the argument from evil reinforces his or her disbelief, making it slightly firmer than it would otherwise have been, this amounts at most to a relatively minor change in doxastic state.[1] Things are far different, however, if a theistic believer reaches a similar conclusion. For the theist a successful argument from evil may force the abandonment of a cherished belief system, or it may have the result that the person continues to believe but does so in such a way that his or her doxastic structure lacks coherence and is threatened with internal collapse. At the very least a successful argument from evil will significantly reduce the amount of epistemic support the theist's belief enjoys in comparison with what it would have been absent the argument in question. Any one of these results is likely to have a profound impact, not only on the person's philosophical views but on his or her life overall.

In view of this and in order to give focus to our discussion, our considerations here will address the problem of evil in the form of *arguments directed at the theistic believer*, aimed at showing that theistic belief is incoherent or otherwise rationally unacceptable. J. L. Mackie put the point nicely. After formulating the famous triad of propositions, "God is omnipotent; God is wholly good; and yet evil exists," Mackie wrote:

> There seems to be some contradiction between these three propositions, so that if any two of them were true the third would be false. But at the same time all three are essential parts of most theological positions: the theologian, it seems, at once *must* adhere, and *cannot consistently* adhere to all three.[2]

Mackie's point is not that theologians (or theistic believers) are persons whose doxastic state is of greater intrinsic interest and importance than that of any other class of persons. But it is after all *their* belief system that is challenged by his argument, so the salient question is whether *from within the resources of that belief system* any cogent response is possible.

Approaching the topic in this way distinguishes the line taken here from another approach, one that is suggested by Hume's Philo when he says, "You must *prove* these pure, unmixt, and uncontrollable attributes [of God] from the present mixed and confused phenomena. A hopeful undertaking! Were the phenomena ever so pure and unmixed, yet, being finite,

---

[1]*Doxastic* means "pertaining to belief" (from Greek *doxa*—belief or opinion).
[2]J. L. Mackie, "Evil and Omnipotence," in *The Problem of Evil*, ed. Marilyn McCord Adams and Robert Merrihew Adams (New York: Oxford University Press, 1990), p. 25.

they would be insufficient for that purpose. How much more, where they are also so jarring and discordant!"[3] Now, no one is likely to take up Philo's challenge precisely in those terms, though Cleanthes, Philo's discussion partner in the *Dialogues*, comes close to doing so. It is evident on any account that the world and human life present a mixed picture morally, so that any attempt at a straight-line induction from these data to a God possessing the traditional attributes has scant chance of success. What Philo in effect invites the theist to do is to put on the table the entirety of his reasons for believing in God, so as to weigh them against the argument from evil and any other counter evidence the skeptic may adduce. Taken in one direction this could lead to the construction of a "cumulative case" argument for theism, or to a comparison of the cumulative case for theism with the cumulative case for atheism or some other alternative to theism. Either of these is a worthy project, but either will of necessity carry the discussion far beyond the problem of evil. And it is that problem to which this book is dedicated.

A somewhat similar issue arises on the other side of the argument, concerning the responsibilities of the philosopher who puts forward an argument from evil. Sometimes it is suggested that before doing this she must provide a general account of the nature of evil. Lying behind this demand there is the suspicion that a naturalistic worldview is unable to support a realist or objectivist account of good and evil, and that this fact undermines the naturalist's attempt to state an argument from evil. I believe this strategy is misguided for several reasons. First, even if the naturalist is unable to give an objectivist account of good and evil, it is undeniable that good, evil and moral obligation have an objective status *within the theistic worldview,* and this fact by itself suffices to provide a basis for the charge that the facts about evil are in conflict with other elements of that worldview. Furthermore, it is well known that objectivist and moral realist views are defended by some philosophical naturalists. Whether such defenses are successful cannot be decided here; the contention that they are not successful can form a part of that enterprise known as "moral arguments for the existence of God." These considerations will no doubt form a part of one's

---

[3]David Hume, *Dialogues Concerning Natural Religion,* pt. 10 (New York: Hafner, 1948), p. 69.

overall evaluation of theism in relation to naturalism, but they are not strictly a part of the consideration of the problem of evil.

But if no general account of the nature of evil is required, what is the "evil" that may be appealed to in arguments from evil? The answer is simple: the proponent of such an argument can appeal to any of the negative phenomena of life which in his or her estimation provide reason to doubt the existence of a loving and all-powerful God. No doubt these phenomena will include human and animal pain, disease, suffering, and death, especially deaths that are violent, extremely painful or premature. It will include natural disasters and emotional suffering of all kinds. And it will include moral evil, the wrong and the harm willingly done by moral agents. The theist in responding will then contend either that God has adequate reason (or has not been shown not to have adequate reason) for permitting the evil in question, or else that the phenomena appealed to are not seriously evil in the first place; in any case, it will be argued that they do not provide compelling reason for disbelief in God. By proceeding in this way it is possible to address the problem of evil directly rather than postponing it indefinitely in the (no doubt vain) hope of first establishing a common understanding of the ultimate nature of good and evil.

This liberality with regard to what can be adduced as "evil" should be matched with a similar liberality concerning the sorts of considerations that are allowable in constructing a response to an argument from evil. Put briefly, *such a response may include any propositions judged to be congruent with the theistic belief system that is under attack.* It is important to say this because it is not uncommon that a response to a problem of evil is met by the protest "But that begs the question!" In most cases this protest is beside the point. The proposition may well be one that the nontheist propounding the argument from evil does not accept, but what of that? The question being investigated is whether the argument discloses a flaw *in the theistic belief system*, so a reply to the argument is free to invoke in response any proposition that forms a part of that belief system. To be sure, any such proposition may itself be taken by the critic as a target for attack, and such an attack, if successful, will undermine that part of the response to the argument from evil. But the responsibility falls to the critic to show that the proposition adduced is unacceptable; it is not the case that the believer must first provide evidence of its truth before employing it in his response. (One of the merits of the approach taken here is that it helps to clarify, in many cases, the vexed question of the burden of proof.)

Supposing that an argument from evil is on the table, what forms may a response to this argument take? Since the publication of Alvin Plantinga's *The Nature of Necessity*,[4] it has become customary to distinguish between "theodicies" and "defenses." A theodicy—literally, a "justification of God"—seeks to provide a *justifying reason* for the existence of the evil in the world, a reason such that, if it obtains, God is not morally at fault for permitting the evil. One example of such a theodicy (though not one that enjoys much popularity at present) is Leibniz's claim that this, the actual world, is the best of all possible worlds, and that all of the evils the world contains are necessary for its being the best possible. This example, in fact, brings out vividly the reasons why, in some theistic quarters, the enterprise of theodicy has little by way of prestige or credibility. There are, however, a number of more promising candidates than this one of Leibniz, and we shall be examining some of them in due course.

Plantinga's free-will defense was so called to distinguish it from a theodicy, a task Plantinga did not choose to undertake. The purpose of the defense is to demonstrate that, contrary to the assertion of Mackie and others, the triad of propositions, "God is omnipotent; God is wholly good; and yet evil exists," is not logically inconsistent. Some writers, accordingly, have taken the term *defense* in this context to refer to an argument that does just that: show the logical consistency between God's existence and the presence of evil in the world. However, I submit that there is another and better way of understanding *defense*. Suppose we understand this to refer not only to demonstrations of logical compatibility but to any counter-argument that attempts to defeat or neutralize an argument from evil *without* claiming to give God's reasons for allowing the evil in question. This allows for a dichotomy of responses to arguments from evil: there are theodicies, which respond by giving possible reasons for God to permit the evils, and defenses, which do not provide such reasons. Using the more restrictive definition of *defense*, on the other hand, means that some re-

---

[4]Alvin Plantinga, *The Nature of Necessity* (New York: Oxford University Press, 1974).

sponses will be neither theodicies nor defenses, and we will need yet another category if we are to account for them. For instance, Plantinga's own response to the probabilistic argument from evil is neither a theodicy nor a demonstration of logical consistency.[5]

There is one further point that is worth making here. Experience has shown that theists who offer defenses need to take special pains in order to prevent, if possible, their defenses from being misunderstood as theodicies. I would not like to estimate the number of articles and books that have criticized Plantinga's defense as if it were a theodicy, in spite of the fact that he makes his intentions quite clear. And Plantinga's experience in this regard is not unique. Not only do authors need to exert themselves to prevent readers from making this mistake, but readers also need to be on guard and make sure that they are not interpreting an argument as claiming more than its author intended to claim. Perhaps what this shows is the depth of the natural human desire to achieve an understanding of the phenomena of evil that so greatly perplex us. Nevertheless, authors who address this topic must be judged on what they are attempting and claiming to do, and not on the basis of what the reader would like to have them be able to do.

THE EXISTENTIAL PROBLEM AND THE PHILOSOPHICAL PROBLEM

So far our attention has been focused on the formal structure of arguments from evil and responses to those arguments, but there is another, more human, dimension to be considered. In order to bring this into view, we may distinguish between the *philosophical* problem of evil and the *existential* or, as it is sometimes called, the *pastoral* problem of evil. The philosophical problem of evil asks whether the evil in the world provides rationally compelling reasons to disbelieve in the God of theism. The existential or pastoral problem, on the other hand, deals with the impact of evil on a personal and emotional level; this applies especially, though not exclusively, to those who are personally suffering from terrible evil of some kind. Both of these represent legitimate and important concerns, but they are very different concerns, and conflating the two is a source of trouble. Not everything that may legitimately be said in a philosophical discussion of evil is

---

[5]Alvin Plantinga, "The Probabilistic Argument from Evil," *Philosophical Studies* 35 (1979): 1-35.

appropriate or helpful for use in a grief-counseling session, and vice versa; to take things said in one of these contexts and evaluate them in the other context is inappropriate and unfair.

An interesting and moving illustration of the difference is found in two books by C. S. Lewis, *The Problem of Pain* and *A Grief Observed*.[6] In the first of these Lewis says many of the things about the problem of evil that had been said by philosophers before him, adapted with his customary stylistic brilliance for a nonphilosophical audience. The second book, which at first was published under a pseudonym, was written in the throes of his intense grief over the death from cancer of his wife, Joy. As one might expect, the two books read very differently. Some critics have supposed that when he encountered great personal grief, Lewis realized that his former reflections on evil were worthless, but this is not the case. Lewis by no means lost his faith as a result of the grief experience (though isolated quotations might suggest this), and many of the main arguments featured in *The Problem of Pain* make their appearance again, in a different form, in *A Grief Observed*. But the context is very different, and it is evident that the intellectual reflections of the earlier book did not by any means save him from terrible emotional suffering when his wife passed away. Should anyone expect that they would have had this effect?

But perhaps the enormity of actual suffering means that philosophical discussions of the problem of evil are simply a mistake—at best irrelevant, but often expressive of gross moral insensitivity. This is one possible interpretation of the oft-quoted remark "No statement, theological or otherwise, should be made that would not be credible in the presence of the burning children."[7] Taken at face value, this would mean the end for discussions about the problem of evil and about much else besides. Who would be so callous as to undertake *any* theoretical discussion, of any

---

[6]C. S. Lewis, *The Problem of Pain* (New York: Macmillan, 1947), and *A Grief Observed* (New York: Seabury Press, 1961).

[7]The remark comes from Irving Greenberg, "Cloud of Smoke, Pillar of Fire," in *Holocaust: Religious and Philosophical Implications*, ed. John K. Roth and Michael Berenbaum (New York: Paragon House, 1989), p. 315. Greenberg himself, however, does not use the remark in the ways criticized in the text. What he seems to be advocating is a religious and philosophical stance that finds itself in a perpetual dialectical confrontation with the Holocaust, which he suggests should be taken by both Jews and Christians as a "new revelatory event in our time" (ibid., pp. 314-17).

topic whatsoever, while standing literally in the presence of children being burned to death? If unable to interfere physically in such a situation
one might pray or burst into tears or remain in a stunned silence, but any
sort of disinterested intellectual inquiry would be wholly out of the question. Often, however, this is not the conclusion drawn from the remark,
as shown by the fact that the person citing it goes on to offer his own assessment of the problem of evil. I suspect, in fact, that the remark is
sometimes employed as a means of emotional intimidation, designed to
silence responses to the problem that the speaker dislikes. The speaker
thereby claims for him- or herself a moral seriousness which is supposedly lacking in the opponent. Such attempts at intimidation should, I
think, be disregarded.

But is it perhaps the case that the enormity of actual evil should silence
all attempts at theoretical reflection on the topic? For some, this may be
the appropriate response. If anyone is so overcome by personal suffering or
so immersed in efforts to relieve suffering that no time, energy or inclination is left for reflection, I shall say nothing in criticism. But not everyone
is in this situation. The question as to how the world's evil can be recon-
ciled with the goodness, wisdom and power of God seems important, even
urgent, to many who are not at the moment experiencing great personal
suffering. I have already mentioned that this topic seems to be one that
above all others is able to gain and hold the attention of almost any audience, from seasoned professional philosophers to those innocent of philosophical sophistication. Sometimes the topic will be brought up in the
midst of a discussion of some other subject only distantly related to it; this
I take to be yet another evidence of the hold the question has on the minds
of many of us. It would be of great interest to understand more clearly why
the topic looms so much larger for us today than it has in most past eras,
but I have no definitive answer to offer on this point.

It would be wrong to assume, furthermore, that one's theoretical perspective on evil makes no difference when one is in the midst of personal
suffering. Theologian John Sanders recalls two separate incidents that illustrate this fact:

One colleague told me that he would have a difficult time trusting God if he did not believe that God ordained his mother's death when he was a small child. Believing that God had his best interest in mind gave him comfort. On the other hand, a different colleague was angry at God because he blamed God for what was happening to his wife (she had breast cancer and then needed a heart transplant). One day he pressed me on the topic, so I told him that, in my view, God was not doing this to his wife. He resolved his struggle with God when he came to believe that God was not micro-managing the situation—that it was not God's will for his wife to suffer as she was.[8]

Note that it is not claimed by Sanders that one, and only one, theistic perspective on suffering is capable of giving comfort to the sufferers. The reactions of believers in these matters are diverse and can be taken as supporting a number of different theological perspectives. However, he goes on to state:

> It is my conviction that the understanding of divine providence affirmed by open theism (where God does not exercise tight control over the world) offers greater comfort to those experiencing tragedy. However, I will not claim this is the only theological perspective that can provide comfort, even if I do not see how it is comforting to claim that God desired the deaths of people in a tsunami.[9]

I believe, furthermore, that in view of the importance many of us attribute to the problem of evil, success in addressing this problem has become an important part of the basis for evaluating theological views. In any case, the examples show clearly the existential and human significance of various ways of approaching the problem.

A THEOLOGICAL PERSPECTIVE: OPEN THEISM

The points made here come together to raise a question concerning the present enterprise, namely, what theological conception will inform our discussion? I have argued that the problem of evil should be seen as a chal-

---

[8]John Sanders, "How Do We Decide What God Is Like?" in *And God Saw That It Was Good: Essays on Creation and God in Honor of Terence E. Fretheim*, ed. Fred Gaiser, *Word and World* Supplement Series 5 (St. Paul: Luther Seminary, 2006), p. 160. For a moving account of the faith struggles of the second faculty member mentioned, see James O'Donnell, *Letters for Lizzie: A Story of Love, Friendship and a Battle for Life* (Chicago: Northfield, 2004).

[9]Sanders, "How Do We Decide What God Is Like?" p. 160.

lenge to the viability of a theistic worldview, so some variety of theism must be presupposed as the target of the various arguments from evil. But there are many versions of theism on offer, and even specifying the view in question as Christian theism goes only part way in reducing the ambiguity. It stands to reason (and will become apparent in the subsequent discussion) that the different versions of theism bring with them somewhat different resources for addressing the arguments from evil. And I have just pointed out that different versions also make a difference experientially for persons suffering as a result of serious evils—though to be sure, it is not clear that the differences point unambiguously to a single preferred solution. So the question naturally and properly arises: What theological vision lies behind the present work?

The answer to this can be simply stated, but then again can be elaborated indefinitely. The position taken here is that of the "openness of God" or "open theism" alluded to in the previous quotation from John Sanders.[10] This is a version of orthodox Christian theism according to which God is perfect in wisdom, goodness and power, and is the unique, self-sufficient Creator of the universe, including all concrete entities other than God. God exists eternally as the Trinity of Father, Son and Holy Spirit; God the Son became a human being as Jesus of Nazareth, and as such lived a human life, died, and rose again from the dead for the salvation of humankind. Some aspects of the problem of evil can be discussed without invoking these distinctively Christian doctrines, but they are essential parts of the total theological package and are available for use if called upon.

But open theism is not merely generic theism, not even generic Christian theism. Open theism has distinctive implications concerning the nature of God and God's relationships with the world and with humankind that distinguish it from other versions of theism in ways that are important for our topic. The central idea of open theism is that God is "open," that

---

[10]For open theism see Clark Pinnock et al., *The Openness of God: A Biblical Challenge to the Traditional Understanding of God* (Downers Grove, Ill.: InterVarsity Press, 1994). The theological implications of open theism are further developed in John Sanders, *The God Who Risks: A Theology of Providence,* 2nd ed. (Downers Grove, Ill.: InterVarsity Press, 2007), and Clark H. Pinnock, *Most Moved Mover: A Theology of God's Openness* (Carlisle, U.K.: Paternoster, 2001). For essays discussing some of the implications of open theism for the problem of evil, see William Hasker, *Providence, Evil and the Openness of God* (London: Routledge, 2004).

is, affected by and responsive, to the world God has made and especially to free and rational creatures, such as human beings. In contrast with Aristotle's Unmoved Mover, the God of open theism has been characterized by Clark Pinnock as the "Most Moved Mover"; God is more deeply affected by what occurs in his creation than we can ever imagine. Also included is the idea that God is open to the future, which is itself open, indeterminate in many respects and waiting to be determined both by God and by human beings. A brief discussion of some specific implications of this will enable the reader to obtain at least a preliminary grasp of the significance of open theism.

It will be helpful to introduce these implications by way of a comparison with a view that has come to be known as "classical theism." But in order to avoid misunderstanding, it is necessary to say something about this term. The term *classical theism* was introduced by philosopher Charles Hartshorne as a label for a position he wanted to contrast with his own view of God, a view which he termed *neoclassical theism* and which was strongly influenced by the philosophy of A. N. Whitehead.[11] I am using the term as Hartshorne used it, as a shorthand way of referring to a cluster of theological doctrines found in the writings of stalwarts such as Augustine, Aquinas and Calvin. Classical theism so defined is not a straw man; it has been and continues to be influential in Christian theological thinking. On the other hand, it by no means represents a consensus view of all Christian theologians, in either the past or the present.[12] My purpose in introducing it here is not to imply that this is the only alternative to open theism; that would be far from the truth.[13] However, it is useful for our purposes precisely because it contrasts so clearly with open theism in a number of respects.

---

[11]See Charles Hartshorne, *Man's Vision of God* (Hamden, Conn.: Archon, 1964); for discussion see William P. Alston, *Divine Nature and Human Language* (Ithaca, N.Y.: Cornell University Press, 1989), pp. 121-43.

[12]It should perhaps be pointed out that a number of theologians have sought to claim the title "classical" for their own views of God, while modifying the classical package of attributes in various ways. The motivation for this is understandable, but once this is done the term *classical theism* really ceases to have any definite meaning.

[13]An interesting book in this connection is Jay Wesley Richards, *The Untamed God: A Philosophical Exploration of Divine Perfection, Simplicity and Immutability* (Downers Grove, Ill.: InterVarsity Press, 2003). Richards is not an open theist; he writes within the Reformed tradition and gives serious and respectful attention to classical theism as defined here. However, so far as I can see, there is nothing in Richards's positive assertions about God that an open theist need disagree with.

According to classical theism, a perfect, divine being must be *unchangeable* because any change would be either for the better or the worse, and neither of these is compatible with perfection. Thus *absolute immutability* becomes an ingredient in divine perfection. Now the way in which immutability can be most securely guaranteed is if the divine being is *timeless*, "outside of time" as well as outside of space. If God is timeless, then the category of change is simply inapplicable to God. It was further considered that the divine being must be *impassible*; for God to be in any way affected by his creatures is to render God, in a sense, dependent on the creatures; it is to compromise the absolute autonomy and self-sufficiency that must pertain to a supremely perfect being. Nevertheless, God knows everything that there is to know about the creatures; classical theism takes this to imply complete and utterly detailed knowledge of the future as of the past. Beyond this, a proper respect for God's power and God's sovereign rule over the world entails that God absolutely controls everything that takes place in the world. Thus divine *omniscience* means that God knows all truths without exception, and divine *omnipotence* and *sovereignty* mean that God is not only all-knowing but also all-determining.

Open theism rejects all of the ingredients of this synthesis, even while it continues to insist that God is supremely perfect in power, knowledge and goodness. (The issue is not *whether* God is perfect but rather in what this perfection consists.) God is temporal, not timeless; God's eternity does not mean that temporal categories are inapplicable to God, but rather that God is *everlasting:* unlike the creatures, God always has existed and always will exist. Time is not an alien medium within which God is "trapped" or "limited"; rather time, in the sense of a changeful succession of states, is inherent in God's own nature. God is unchanging in his nature and character; his wisdom, power and faithfulness to us never alter in the slightest degree. But God's experience does vary from time to time, as indeed it must if he is aware of what occurs and changes in the world, and if God responds to the creatures in the way the Bible and Christian tradition insist that he does. One of the most profound differences between open theism and classical theism concerns the doctrine of divine impassibility. Open theism insists that God, far from being impassible, is profoundly affected by events in the lives of his creatures: he suffers with us when we are afflicted and rejoices when we find true happiness. To be sure, God is not controlled or overpowered by emotion in the way that often happens to us; rather, God has chosen to sympathize with us, to share our joys and sorrows. For Christians, the supreme instance of this is the incarnation of God in Jesus Christ, but open theists insist that God's "openness" to sharing our experiences is not limited to this; rather, God's presence in Jesus is a revelation of what God in his essential nature truly is and thinks and feels.

Open theists recognize God as having the power that would enable him to exert his rule over the world by unilaterally controlling everything that takes place. They believe, however, that God has not chosen to do this but has instead bestowed upon his human creatures a genuine power to make decisions of their own, including decisions as to whether or not to cooperate with God's loving purposes toward them. This creates a real possibility of tragedy in the world, as our actual history illustrates all too vividly, but also makes possible a genuine, spontaneous response of love toward God that would be precluded were we totally controlled by God in thought, word and deed.

It is important to point out here that open theists reject one fairly common strategy for addressing the problem of evil. They refuse to go along with the idea that God's goodness is of a radically different kind than human goodness, in such a way that we can draw no conclusions about what a good God would do on the basis of what we would expect of good and morally admirable human beings. Most philosophers and theologians recognize that to say that God is "good" in some unique, divine way that is entirely unlike human goodness is to say, in effect, that God is *not* good in the sense of the only kind of goodness we humans understand or know anything about. And saying *that* is far too heavy a price to pay for a solution to the problem of evil! It should be said that the strategy rejected here is not one that is commonly adopted by classical theists or indeed by thoughtful and reflective Christians of any stripe. But it shows up frequently enough in popular thought about God that it is important to mention it here and to make it clear that this is not a line of thought that will be pursued in this book.

One final position taken by open theists is at once the most clearly distinctive feature of their view and the most controversial. Open theism holds that creatures are "free" in the libertarian sense, meaning that it is really possible, in a given situation, for the creature to do something different than the thing it actually does.[14] Furthermore, the choices of this sort that will be made in the future *do not now exist* and as such are unknowable for any being, God included. It is not a matter of God's knowledge being less than perfect; rather, with regard to these undetermined future events, there is simply nothing for God to know. Open theists argue (as we will see) that the lack of this sort of knowledge does not impede God in his providential governance of the world, though it does lead us to understand that governance in a different way than is typical of classical theism.

Each of the elements of open theism discussed here can be argued for separately, and this has been done on many occasions. A few arguments on specific points will make their appearance later on in this book. For the present, however, the reader is asked simply to take this as a statement of the theistic view affirmed and defended here, in order to see what its implications may be concerning the problem of evil.

This chapter began with a question about the state of play in discussions of the problem of evil. By now it should be apparent that this question can be answered only by the book as a whole. There are arguments from evil, and there are defenses and theodicies that have been offered as responses to those arguments, so we will need to assess many of these arguments and responses in detail. Beyond that, there are human beings, philosophers and otherwise, who are struggling to make sense of a world containing vast amounts of evil, either with or without religious faith. In the chapters to come we will do our best not to forget this struggle, even as we wrestle with the technicalities of the various arguments.

---

[14]Of course this is not true in *all* situations. Sensible libertarians recognize that there are a great many limitations and obstructions to human action that prevent us from being entirely free.

2

Does Auschwitz Change Everything?

Never shall I forget that night, the first night in camp. . . . Never shall I forget that smoke. Never shall I forget the little faces of the children, whose bodies I saw turned into wreaths of smoke beneath a silent blue sky.

Never shall I forget those flames which consumed my faith forever.

Never shall I forget that nocturnal silence which deprived me, for all eternity, of the desire to live. Never shall I forget those moments which murdered my God and my soul and turned my dreams to dust. Never shall I forget these things, even if I am condemned to live as long as God Himself. Never.

ELIE WIESEL, *NIGHT*

Since the middle of the twentieth century, thinking about the problem of evil encounters a massive roadblock, one that threatens to doom the entire enterprise before it is begun. I refer, of course, to the Holocaust. The cold-blooded, state-sponsored murders of six million people, often after treatment that degraded and dehumanized them almost beyond belief, leaves a dark and ineradicable stain on a history of modern Europe that was already anything but lovely. Not surprisingly, debate about the causes and the implications of this overwhelming evil persists more than sixty years later and will no doubt continue for the foreseeable future. Of particular concern to Christians are questions about their collective responsibility for these horrendous events. The regime that carried out the killings was, to be sure, anything but Christian. But it is widely believed that the Holocaust would not have been possible apart from the long history of Christian anti-Semitism, stretching back for hundreds of years. And the failure of Christians in general to resist the program of extermination of Jews, or even forcefully to object to it, is deeply troubling.

Many of these questions are not our present concern. What we do have to grapple with are the implications of the Holocaust for religious thought, specifically for the problem of evil. It has seemed to some that even to attempt to justify affirming the love and the justice of God in the face of these tremendous evils is already a confession of one's moral failure and bankruptcy. If this issue is not squarely addressed, the rest of what we have to say on the subject may resonate as a "noisy gong or a clanging cymbal" (1 Corinthians 13:1).

As one would expect, much of the reflection on the Holocaust has been carried out by Jewish thinkers, resulting in a large and diverse body of "Holocaust theology."[1] After some thought, I have decided to focus here on two thinkers in the Christian tradition who have made the Holocaust central to their own reflections on the problem of evil. There are several reasons for this. Given the huge volume and diversity of material available, some narrower focus is essential if this topic is not to take over the entire book. Some of the issues that are central for Jewish thinkers—for example, the questions of the chosen people and of the future of the state of Israel—though they are far from unimportant, can be left to one side for our present purposes. And on the other hand, I have more points of reference in common with the Christian thinkers, though these will not necessarily lead to substantive agreement. In any case, one of the Christians has developed his own position with close reference to Jewish thinking on the topic, so the latter will by no means be ignored in what follows.

JOHN ROTH: A THEODICY OF PROTEST

The first to be considered is philosopher and Holocaust scholar John K.

---

[1]An extensive selection of this material may be found in Dan Cohn-Sherbock, ed., *Holocaust Theology: A Reader* (New York: New York University Press, 2002).

Roth.[2] For each of these thinkers two main questions need to be answered: What is the nature of their objection to traditional attempts to address the problem of evil? And what alternative position do they propose? I begin my exposition of Roth by quoting his own summary:

> My approach underscores God's sovereignty. It allows for God's disappointment with human life gone wrong. It also holds out for the possibility of grace experienced through faith and for the hope of God's salvation. At the same time, and precisely because the accumulated devastation of history is so vast, this perspective echoes voices that are Jewish as well as Christian. . . . The Jewish voices belong to a dissenting spirit that quarrels with God over the use of power. That confrontation is rooted not so much in rejection of God but rather in recognition that such defiance is crucial in struggles against despair. Jewish insight, ancient and contemporary, calls for men and women—particularly Christians—to consider a theodicy of protest, which is a form of antitheodicy.[3]

A "theodicy of protest" or "antitheodicy" (Roth regards the terms as virtually synonymous) is evidently going to be something quite different from theodicy in the traditional sense, which he describes as "human vindications of God's justice in permitting the existence of evil and suffering."[4] Roth's objection to standard theodicies is complex and difficult to summarize, but I hope that the following gives a good approximation of his thinking. An important initial point is that there is simply too much waste in human history. On the one hand, in Genesis "God called the creation good. In some sense, everyone agrees. Corrupted though the world may be, our lives are not without optimism, which persists in the experience that life is worth living."[5] On the other hand, Roth cites Hegel's remark about history as a "slaughter-bench at which the happiness of peoples, the wisdom of states, and the virtue of individuals have been sacrificed."[6] He asks, "if creation is good, and yet history is largely a

---

[2]Material on Roth is drawn from his essay "A Theodicy of Protest," as well as responses and rejoinders in *Encountering Evil: Live Options in Theology*, ed. Stephen T. Davis, 2nd ed. (Louisville: Westminster John Knox Press, 2001).

[3]Ibid., p. 4.

[4]Ibid.

[5]Ibid., p. 7.

[6]G. W. F. Hegel, *Reason in History*, trans. Robert S Hartman (Indianapolis: Bobbs-Merrill, 1953), p. 27, quoted in ibid.

slaughter-bench, how 'cost-effective' are God's decisions?" He concludes, "such a wasteful God cannot be totally benevolent. History itself is God's indictment."[7]

A common response, of course, is that it is human free will that accounts for the vast gap between the way things are and the way they ought to be. Roth affirms free will but denies that it gets God off the hook. "In a word, our freedom is both too much and too little. It is far more an occasion for waste than a defense of God's total goodness can reconcile."[8] It is too little because people are confronted with evils that free will is impotent to prevent or that can be prevented only at the cost of still further evils. "When the fury of Auschwitz was unleashed, the powers at work there were so deeply entrenched that none of humanity's countervailing energy, individual or collective, could halt them before millions perished. Only vast military force and massive killing brought Nazi Germany to its knees and the Holocaust to an end."[9] As an example of the impotence of free will to prevent evil he cites the "choiceless choice" of William Styron's protagonist Sophie Zawistowska, who was allowed to save one of her two children from the gas chamber only at the cost of condemning the other. But on the other hand, "the freedom God gives us is also too much and too soon. . . . Cancer often illustrates that we are free to abuse our bodies until things go too far, and the Holocaust shows that human beings can and will do anything to each other. We have more power and more freedom than is good for us."[10] Such freedom is not the solution to the problem of theodicy; it is itself a major part of the problem.

Is an answer to be found in the redemptive acts of God? Jews and Christians believe that in the exodus God led his people out of bondage in Egypt, and Christians believe that God raised Jesus from the dead. Roth himself shares both of these beliefs. But "God's saving acts in the world are too few and far between. . . . Why," he asks rhetorically, "should anybody bother with a God like this one, who seems so infrequently to do the best that is within God's power?" "Although God could intervene dramatically

---

[7]Roth, "Theodicy of Protest," p. 7.
[8]Ibid., p. 9.
[9]Ibid.
[10]Ibid., p. 10.

at any point in present history, God elects to let freedom work out its own course as it lives in individuals and communities. Thus, God's 'plan' for history is virtually no plan at all. It can release the worst as well as the best that is in us."[11]

So far we have been told that history contains too much waste, too much wanton destruction, to be justifiable; that free will in the form we have it is deeply flawed and does not constitute an excuse for God; and that God's interventions are too few to provide any effective defense for his complete goodness. A final point in Roth's case emerges in response to a challenge from Stephen Davis. Davis had asked, If Roth accepts that God is omnipotent, how can he "rule out the possibility that God can retain perfect goodness by redeeming all evil?"[12] Davis admits that he himself cannot understand how this is to be done, but he cites the affirmation of the apostle Paul that "the sufferings of this present time are not worth comparing with the glory about to be revealed to us" (Romans 8:18).

In his reply Roth cites the words of Jankiel Wiernick, a Jewish carpenter who escaped from the death camp in Treblinka. "Perhaps some day I shall know how to laugh again," wrote Wiernick. "My life is embittered. Phantoms of death haunt me, specters of children, little children, nothing but children. I sacrificed all those nearest and dearest to me. I myself took them to the execution site. I built their death chambers for them."[13] Roth goes on to say:

> The suggestion—with due respect to Davis and St. Paul—that the torment of burning children and their parents is 'not worth comparing to the glory about to be revealed to us' may get high marks as religious hyperbole, but it scarcely seems like solidarity with the victims. A protesting antitheodicy would find it incredible, if not obscene, to utter such words in the presence of the Holocaust's burning children.

He adds, "Should Jankiel Wiernick discover that *anything* pales his past into insignificance, I hope that he laughs . . . madly."[14] Roth's point here seems to

[11]Ibid., pp. 11, 13.
[12]Stephen T. Davis, quoted in Roth, "Theodicy of Protest," p. 21.
[13]Jankiel Wiernick, "One Year in Treblinka," in *The Death Camp Treblinka*, ed. Alexander Donat (New York: Holocaust Library, 1979), p. 149; quoted in Roth, "Theodicy of Protest," p. 31.
[14]Roth, "Theodicy of Protest," p. 33, ellipsis in original.

be that some evils are so horrible that they are intrinsically unredeemable; there is no way compatible with moral integrity that they can be reduced to insignificance. The fatal flaw in most theodicies is that they legitimate evil; Davis's theodicy, for example, "makes the Holocaust acceptable."[15]

What then is Roth's constructive view? In many respects it is surprisingly traditional and orthodox. Roth is a Protestant Christian, a believer in divine grace and in the hope of salvation. He affirms the resurrection of the dead—in particular, the resurrection of Jesus—and the life of the world to come. He sings the doxology—"Praise God from whom all blessings flow"—but he does not believe that "expressions of thanksgiving and awe-filled love are sufficient worship responses."[16] On the contrary, moral integrity as well as solidarity with the sufferers of the Holocaust demand an element of protest, at God's excessively and needlessly wasteful way of running the world. Can God retrieve his reputation by a happier outcome in the future? Roth suggests that "the issue of whether God is without any justification depends on what God does with the future, God's and ours." But in order for the best attainable outcome to occur "human repentance will have to be matched by God's." He even expresses the hope that when dissent is raised for the sake of human well-being, "its rebellious care may grip God's heart."[17] But this will be at best a partial vindication of God's goodness; not even God can erase the harm that God has already done, and some evils are beyond redemption. Yet there is reason for hope: a theodicy of protest, holding that God's "nature is a self-controlled mixture that gives us freedom and that may yet reduce evil's waste, is an option that can set human souls on fire for good."[18]

Any response to Roth must begin with an acknowledgment of his moral integrity and passion, and his determination to maintain solidarity with those who have suffered in the Holocaust and elsewhere. Even God, one thinks, must respond to these qualities, though perhaps not, as Roth hopes, by repenting of sins that God has committed. For the present, though, our respect for Roth's moral stance must take the form of a search-

---

[15]Ibid., p. 36.
[16]Ibid.
[17]Ibid., pp. 13, 6, 16.
[18]Ibid., p. 17.

ing examination of the case he has made and the position he has presented. Speaking now for myself, certain elements in Roth's critique of traditional theodicies seem compelling. Any theodicy that has the effect of legitimating evil—of making the Holocaust acceptable—must for that very reason come into serious question.[19] I will argue, in due course, that there are effective theodicies and defenses that do neither of these things, but I will not anticipate that argument now. The notion that an enormous and outrageous evil such as the Holocaust might be "cost effective" I find repellent; the term is far too suggestive of a cynical calculation that shrugs off as "collateral damage" the terrible harm that one's supposedly well-intentioned plans will do to innocent persons. And there is also considerable force in Roth's insistence that certain experiences of evil *cannot* be allowed to fade into insignificance; for this to happen would be to negate rather than redeem the significance of the life one has lived. This is especially clear in cases where the experience involves some grave fault of one's own; we may hope that God will "forget" our sins, but we ourselves had best not forget them entirely, for that would mean forgetting what it is for which we have been forgiven. (Note that the quotation from Jankiel Wiernick implies that he, like many other inmates of the death camps, was complicit to some degree by cooperating with the executioners, though no doubt under extreme duress and with no real possibility of lessening the carnage should he refuse to cooperate.)

Other claims made by Roth, however, are more problematic. His views concerning free will come most clearly into focus in a confrontation with David Ray Griffin. Griffin had asserted that

> a positive correlation necessarily obtains among the following variables: (1) The capacity to enjoy positive value. (2) The capacity to suffer negative value (evil). (3) The power of self-determination. (4) The power to influence others, for good or evil. To say that a positive correlation exists means that, as one variable increases, all the others increase proportionally.[20]

Roth doubts this, noting that "if this theory is correct, it seems to follow that my potential to experience value is somehow dependent on my capac-

---

[19] I am certain that this was not Davis's intent, but I will not argue this here.
[20] Griffin, quoted in Roth, "Theodicy of Protest," p. 126.

ity to commit murder, or even to help unleash genocide."[21] Griffin responds, "Exactly. No dogs, even no chimpanzees, could unleash genocide. The human capacity for symbolism—the same capacity that allows us to enjoy literature, mathematics, science, philosophy, and all other distinctively human pursuits—gives us the capacity to formulate and carry out genocidal plans."[22] It seems to me that Griffin has the better of this exchange and that Roth's apparent wish that we could enjoy the positive capacities without being enabled thereby to do harm is a wish for what may be literally impossible. Proponents of free-will defenses and theodicies are by no means unaware that free will can be used to do evil as well as good, and that at times we lack the capacity to prevent certain grave evils. One might, in the light of this, conclude that bestowing free will on the creatures was simply too great a risk and should not have been done. What one cannot responsibly conclude is that free will ought to have been given as a power to do good but not to do evil.

On a number of other points Roth seems content merely to assert his own estimate of the situation without providing much argument by way of support. Is the amount of waste in the world's history too great to allow God to be wholly good in spite of it? Roth thinks so, but others disagree. Would a loving God of necessity intervene more often and more forcefully in history than God seems in fact to have done? Roth thinks so, but offers no argument that this is the case. My sympathies on these points lie with Davis, who writes:

> Sadly, Roth and I are at an impasse here. I argue that in the light of the eschaton a perfectly good God morally can allow the waste that we see in human history. To counter this, Roth keeps pointing out how terrible and massive the waste is. And I keep looking for an argument why this admitted amount of waste—whatever amount it is—could not have been allowed by God. He thinks I am looking at the evidence blindly; I think he is not producing an argument.[23]

Viewed in the light of the approach to the problem of evil described in

---

[21]Ibid., p. 127.
[22]Griffin, quoted in ibid., p. 143.
[23]Davis, quoted in Roth, "Theodicy of Protest," p. 104.

the first chapter, it would seem that Roth does need an argument. The sheer fact that in the light of the Holocaust and other evils he is unable to believe in a wholly good God does not, by itself, constitute a reason why Davis, and others who share this belief, should abandon it. Passionate rhetoric is one thing; shouldering the burden of proof is another.

When we turn to Roth's constructive proposals, the difficulties multiply. Both Griffin and Davis note that the prospect that God's disposition will improve in the future seems more wishful thinking than a realistic hope.[24] As Davis says, "If God is partially demonic, the risk that God will be in a testy mood when the eschaton dawns is too much to take."[25] And it is hard to take seriously the idea that our courageous dissent "may grip God's heart" and change it for the better. If God has not changed in response to the protests of Jews over many centuries, why suppose that it will make a difference if a few Protestants come on board with them? Of course, there is another possibility, which is even less appealing: perhaps it is only those protests over the centuries that have "kept God in line" and prevented things from being a great deal worse than they are now. In that case Jesus' parable of the unjust judge, who "neither feared God nor had respect for people" (Luke 18:2) but who gave justice to a poor widow only because she hounded him day after day, is a literally accurate portrayal of the divine character!

I think Roth greatly underestimates the impact on worship of his theodicy of protest, if the latter is taken with full seriousness. When Roth reads in Scripture that "God is light and in him there is no darkness at all" (1 John 1:5), he really ought to be saying to himself, "Yes, that sounds good in your advertising, doesn't it?" When he hears, "be holy, for I am holy" (Leviticus 11:44), he must understand this as "Do as I say and not as I do." Of course, I do not for a moment suppose that Roth actually responds to these pas-

---

[24]It is interesting to note that David Blumenthal, a Jewish "theologian of protest" whom Roth cites and obviously admires, takes a different line here. His conclusion, informed partly by psychoanalysis, is not that God can be expected to improve but that there is a vengeful, abusive side both in human beings and in God that we just have to learn to live with. He crafts prayers in which, after repenting of their sins, the congregation asks God to repent of his sins—but he does not seem to hold out a hope for permanent reformation. A key statement of his is *"God is abusive, but not always."* See David R. Blumenthal, *Facing the Abusing God: A Theology of Protest* (Louisville: Westminster/John Knox Press, 1993), pp. 240-48; quotation from p. 247.

[25]Davis, quoted in Roth, "Theodicy of Protest," p. 22.

sages in such ways. Almost certainly, the "protest" is kept in check until the appropriate moment, so as to keep from ruining the worship experience entirely. We have seen Roth's claim that the theodicy of protest "can set human souls on fire for good." These words were written for the first edition of *Encountering Evil*, published in 1981.[26] I think it is fair to say that, in the quarter-century since they were written, the implied promise has not been fulfilled. Roth's own soul may be on fire, and this may be possibly be true of some of his students, but I see no evidence in the Christian community at large of such a result. It is undeniable that in contemporary philosophical discussions of the problem of evil Roth's option is off the radar screen except for its presence in Davis's anthology. Those religious thinkers who have found it untenable to maintain strong views both of divine power and of God's absolute goodness have, with very few exceptions, elected to curtail the power rather than compromise the goodness. That is not to say that limiting divine power is unproblematic; the opposite is the case. But for most of these thinkers a partially evil God is simply not an option.

At this point I would like to suggest that part of the difficulty stems from the need to discern the proper place of protest in the spiritual life. Many of us, perhaps most of us, have at some time in our lives a strong need to lodge a protest with God. Too many important things go badly, there is too much apparently pointless suffering for it to be otherwise. If we suppress the protest and assure ourselves that everything that happens is God's will and is for the best, the protest is likely to fester and cause spiritual damage in the form of repressed anger against God. Since this is a reality, a question arises concerning the place of such protest in one's religious life. Now it is widely acknowledged that protest is more explicitly recognized in Jewish piety than in Christian, so I propose that we pay attention to the way the Jewish tradition has addressed this topic. Anson Laytner, who has studied the Jewish protest tradition in depth, gives a four-part analysis of the way the rabbis dealt with this theme:

> First, the rabbis emphasized and deepened the anthropopathism of the biblical sources. As a result, the rabbis made the protest argument more explicit than it is in the biblical texts. Second, the rabbis recognized the tradition of

---

[26]Roth, "Theodicy of Protest," p. 20.

explicit protest prayer only when the prayer was executed by especially saintly rabbis and only under restricted circumstances. They also recognized the value of protest in the midrash. Third, by contrast, in the statutory liturgy, the rabbis, under the leadership of Akiva, suppressed protest and adopted the submissive-penitent form of prayer as the official stance. Fourth, the tension between protest prayer and submissive prayer, however, could not be fully repressed, and protest prayer surfaced again in medieval religious poems, many of which were adopted into the liturgy.[27]

I submit that the pattern thus indicated exhibits not merely caution but genuine wisdom. The existential need for protest against God is recognized, but care is taken to keep it in a proper context. "Especially saintly rabbis" could be trusted to utter such prayers because their presumed intimacy with the divine would keep them from carrying the protest to the point where it would become destructive. Protest was excluded, however, from the official liturgy, which as much as anything represented the core beliefs of the community. One way of reading this is to say: Protest against God as existential response can be legitimate and good; protest solidified into a formal belief system—*as it is in a theology of protest or theodicy of protest*—is potentially destructive and should be avoided.[28]

At certain points Roth seems to be signaling that his antitheodicy may in fact be more an existential response than a formal system of belief. He states his wish to reconcile "much, but not all" of the Jewish and Christian tradition with notes of dissonance, and states that "The struggle, more than the result, unfolds here."[29] In closing his essay, he writes, "A theodicy of protest is for those who need it. Like the victims of waste in our own day, who knows how many they may be?"[30] In concluding his response to his critics, he acknowledges the value of each of their contributions, but says,

A problem remains. How, if at all, can these pieces fit together? One possi-

---

[27]Blumenthal, *Facing the Abusing God*, p. 252; Blumenthal is summarizing material from Anson Laytner, *Arguing With God: A Jewish Tradition* (Northvale, N.J.: Jason Arenson, 1990).

[28]A text from Jeremiah gives a marvelous statement of a particular biblical attitude toward protest: "You will be in the right, O LORD, when I lay charges against you; but let me put my case to you" (Jeremiah 12:1).

[29]Roth, "Theodicy of Protest," p. 13.

[30]Ibid., p. 20.

bility is shown, more than said, by this book. Its words have taken the writers on more than one journey. All of us—I hope—have been stretched, changed by being prodded. Where theodicy, or antitheodicy, is concerned, perhaps that outcome is the point: Do not sit tight, but instead question and move.[31]

This is well said, but it cannot be the final word. What we most want to know about Roth's theodicy of protest—at least, what I most want to know—is not whether it meets certain needs for certain persons, but quite simply whether or not it is true.

Finally, a word concerning solidarity. I think we should acknowledge and respect Roth's commitment to solidarity with those who suffered in the Holocaust, in spite of the fact the he has not personally gone through those experiences. What should not be accepted, however, is the claim that such solidarity dictates some particular theological response or interpretation of the Holocaust. In fact, the sufferers came from a wide range of religious backgrounds and evinced a wide variety of religious and nonreligious responses. Some simply abandoned faith altogether, while others lived and died strong in their faith, and there were all sorts of responses in between. Jewish religious interpretations of the Holocaust have ranged from Richard Rubenstein's embrace of a Jewish version of death-of-God theology (in spite of his dislike for the Christian-inspired name of the movement) to more or less traditional theodicies that attempt to explain the role of the Holocaust in God's historical plan.[32] Also common has been the view that God's purposes in the Holocaust are entirely incomprehensible, but Jewish people should remain faithful in spite of that.[33] A theology or theodicy of protest is merely one strand in this complex tapestry; it has by no means established itself as the required path for anyone claiming solidarity with the victims.[34]

---

[31]Ibid., p. 37.

[32]See Richard L. Rubenstein, *After Auschwitz: Radical Theology and Contemporary Judaism* (Indianapolis: Bobbs-Merrill, 1966).

[33]For examples, see Cohn-Sherbock., *Holocaust Theology.*

[34]I am told that a theology of protest such as Blumenthal's, in which God is held to be guilty of sinning, plays no significant role in the American Jewish religious community.

D. Z. PHILLIPS: DOING WITHOUT THEODICY

The other thinker to be featured in this chapter is the Wittgensteinian philosopher of religion D. Z. Phillips.[35] As with Roth, we will begin with his objections to standard theodicies and then go on to consider his constructive view. Like Roth, Phillips has multiple, complex objections. He devotes a number of pages to objections to specific proposals for theodicy, with Richard Swinburne a favorite target.[36] Of greatest interest here, however, are two arguments that if successful strike at the heart of the entire enterprise and not merely at specific proposals. In *The Problem of Evil and the Problem of God* Phillips begins from the famous formulation of the logical problem of evil by J. L. Mackie in terms of the triad of propositions, "God is omnipotent; God is wholly good; and yet evil exists." According to Mackie:

> There seems to be some contradiction between these three propositions, so that if any two of them were true the third would be false. But at the same time all three are essential parts of most theological positions: the theologian, it seems, at once *must* adhere, and *cannot consistently* adhere to all three.[37]

There is at present a widespread philosophical consensus, shared by atheists as well as theists, that this problem has been satisfactorily answered by Alvin Plantinga's free-will defense. Accordingly, philosophical attention has shifted to other forms of the problem of evil, forms which do not involve a charge of logical inconsistency. Phillips asks, "Is this confident philosophical change of heart justified?"[38] The answer is no—but this is not because the problem, as Mackie stated it, can be rehabilitated in the face of Plantinga's defense. On the contrary, the very terms in which the

---

[35]Material on Phillips is drawn from his essay "Theism Without Theodicy" and responses and rejoinders in Davis's *Encountering Evil*, as well as from his recent book *The Problem of Evil and the Problem of God* (London: SCM Press, 2004). Some of the material in this section is drawn from my review essay "D. Z. Phillips' Problems with Evil and with God," *International Journal for the Philosophy of Religion* 61 (2007): 151-60. Shortly before his death in the summer of 2006 Phillips wrote a response to this article, published as "William Hasker's Avoidance of the Problems of Evil and God (or: On Looking Outside the Igloo)," *International Journal for the Philosophy of Religion* 62 (2007): 33-42.
[36]Phillips, "Theism Without Theodicy," pp. 147-52, and *Problem of Evil and the Problem of God*, pp. 49-94.
[37]Mackie, "Evil and Omnipotence," p. 25; cited in Phillips, *Problem of Evil and the Problem of God*, p. 3.
[38]Phillips, *Problem of Evil and the Problem of God*, p. 5.

problem is cast are misconceived, and this means that the answer also is misconceived. Phillips states, "if we stay *within* the terms of reference in which the logical problem of evil is usually discussed, we shall find that neither the proposition 'God is omnipotent', nor the proposition 'God is perfectly good', can get off the ground—and that for logical reasons."[39] In view of this, the problem of evil leads to the "problem of God."

Phillips's objection to omnipotence begins with a common definition of that attribute, here quoted from Swinburne: "An omnipotent being is one who can do anything logically possible, anything, that is, the description of which does not involve a contradiction."[40] Phillips makes the familiar Wittgensteinian point that words and sentences have their meaning only in the context of a linguistic practice within which they are employed, and in view of this he paraphrases the definition as follows: "To say that God is omnipotent is to say that God can do anything describable in any practice without contradiction." But, he says, it's obvious that God fails this test: as counterexamples he proposes "riding a bicycle, licking and savouring a Häagen-Dazs ice-cream, bumping one's head, having sexual intercourse, learning a language and so on and on."[41]

An interesting list, without any doubt! But orthodox Christians would suppose that God did learn a language, did bump his head and probably mashed his own fingers with his carpenter's mallet a few times while he was learning the trade! Ice cream and bicycles were not available, but if they had been he would no doubt have enjoyed both. And they believe he did not engage in sexual intercourse, but not because the idea does not make sense.

It seems likely, though, that Phillips was not thinking about what could or couldn't be done by God the Son incarnate, but rather what God could do through his own divine nature, as opposed to an assumed creaturely nature. In that case, the task to be performed, in the case of bumping one's

---

[39]Ibid.

[40]Richard Swinburne, *Providence and the Problem of Evil* (Oxford: Clarendon Press, 1998), p. 3; cited in ibid., p. 6. Aquinas could also have been referenced: "If, however, we consider the matter aright, since power is said in reference to possible things, this phrase, *God can do all things*, is rightly understood to mean that God can do all things that are possible; and for this reason He is said to be omnipotent" (*Summa Theologica* 1.25.3).

[41]Phillips, *Problem of Evil and the Problem of God*, pp. 11, 12.

head, would be to "bring it about that God bumps God's head." But given that the divine nature is essentially immaterial (as it is on all standard conceptions), this is *not* something that is describable without contradiction—and so also for the rest of the items on Phillips's list. This point is perhaps more readily grasped in the light of another statement from Swinburne: "God cannot do what is logically impossible *for him* to do, whatever the reason for that logical impossibility."[42] Phillips quotes this from Swinburne, and a similar qualification from Stephen Davis—but oddly enough, he ignores the point completely in the rest of his discussion. Phillips's attempt to show that omnipotence is incoherent is completely unsuccessful.[43]

But what of perfect goodness? Phillips's main point about this is that, given the tradition's view of divine power, the problem of evil logically rules out ascribing perfect goodness to God. His statement of his program is striking:

> What I am going to argue is that even if we grant that things are as theodicies and defences depict them, even if the ultimate good did necessitate all the evil in the world, and even if the ultimate good somehow redeems all evil, it would still be impossible to attribute perfect goodness to God.[44]

Stripped to essentials, the central idea is that it is morally outrageous to suppose that God might have a morally adequate reason for permitting the Holocaust, assuming that it was in his power to prevent it. It's not that the believer is unreasonable or straining faith too far in asserting that God has such a reason. On the contrary: even to contemplate the possibility that there might be such a reason is morally unacceptable, showing great ethical insensitivity (at the least) on the part of one who puts forward such an idea. Phillips does suggest, in his comments on Stephen Davis, that Davis is not as morally insensitive in real life as he is in his endorsement of the free-will defense. But "to describe redemption [from evils] in the way Davis suggests is to include in its effects a dulling of the most elementary moral reactions to horrendous evils, a result which, when not philosophizing,

---

[42]Swinburne, *Providence and the Problem of Evil,* p. 3; cited in ibid., p. 12.

[43]Not everyone would agree that Swinburne's definition of omnipotence is adequate; there has been a vigorous discussion on this subject, and a number of alternative definitions have been proposed. This fact does nothing, however, to rescue Phillips's critique or the sweeping negative conclusion he derives from it.

[44]Phillips, *Problem of Evil and the Problem of God,* p. 35.

Davis would deplore as much as anyone else."[45]

I think this claim to moral superiority should be rejected. I see no evidence that those who reject belief in God as understood by the theistic tradition are morally superior to believers in the way assumed by Phillips, and I see little promise in this approach as a constructive means of resolving philosophical disagreement. Phillips, however, attempts to support his case on logical grounds, and his argument must be examined. The centerpiece of the argument is the fictional case of Sophie Zawistowska, made famous in William Styron's novel *Sophie's Choice* and the movie based on it. Forced to choose one of her two children to be spared from the gas chamber (if she had refused to choose, both would have died), she "let Eva go" and saved her son Jan. But although the horrible choice was forced upon her, "Sophie never thinks of handing Eva over as an act to be excused in the light of the total situation."[46] In 1947, two years after her release from the death camp, she took her own life.

Phillips is quite clear that we, as bystanders, would not blame or condemn Sophie for her choice. He asks, "Who could blame Sophie? Who would want to make that third-person judgment?" Yet at the same time he thinks we should endorse[47] her self-judgment of moral condemnation:

---

[45]Ibid., p. 39. I believe Phillips is seriously unfair in his use of quotations from Davis. In citing Davis's remarks about the redemption of evils, he omits a crucial sentence: "The biblical vision is that despite the pain that all people have endured, and despite the horrible pain that some people have endured, the vision of the face of God that we will then experience will make all previous suffering such that the pain will no longer matter" (Davis, cited in ibid., p. 85). This statement hardly minimizes suffering! The trivial example Davis gives (of being forced to wear an excruciatingly awful pair of pants to junior high school) is not selected because it is comparable to the Holocaust (which would be absurd) but because this is a case in which we can readily see how pain and suffering can be overcome so that it is no longer troubling—something we admittedly cannot now see in the case of truly horrendous evils. Finally, Phillips claims that "this language is meant to have a beneficial effect *now* on those who have suffered the horrendous evil" (*Problem of Evil and the Problem of God*, p. 59), but I see nothing in the text that justifies attributing this intention to Davis. Not everything that can properly be said in a philosophical discussion of the problem of evil is suitable for use in grief counseling, and I believe Davis is well aware of this fact. (I do not deny that in attempting the difficult task of theodicy philosophers have sometimes said morally objectionable things. Davis, however, is not deserving of the harsh treatment he receives from Phillips; on this see especially his response to Roth in his "Theism Without Theodicy," pp. 20-23.)

[46]Phillips, *Problem of Evil and the Problem of God*, p. 42.

[47]What he actually says is that "it is *possible to understand* the personal judgment she makes at the end" (ibid., emphasis added). This much is surely true, but if that were all he was claiming such "understanding" on our part would be consistent with the further judgment, "but she was mistaken in thinking she was morally at fault over Eva's death." Phillips's argument requires us to reject this further judgment, so he is committed to endorsing (and not merely "understanding") her self-judgment.

"She cannot eliminate the moral significance of letting Eva go."[48] The lesson drawn from this is that one who consents to the occurrence of great evil, even in order to avoid a still greater evil or to secure a commensurately great good, cannot emerge morally unscathed. Sophie is morally stained by the choice she was forced to make; *a fortiori*, God is morally stained for having allowed the Holocaust and other horrendous evils to occur, *even if* the most extravagant claims of the theodicists are correct and all of this evil is strictly necessary for enormously valuable goods that could not be obtained in any other way. And this is why the claim that God is morally perfect (given the belief in omnipotence) doesn't get off the ground.

It seems to me that Sophie's choice, and the judgment Phillips would have us make about it, is an extraordinarily fragile basis for his conclusion that the notion of divine moral perfection is logically incoherent. One can, as he says, perfectly well understand how Sophie "could never forgive herself" for having given up her daughter to the gas chamber. But this is consistent with holding, as one might very well hold, that Sophie was *in no way* morally at fault or morally defective for her conduct in that horrendously evil situation. In discussion, Phillips declined to say what Sophie ought to have done, instead of making the choice she actually made.[49] But he continued to insist that her choice was morally horrendous and that she was morally tainted by what she had done. I submit that one can perfectly well dissent from these judgments without being guilty of either logical confusion or moral turpitude. And it is precisely the generalization of these judgments to divine action that is the nerve of Phillips's argument.[50]

But perhaps we can press the point a little farther, and doing so may lead us to another quite general argument against the possibility of theodicy. Why does it seem self-evident to Phillips that Sophie is morally guilty for handing Eva over, and God is morally guilty for permitting

---

[48]Ibid.

[49]The discussion was at the Society for Philosophy of Religion in Charleston, South Carolina, on February 25, 2006; Phillips was responding to questions raised by George Mavrodes.

[50]Another case cited by Phillips, of a pacifist who killed a gangster who was about to murder an innocent girl, strikes me as less problematic. One might perfectly well conclude that the man's pacifist belief was mistaken and that his action in defense of innocent life was entirely justified and proper. If on the other hand we endorse his absolute pacifism, we would think he was wrong to use deadly force even in such a situation, while feeling deep compassion over the intolerable circumstance in which he found himself.

the Holocaust, *even if* any other course of action, in either case, would have resulted in an outcome worse than the one that actually occurred? (Phillips, of course, does not believe that God's preventing the Holocaust would have led to an even worse result, but in the discussion of this objection he is committed to accepting that assumption.) The answer is that Phillips has an extreme aversion to allowing for any kind of consequentialist reasoning as providing a justification for serious evils. This aversion runs as a thread through all his discussions of this topic, and if we do not take it into account we will fall short of grasping his thought on the subject.

Phillips's remarks about this are spread throughout his writings on the problem of evil, and it is out of the question to examine all of them here. Because of this I will focus on one theme that recurs in a number of passages, the idea that God permits certain evils at least partly in order to allow us the opportunity to develop morally. Phillips writes:

> We are told that in allowing evils to exist, God is providing the conditions needed to give us the choice of moulding our characters in one direction or another. This offer of God's morally sufficient reason suffers from a fatal objection. *To make the development of one's character an aim is to ensure that the development will not take place.* This is because the endeavor so conceived is self-defeating: *it lacks character.* . . . It seems to be both a logical and moral truth that to seek one's character development is to lose it.[51]

Unfortunately for Phillips's argument, his generalization about character development is simply false. For consider the New Testament: When the apostle Paul wrote about the fruits of the Spirit, he was most assuredly speaking of a set of moral virtues that the faithful are urged to cultivate.[52] For a more recent example, consider the novels of Jane Austen. Does Phillips really mean for us to understand that these writers lacked any grasp of moral development? It is true, of course, that an excessive preoccupation with one's own virtue can be an obstacle rather than an aid to character development. It is also true that some people go through life with never a

---

[51]Phillips, *Problem of Evil and the Problem of God,* p. 57.

[52]"By contrast, the fruit of the Spirit is love, joy, peace, patience, kindness, generosity, faithfulness, gentleness, and self-control. There is no law against such things" (Galatians 5:22-23).

thought to issues of virtue and vice, at least until some fault of character leads them into serious trouble. I will leave it to the reader to consider which of these opposite moral errors is more characteristic of our present society.

There is, however, another point in the neighborhood that has more substance: It is morally questionable, to say the least, for us to regard the misfortunes of others primarily in the light of the opportunities for character development they afford to us. We do not want "the Good Samaritan to say, on coming across the victim of the robbers, 'Thank you, God, for another opportunity to be responsible.' "[53] There is, however, an obvious counter to this objection, which Phillips considers:

> It may be said that my criticisms are misdirected. This is because the morally sufficient reason being discussed is God's reason for acting, not ours, and thus was never advanced as a thesis about human moral motivation. Two responses can be made to this objection. First, if God's reasons are confused and morally objectionable, this would have the unhappy consequence, for the theodicist, of making God inferior to human beings.[54]

This is very strange. The arguments Phillips has given, even if otherwise impeccable, show at most that it would be confused and morally objectionable for the *human agents* to view the situations in question primarily as means to their own moral development. It by no means follows that it would be confused and morally objectionable for *God* to view the situations in that way; that is precisely what needs to be shown. This response by Phillips is thoroughly question-begging. But let us go on to his second response:

> Second, however, one need not accept the view that the issue of our own moral motivation is not involved in God's morally sufficient reason for allowing evils to exist. After all, it is we who want to know that reason, when those evils threaten our belief in God's perfect goodness. Theodicies are for our benefit, not God's. We are told that the evils exist as opportunities for our character development. If we understand the evils in these terms, this will obviously determine what we think we are doing when we respond to

---

[53]Phillips, *Problem of Evil and the Problem of God,* p. 58.
[54]Ibid., p. 57.

them, namely, that we are developing our characters. In this way, God's morally sufficient reason clearly affects our own motivation.[55]

Here I think Phillips is on to something important. It is quite true that theodicies are intended for human consumption and can have an effect on our practical views concerning the evils in question. If what I learn from a theodicy concerning God's reasons for allowing some evil has the effect of undermining or corrupting my own moral motivations in that situation, the theodicy is counterproductive and something has gone seriously wrong. I will be arguing later on that some widely entertained theodicies and defenses do suffer from this flaw and that the consequences of our accepting them and taking them with full seriousness would be morally harmful.

But Phillips is attempting to make an entirely general point with his argument, which prompts the following question: Will it *always and necessarily* be the case that if we accept a theodicy according to which God allows certain evils in part as a means to our moral development, this will undermine or corrupt our moral motivation to respond to these evils? I believe the answer to this is negative, and I will illustrate the point with a hypothetical example. Suppose some acquaintance of mine is suffering and is in severe financial need, a need which if not supplied will have serious negative consequences for his future life. I have the resources to meet the need, but doing so will require considerable sacrifice on my own part. So far as I can tell, if I do not meet the need no one else is likely to do so. Finally, we add the following fact: Part of God's reason for allowing this situation to develop is precisely to shake me out of my usual moral lethargy and spur me to an unaccustomed exercise of the virtue of generosity.

Now, suppose also that I accept a theodicy according to which some evils are permitted by God in order to provide people with opportunities for moral development. Will this have a negative effect on my motivation in this situation? I see no reason why it should. First, I may be quite unaware that this was God's reason for allowing the situation to develop. (My theodicy tells me that *in general* God sometimes acts for such a reason; it does not specify God's reasons in particular cases.) But suppose I do come

---

[55]Ibid., pp. 57-58.

to believe that God has allowed this situation to develop in part for the purpose of challenging me to act generously. Will this undermine or corrupt my motivation? It is hard to see why it should. I am still confronted by my acquaintance in his state of severe financial need; it is still the case that he will suffer greatly if the need is not met, as it apparently will not be unless I step forward to help. But now I have come to believe that God specifically intended this situation as one in which I should exercise an unaccustomed generosity. This belief should, if anything, encourage and reinforce my inclination to provide the needed assistance; I may indeed come to see this as part of my moral "vocation."[56] The corrupting effect feared by Phillips seems entirely absent.

What my example shows, if it succeeds, is that Phillips's concern, though real, is not fully general in that it does not apply to all cases of the kind he describes. I believe, however, that he would not be satisfied with the example. He may think that my moral motivation has after all been corrupted, and he may also think it is morally unacceptable for God to "use" my acquaintance in this way as a means to my moral development. In the end I suspect that opposition to a teleological justification of suffering has for Phillips the status of an ultimate moral principle to which counterexamples are simply inadmissible.

This observation, however, leads to another interesting question about Phillips's view. It would seem, on the surface, that the difference between Phillips and his opponents hinges in large part on certain moral views about which they differ. So it seemed to Brian Davies, who wrote, "What is now at stake is a fundamental *moral* option. . . . One side is saying that the whole attempt to justify God in terms of consequences is simply intolerable. . . . The other side holds that it is not intolerable."[57] Phillips rejects this, insisting, "But what is at issue is not a moral dispute, but whether conceptual justice has been done to the notion of moral responsibility."[58] What is it that leads Phillips to insist that the difference between him and

---

[56]For an illuminating discussion of vocation, see Robert Merrihew Adams, *Finite and Infinite Goods: A Framework for Ethics* (Oxford: Oxford University Press, 1999), chap. 13.

[57]Brian Davies, *An Introduction to the Philosophy of Religion* (New York: Oxford University Press, 1993), p. 38; cited in Phillips, "Theism Without Theodicy," p. 148.

[58]Phillips, "Theism Without Theodicy," p. 148.

his critics is conceptual rather than moral? I believe this insistence is forced on him by his view of the nature of philosophy. He begins his reply to his critics in *Encountering Evil* by saying, "In *Philosophy's Cool Place*, I argue that philosophy has the contemplative task of doing conceptual justice to the world in all its variety. I discussed the temptation to go beyond this task in claiming that philosophy can tell us what to believe, or how to behave."[59] Now, espousing substantive ethical principles would undoubtedly fall under the rubric of "telling us how to behave," so Phillips's conception of philosophy rules it out. In order to fit within that view of philosophy, the ethical principles he insists upon must be placed under the rubric of conceptual analysis, and that is just what he has done.

But it is one thing to show that classifying the principles in question as conceptual analysis is required by Phillips's view of philosophy; it is another to show that such a classification is justified. I do not believe that it is. One thing I do hope we have learned from Wittgenstein is that the meaning of expressions is determined by the way they are used. This means that if Phillips is right to hold that it is conceptually confused to say that God is justified in permitting some evils because they create the opportunity for moral growth, this confusion arises because of the implicit rules for the way the terms in question are used in our linguistic practice. And this in turn means that competent users of the language should be able to recognize the aberrant uses as nonstandard. Here, however, that is evidently not the case, as is shown by Davies, Hick, Davis, Swinburne and innumerable others who have found the assertions of theodicists to be readily intelligible (whether or not they are true) and by no means ungrammatical or ill-formed. Phillips does argue against the theodicists' assertions, but he does so by appealing to what he takes to be common moral intuitions, not by any sort of rigorous attempt to demonstrate logical incoherence. And this is just what we should expect, if the principles in question really are moral rules.[60]

---

[59]Ibid., p. 174.

[60]Readers should keep in mind that at this point I have not put forward any proposals of my own for theodicy, nor am I committed to defending the proposals from Swinburne and others that Phillips has criticized. What I have been trying to show is that Phillips's general arguments against the possibility of theodicy do not succeed.

So much then for Phillips's critique of theodicy. What of his constructive views? Here I encounter a considerable difficulty—one that is not limited to me—in saying just what those views amount to. Each of the four respondents in *Encountering Evil* expresses some degree of puzzlement as to what Phillips's view of God involves. (By way of contrast, the four seem to have relatively little difficulty in comprehending one another's views, even though those views differ significantly among themselves.) Phillips complains of being misunderstood, but does not seem to consider whether the fault for this may be his own. I believe the confusion does result in large part from the way that Phillips expresses himself. The difficulty is that he uses many familiar-sounding expressions in talking about God—expressions which seem to retain, in his use of them, much of their familiar connotations and emotional resonance—and yet, in the light of other things he says, it is evident that the expressions cannot possibly mean, for him, what they seem to be saying.

After consideration I have concluded that it may be best to summarize somewhat baldly my conclusions about Phillips's constructive views. Some textual support will be provided for these conclusions, but for a more extensive discussion the reader should consult my review essay on Phillips's book. At one point Phillips claims to have shown, by conceptual analysis, *"what God cannot be,"*[61] and I think it will be helpful to start with that before going on to see, as best we can, what according to Phillips God *is*. A point repeatedly emphasized by Phillips is that God is not "a member of the same moral community" with ourselves. (According to him, it is one of the major mistakes in the theodicy project to assume the contrary.) This means that God is not an agent who performs particular acts at particular times, and whose acts can be described in terms implying moral evaluation (e.g., as keeping promises, treating persons justly or the like). It may seem astonishing that Phillips should hold this, in view of the myriad biblical descriptions of God as doing just these sorts of things. Nevertheless he does hold it, and it is impossible to make sense of what he says without taking note of it.[62]

---

[61]Phillips, *Problem of Evil and the Problem of God*, p. 156.
[62]On this topic see Phillips's use of the quotations from R. F. Holland and Rowan Williams in ibid., pp. 148-51, and the discussion in Hasker, "D. Z. Phillips' Problems with Evil and with God," pp. 155-56.

Phillips's account of *"what God cannot be"* goes even further. Following some ideas of Wittgenstein, Phillips holds that the notion of God as a nonembodied consciousness does not make sense.[63] We are not, of course, to entertain the idea of God's having a physical body, so it becomes evident that whatever else he (or she or it) may be, God is not any sort of conscious entity at all. But now, surely, we will find ourselves asking, What then *is* God, according to Phillips? According to Phillips, this question is misconceived! He writes:

> In "God is love," is the "is" one of predication as in "Tony Blair is Prime Minister"? In the latter case, I can refer to Tony Blair without knowing that fact. . . . But when I say "God is love," or "God is gracious," what is the "it" to which the love or grace are attributed? There is none. That is "the metaphysical subject" which, as Feuerbach says, is an illusion.[64]

This could hardly be plainer: the "metaphysical subject"—that is, God as an active, personal being, indeed as a being of any kind—is an illusion. So we should not ask, What is God? The question that does arise is: What is signified by God talk, given that there is no such being as God? At this point, however, I have to say with regret that I am unable to give a clear and convincing explanation of Phillips's answer to that question; interested readers are invited to peruse his numerous books for themselves.

In any case, it is now apparent why Phillips is untouched by the problem of evil as ordinarily conceived. If there is literally no such being as God, then the question of why God permits so much evil in the world cannot arise. This does not mean, to be sure, that evil is not a problem for Phillips: it is a profoundly existential problem for him as for each one of us. But the problem of evil addressed in this book is not among his concerns.

We began this chapter by addressing the Holocaust, arguably the most overwhelming instance of evil in our time. It may seem that in recent pages this emphasis has been left behind as we discussed general features of Phillips's analysis of religious concepts. If so, a corrective is in order. We cannot

---

[63] This, of course, is an application to God of Wittgenstein's "private language argument," which Phillips appeals to with confidence despite the fact that most philosophers have now concluded that it is unsuccessful. For Phillips's brief summary of the argument, as it applies to God, see Phillips, "Theism Without Theodicy," p. 176.

[64] Ibid., p. 155.

and must not forget such an egregious example of horrible evil. The Holocaust does indeed cause us to raise questions concerning the love and justice of God, and concerning his ability or inability to avert such terrible suffering. *These questions remain to be addressed.* We have not by any means "disposed of" the Holocaust; we have, however, tried to address claims that, in view of the Holocaust, any attempt at theodicy or defense with respect to the problem of evil is doomed from the outset. Roth insists that this is so but gives no compelling reasons for his insistence. Phillips presents more by way of argument, but his arguments are flawed and fail to establish their intended conclusion. And the positive alternatives presented by the two men are gravely lacking. Roth modifies belief in God in a way that has been found unacceptable by believers almost without exception. Phillips goes further and abandons belief in God in anything remotely like the ordinary sense. But if Roth and Phillips cannot be our guides, we must nevertheless keep their concerns, especially their concern with the Holocaust, very much in mind as we press onward for what we hope will be a better solution to the question of the triumph of God over evil.

3

Are God and Evil Compatible?

Epicurus' old questions are yet unanswered. Is he willing to prevent evil, but not able? Then is he impotent. Is he able, but not willing? Then is he malevolent. Is he both able and willing? whence then is evil?

DAVID HUME, *DIALOGUES CONCERNING NATURAL RELIGION*

Is the existence of any evil at all logically consistent with the existence of God? For most religious believers, the answer is obvious. The existence of both God and the evil from which God is entreated to deliver us are integral and central ingredients in their religious worldview; the notion that there might be some logical incompatibility between the two simply does not come to mind. Nevertheless, the compatibility has been questioned, most famously by Hume, as seen in the epigraph to this chapter. More recently, center stage has been occupied by a challenge from J. L. Mackie, already cited in each of the previous two chapters:

> In its simplest form the problem is this: God is omnipotent; God is wholly good; and yet evil exists. There seems to be some contradiction between these three propositions, so that if any two of them were true the third would be false. But at the same time all three are essential parts of most

theological positions: the theologian, it seems, at once *must* adhere, and *cannot consistently* adhere to all three.[1]

Mackie does recognize that something more needs to be said:

> However, the contradiction does not arise immediately; to show it we need some additional premises, or perhaps some quasi-logical rules connecting the terms "good," "evil," and "omnipotent." These additional principles are that good is opposed to evil, in such a way that a good thing always eliminates evils as far as it can, and that there are no limits to what an omnipotent thing can do. From these it follows that a good omnipotent thing eliminates evil completely, and then the propositions that a good omnipotent thing exists, and that evil exists, are incompatible.[2]

Now in order to show that the theological positions in question are contradictory the "additional premises" must be necessary truths, but these particular (alleged) necessary truths require further examination.[3] Mackie in effect recognizes this; he examines a number of ways in which his original premises might be modified and acknowledges that at least some of them might be acceptable to theists. So he considers a number of proposed solutions along these lines and argues that each of them is unsatisfactory. He allows that the claim that evil is due to human free will is "perhaps the most important proposed solution of the problem of evil."[4] He envisions the solution working in the following way: "first order evil (*e.g.* pain) may be justified as a logically necessary component in a second order good (*e.g.* sympathy) while second order evil (*e.g.* cruelty) is not *justified*, but is so ascribed to human beings that God cannot be held responsible for it." Mackie states, "I think this solution is unsatisfactory primarily because of the incoherence of the notion of freedom of the will: but I cannot discuss this topic adequately here."[5] (I should state here that I will assume in my

---

[1]J. L. Mackie, "Evil and Omnipotence," in *The Problem of Evil*, ed. Marilyn McCord Adams and Robert Merrihew Adams (New York: Oxford University Press, 1990), p. 25.

[2]Ibid., p. 26.

[3]Much of what will be said in the following pages is familiar to philosophers interested in the topic, and they should feel free to skip ahead. However, discussion of the logical problem occupies an important role in the recent history of our subject, and I think it still can yield useful insights. For Plantinga's reflections on the unfolding of the story, see Alvin Plantinga, "Self-Profile," in *Alvin Plantinga*, ed. James E. Tomberlin and Peter van Inwagen (Dordrecht: D. Riedel, 1985).

[4]Mackie, "Evil and Omnipotence," p. 33.

[5]Ibid.

discussion that the notion of [libertarian] free will is coherent and intelligible, but I will not attempt a full defense of this assumption.)[6] He goes on to raise a number of more particular criticisms of this defense.

THE FREE-WILL DEFENSE

Enter Alvin Plantinga, stage right, with his free-will defense. (An entrance from the left would of course be wholly out of character.) He argues at some length and in minute analytical detail that no one has produced plausible candidates for the additional premises that are required in order to show theism incoherent. The candidates proposed by Mackie are unsatisfactory, and revisions that suggest themselves fail to accomplish the job.[7] In view of this the logical argument from evil has failed to accomplish its announced intention of showing theistic belief to be self-contradictory.

Plantinga, however, is after bigger game. He is not content merely to show that objectors have so far failed to show that the existence of God is logically inconsistent with evil; this, after all, could leave us wondering whether the next issue of a philosophical journal might contain a successful proof of the inconsistency. His aim, in contrast, is to show positively that the existence of God *is* consistent with that of evil. In order to do this he makes use of an important but nonobvious principle of modal logic (the logic of necessity and possibility). The principle is this: If two propositions are logically consistent with each other, so that it is possible for both of them to be true, *and* these two propositions together entail a third proposition, then that third proposition is itself logically consistent with each of the first two propositions.[8] A little thought shows this to be correct. If the first two propositions together entail the third, then those two propositions cannot both be true unless the third is also true. So if it is possible that the first two propositions are true together, it is possible for all three

---

[6]See Timothy O'Connor, *Persons and Causes: The Metaphysics of Free Will* (New York: Oxford, 2000); and Derk Pereboom, *Living Without Free Will* (Cambridge: Cambridge University Press, 2001). As the title indicates, Pereboom does not in the end affirm free will, but he gives an excellent conceptual analysis on the way to rejecting it. The rejection is not because of conceptual difficulties but is due to a perceived conflict with the deliverances of science.

[7]See Alvin Plantinga, *God and Other Minds: A Study of the Rational Justification of Belief in God* (Ithaca, N.Y.: Cornell University Press, 1967), pp. 115-30.

[8]In symbols, $(\Diamond(p \,\&\, q) \,\&\, \Box((p \,\&\, q) \to r)) \to (\Diamond(p \,\&\, r) \,\&\, \Diamond(q \,\&\, r))$.

to be true together; there is no contradiction between any of them. It is essential to recognize here that what is to be proved is the *logical consistency* of various propositions—that is, their freedom from contradiction. It is no part of Plantinga's project to prove or even to claim that any one of the propositions he is presenting is actually *true*. (To be sure, he *believes* some of the propositions to be true—but this fact is strictly irrelevant to the free-will defense as he presents it.) Plantinga himself is perfectly clear on this point, but it is necessary to emphasize it because it is easily overlooked and has in fact been frequently overlooked.

Now the first of the three propositions in question is simply theism—that there is a God who is omnipotent, omniscient and perfectly good. The third proposition is that evil exists. So the task Plantinga sets for himself is to find a second proposition, one that is itself consistent with theism and that, taken together with the truth of theism, entails the existence of evil. It is by no means necessary, however (to repeat this one more time), that this second proposition be true, only that it is logically consistent with theism and, together with the truth of theism, entails the existence of evil.

It is the search for this second proposition, then, that leads Plantinga to the free-will defense. The basic outlines of such a defense are of course not new; the idea has been frequently invoked in the history of Christian theology and philosophy. Plantinga in explaining his defense introduces the notion of "significant freedom" as follows: "a person is *significantly free*, on a given occasion, if he is then free with respect to an action that is morally significant for him"—that is, if "it would be wrong for him to perform the action but right to refrain, or vice versa."[9] He then gives the following as a preliminary statement of the defense:

> A world containing creatures who are sometimes significantly free (and freely perform more good than evil actions) is more valuable, all else being

---

[9]Alvin Plantinga, *The Nature of Necessity* (New York: Oxford University Press, 1974), p. 166. I believe the choice of the term "significant freedom" was unfortunate. This was introduced as a technical term, but it unavoidably carries the implication (which Plantinga may not have intended) that exercises of free will that are not choices between moral right and wrong are insignificant. But this is clearly false: there are many exercises of free will in the process of artistic creation (for example) that are extremely significant, and yet are not choices between moral right and wrong. More importantly, God is held by most theists to be incapable of doing wrong, so it will follow on this definition that God's exercise of free choice is insignificant!

equal, than a world containing no free creatures at all. Now God can create free creatures, but he cannot *cause* or *determine* them to do only what is right. For if he does so, then they are not significantly free after all; they do not do what is right *freely*. To create creatures capable of *moral good*, therefore, he must create creatures capable of moral evil; and he cannot leave these creatures *free* to perform evil and at the same time prevent them from doing so. God did in fact create significantly free creatures; but some of them went wrong in the exercise of their freedom: this is the source of moral evil. The fact that these free creatures sometimes go wrong, however, counts neither against God's omnipotence nor against his goodness; for he could have forestalled the occurrence of moral evil only by excising the possibility of moral good.[10]

Now, Mackie was not unaware of the possibility of such a defense, and he offers an ingenious objection to it:

If God has made men such that in their free choices they sometimes prefer what is good and sometimes what is evil, why could he not have made men such that they always freely choose the good? If there is no logical impossibility in a man's freely choosing the good on one, or on several occasions, there cannot be a logical impossibility in his freely choosing the good on every occasion. God was not, then, faced with a choice between making innocent automata and making beings who, in acting freely, would sometimes go wrong: there was open to him the obviously better possibility of making beings who would act freely but always go right. Clearly, his failure to avail himself of this possibility is inconsistent with his being both omnipotent and wholly good.[11]

In responding to this Plantinga took what has proved to be a fateful turn. He might have said simply that (as seems to be implied in his own preliminary statement of the defense) it is inconsistent to suppose that God could create free creatures and allow them to exercise their freedom, and at the same time guarantee that they would choose only good and not evil. Instead, however, he took some pains to develop a method by which God apparently could have done exactly what Mackie says a good God ought to have done: create free creatures and permit them to exercise their

---

[10]Ibid., pp. 166-67.
[11]Mackie, "Evil and Omnipotence," p. 33.

freedom in choices between right and wrong, and yet guarantee that they would in fact choose only what is right. To illustrate this method, take the case of Adam, who according to the biblical story committed the primal sin and by so doing brought sin and moral evil into the world. (This however is merely an illustration; for in what we are now discussing nothing hangs on whether the story is taken to represent an actual event.) God knew, we might suppose, that if Adam was placed in exactly the circumstances in which he in fact found himself, with his mental state and constitution exactly as it was, Adam would take the fruit and freely sin against God. (Propositions of this sort, concerning what a free creature would freely choose to do under one or another set of circumstances, have come to be called *counterfactuals of creaturely freedom*.) No doubt God also knew that there were many other possible sets of circumstances in which Adam might find himself from time to time in which he would freely choose to do right and would not sin. But this leads to the following question: Couldn't God simply have arranged things in such a way that Adam would always find himself in circumstances of the latter sort—circumstances in which he would freely choose to do right—rather than in circumstances of the former sort, in which God knew that he would fall into sin? And if God could have done this, then is it not, as Mackie would insist, a stain on God's character that he did not in fact do it?

But now another, more ominous, possibility comes into view. God, we are supposing, knew before he created Adam a complete set of Adam's "counterfactuals of freedom"—that is to say, he knew exactly what Adam would do in any of the extremely (perhaps infinitely) large number of possible situations in which Adam might find himself. But suppose that part of what God knew about Adam was this: No matter how God might arrange things in Adam's life—no matter which combinations of circumstances and surroundings Adam might find himself in—it would happen *at least once* in Adam's life that he would commit some moral evil. In this (admittedly grim) situation, there would be simply no way in which God could create Adam and leave him free with respect to good and evil without Adam's sooner or later falling into sin. If this is the case, Adam suffers from *transworld depravity:* no matter what set of circumstances occur in Adam's life—no matter what "possible world" he inhabits—he will at least once in his life *freely choose* to do evil, provided that he is allowed to choose between good and evil at all.[12]

There is an additional interesting point concerning transworld depravity: It seems that anyone who suffers from it must of necessity go wrong morally on *the very first occasion* on which that person makes a choice between moral good and evil. For suppose this is not so; suppose someone who suffers from transworld depravity makes her very first moral choice a choice for the good. This poses no problem, you might think; that person will have plenty of additional chances to go wrong. But suppose she doesn't have any more chances? It seems entirely possible that, having made one free choice for the good, the person might have no further opportunities at all: perhaps her existence comes to an end at that point or circumstances change in some way such that she never again chooses between moral right and wrong. If this were to occur, then the person would have been given freedom to choose between good and evil, and yet would never have chosen to do evil—but that would mean that, contrary to our supposition, the person was not transworldly depraved after all. Indeed, if this scenario is even *possible*, it follows that she is not transworldly depraved, for transworld depravity means that *in any possible set of circumstances* in which the person is free to choose between good and evil (*including* the scenario in which the person makes only one morally significant choice in her lifetime), she chooses evil at least once. So if the person is in fact transworldly depraved, she will choose evil on the very first opportunity that presents itself to her.

But let us leave these matters to one side and return to the main line of argument. We have seen that God's knowledge of Adam's counterfactuals of freedom might seem to offer a way in which God could create Adam with free will and leave him free to choose between moral right and wrong, and yet guarantee that Adam would choose only what is right. But then we saw that, on the supposition that Adam suffers from transworld depravity,

---

[12]A *possible world*, as Plantinga and many others use the expression, is an absolutely comprehensive "way things could be." The *actual world* is that world from among all the possible worlds that is the way things actually are, so that a complete description of the actual world would include all of the truths that there are. For a full analysis of these and related concepts see Plantinga, *The Nature of Necessity*.

God could do no such thing: no matter what circumstances God arranges for Adam, Adam will go wrong morally at least once in his life. Well then, we might think, God could just create someone else instead of Adam. But suppose that everyone else God might have created is like Adam in the respect under consideration? Suppose, that is, that *all possible persons suffer from transworld depravity?*[13] This means that regardless of which persons God chooses to create each of them, if allowed to choose freely between right and wrong, will go wrong morally at least once in his or her life. In this case the window of opportunity that seemed to be opened through God's knowledge of the counterfactuals of creaturely freedom slams shut for good. God simply *cannot* create free creatures and allow them to choose freely between moral right and wrong, and at the same time guarantee that they will never choose to do evil.

And now, finally, we are almost within reach of the proposition needed to complete the free-will defense—the proposition that is consistent with the existence of God and that, together with God's existence, entails the existence of evil, thus proving that God's existence and that of evil are logically consistent with each other. One additional point needs to be made however; namely, that *the counterfactuals of freedom are not under God's control.* That this must be so is apparent when we consider that these counterfactuals concern what creatures *freely* choose to do. Now if God could determine which counterfactuals are to be true of Adam, then God would in effect be *deciding for* Adam what Adam would freely choose to do in each of infinitely many sets of circumstances—but then the notion that Adam is *free* in making his choices becomes meaningless. But since Adam *is* free, the counterfactuals that state what Adam will freely do can't be made true by God; God *knows* that they are true but has no say concerning *which* ones are true.

And now the free-will defense is ready to proceed.[14] We are considering the propositions

---

[13]Plantinga speaks not of possible persons but of creaturely essences. I have employed the former expression here in order to avoid having to explain Plantinga's theory of essences.

[14]I should say that my formulations will differ from Plantinga's at a number of points in the interest of avoiding the logical technicalities that are pervasive in his version. I believe, however, that the argument as presented here closely tracks the logical structure of his argument.

(1) God exists and is omnipotent, omniscient and perfectly good.

and

(3) Evil exists.

We need to find a proposition that is consistent with proposition (1) and that together with proposition 1 entails proposition (3). Now let us suppose that, in view of the great value of moral goodness, God decides to create a universe containing such goodness. However, it is also true that all possible persons (persons God might create) suffer from transworld depravity. This means that if God creates any one of them (which he must do if the universe is to contain moral good), there will be moral evil as well, since each of them will do what is wrong at least once in her or his lifetime. Given all this, we have a proposition that does what we have been looking for:

(2) God creates a world containing moral good, and all possible persons suffer from transworld depravity.

Taken together with proposition (1), which affirms the existence and perfection of God, this proposition entails the existence of evil and thus shows that propositions (1) and (3) are consistent. Not for nothing does Plantinga title this section in his book "The Free Will Defense Triumphant." But keep this firmly in mind: Nowhere does Plantinga assert that everyone, or for that matter that anyone, actually does suffer from transworld depravity. There is no requirement whatsoever that proposition (2) should be *true*, only that it is *logically possible* and consistent with proposition (1).

Somewhat amazingly, Plantinga has actually succeeded in convincing most philosophers that his defense is successful. (This is amazing because it is really quite a rare occurrence that philosophers who initially disagree come to agreement on such a point of contention.) Most philosophers, that is to say, agree (with one possible reservation to be addressed presently) that proposition (2) is logically possible and is consistent with proposition (1), and thus that the existence of God and the existence of evil are logically compatible. This however is by no means the end of the story; there are a number of additional complications that need to be discussed.

THE DEFENSE AND NATURAL EVIL

Here is one complication: the free-will defense has shown, we will assume, that the existence of God is consistent with the existence of *moral* evil; that is, with morally wrong choices and actions, and the pain and suffering that flow from them. But what about *natural* evil, evil arising from disease, floods, hurricanes, tornadoes and the like, much of which does not seem to be caused in any way we can understand by human wrongdoing? Is the existence of God consistent with this sort of evil as well?

This is a good question, but we must not lose sight of the issue concerning the burden of proof. The proponent of the logical argument from evil has undertaken (as we saw in the case of Mackie) to show that the existence of God is logically inconsistent with the existence of evil. Mackie's attempt to do this, we may now agree, was unsuccessful. Now, if someone wants to claim that natural evil, unlike moral evil, is indeed inconsistent with God's existence, it is incumbent on such a person to come forward with a plausible candidate for an argument that will show the inconsistency. No one, to my knowledge, has done this—but until someone does it, there is no logical argument from natural evil to be answered.

Still, it might be said, Plantinga has raised the bar for himself, by undertaking to prove positively that the existence of God is consistent with that of evil. Can this more ambitious undertaking be extended to cover natural evil as well as moral evil? According to Plantinga, the answer is yes. He explores a couple of possibilities here, but the most intriguing of these appeals to the free activity of *nonhuman persons*—in theological terms, the devil and his fallen angels. It is possible, Plantinga proposes, that all of the natural evil in the world is in fact "broadly moral" evil, in that it results from the free activity of these nonhuman persons. If so, then we have the following candidate proposition:

> (2*) God creates a world containing moral good brought about by nonhuman persons, and all possible nonhuman persons suffer from transworld depravity; the natural evil that exists results from morally wrong choices made by these nonhuman persons.

This certainly seems to be logically possible and consistent with the existence of God. (Who can say what mysterious reasons God might have for creating such nonhuman persons?) And together with the existence of God it entails

> (3*) Natural evil exists.

This shows the consistency of God's existence with that of natural evil.

It seems, once again, that this defense is entirely successful. It should be kept in mind, however, that it is *wholly irrelevant* to the success of the defense whether or not it is *true* that natural evil is due to the activity of non-human created persons or even that such persons exist at all. All that is required is that these things be logically possible, and this they do seem to be.

Plantinga, however, wishes to take matters one small step further and to claim that the idea that natural evil, evil that is not due to free human agency, is due to the free agency of other rational creatures is *plausible*, or *not improbable*, as an explanation for such evil. He recognizes, to be sure, that this idea does not enjoy much popularity at present and is regarded as preposterous by many people. Nevertheless he insists, "I cannot see that our total evidence disconfirms the idea that natural evil results from the activity of rational and significantly free creatures."[15] I am not sure whether to describe this statement as outrageously funny or as just plain outrageous. Suffice it to say that we do have abundant evidence that many sorts of evil arise from natural causes in such a way that to insert the agency of nonhuman persons into the causal chain is monumentally implausible. (Earthquakes, for instance, arise from shifts in the crustal plates of the earth which are fairly well understood through the discipline of plate tectonics.) The idea that natural evil is due to the agency of nonhuman free creatures is best regarded as part of a demonstration of logical consistency and left at that—or so I say. Plantinga, however, has recently reaffirmed this idea as a component in his *felix culpa* theodicy.[16]

THE DEFENSE WITH AND WITHOUT MIDDLE KNOWLEDGE

A while back I described as a "fateful turn" Plantinga's response to Mackie's argument that a good God would have created persons who would always freely choose to do good. The reason is that in responding as he did Plantinga rediscovered, or rather reinvented, a view of divine knowledge that dates back to the sixteenth century but had faded from view in twentieth-century philosophy of religion. The view in question is the theory of divine

---

[15]Plantinga, *Nature of Necessity*, p. 195.

[16]Alvin Plantinga, "Supralapsarianism, or 'O Felix Culpa,'" in *Christian Faith and the Problem of Evil*, ed. Peter van Inwagen (Grand Rapids: Eerdmans, 2004), pp. 1-25. For further discussion see chapter 5 and the appendix to chapter 6.

"middle knowledge" (in Latin, *scientia media*), also called Molinism because of its originator, the Jesuit theologian Luis de Molina.[17] As a result of Plantinga's rediscovery, Molinism has enjoyed a significant revival among philosophers of religion and has played an important role in recent discussions concerning divine foreknowledge and divine providence.[18] Some of these developments will occupy us in later chapters.

What is important at this juncture, however, is that middle knowledge always has been and remains today a seriously controversial theory. It has always been a minority view in theology (mainly Roman Catholic theology but also classical Arminianism), and it is certainly a minority view among philosophers of religion today, though it has stalwart defenders. But this means that the free-will defense, insofar as it relies on middle knowledge, may not be as clearly successful as it otherwise seems to be. (This is the source of the reservation mentioned earlier concerning the success of the defense.) So we need to look further at this controversy.

The central point at issue in the controversy over middle knowledge is the very existence of the truths God is supposed to know—the "counterfactuals of creaturely freedom."[19] To see why this is a problem (or at least, appears to many to be a problem), consider an example of a free choice that might have been made by you but is never actually made. Suppose, for example, that you were to receive two different job offers, each fairly attractive, but each with some significant drawbacks. After weighing the pros and cons, neither offer seems clearly better than the other. Now according to the theory of middle knowledge, there is some definite fact about which of the offers you would accept. But why is this so? What makes it the case that you would have accepted offer A rather than offer B? We have stipulated that the choice is free, and this means that it is *really possible* for you to accept either of the offers. Overall, neither of the two offers is clearly

---

[17] According to Plantinga, it was Anthony Kenny who first informed him that he, Plantinga, was a Molinist ("Self-Profile," p. 50.)

[18] The two most important contemporary sources for Molinism are Luis de Molina, *On Divine Foreknowledge: Concordia* 4, trans. Alfred J. Freddoso (Ithaca, N.Y.: Cornell University Press, 1988); and Thomas P. Flint, *Divine Providence: The Molinist Account* (Ithaca, N.Y.: Cornell University Press, 1998).

[19] This issue was first raised by Robert M. Adams in "Middle Knowledge and the Problem of Evil," *American Philosophical Quarterly* 14 (1977), reprinted in *The Problem of Evil*, ed. Marilyn McCord Adams and Robert Merrihew Adams (New York: Oxford University Press, 1990), pp. 110-25.

superior to the other. Nothing about your character, your past history or your state of mind as you consider the offers guarantees that you will make one particular choice rather than the other. Nor, we are assuming, has God efficaciously decreed that you will make that particular choice. If you were actually to make the decision, then it would be *you yourself* who would determine the outcome—as we say, you would "make up your mind" what to do. But since this choice is never actually made, you never make up your mind about it either. So again, what makes it the case that you would choose A rather than B? This has become known as the "grounding problem" for counterfactuals of freedom, and it has led many to the following conclusion: There simply is no fact of the matter as to what you *would* do if you were to find yourself in that situation. The truth rather is that you *might* choose to accept offer A, and you *might* choose to accept offer B, but it is not true either that you *would* (definitely) choose A or that you *would* choose B.[20]

Other philosophers, to be sure, do not find this reasoning compelling. The debate over the counterfactuals of creaturely freedom has become extremely complex, and I am not attempting to resolve it here.[21] My point is simply to underscore the highly controversial nature of the theory of divine middle knowledge. And this leads me to pose the question, Is the free-will defense really dependent on this controversial theory? With regard to the version of the defense presented earlier (see pp. 57-63), the answer is clearly yes. If there are no true counterfactuals of freedom, there is no such condition as transworld depravity, and propositions (2) and (2*) will be false. Indeed, they will be *necessarily* false; they *could not possibly* be true. (It doesn't just "happen to be the case" that there are or that there are not these truths;

---

[20]In the logic of counterfactual conditionals the proposition "The agent *might* choose A" is the contradictory of the proposition "The agent *would* refrain from choosing A"; one or the other must be true, but they cannot both be true together.

[21]Additional objections are given in Robert M. Adams, "An Anti-Molinist Argument," *Philosophical Perspectives* 5 (1991); and also in William Hasker, *God, Time, and Knowledge* (Ithaca, N.Y.: Cornell University Press, 1989), chap. 2; "Middle Knowledge: A Refutation Revisited," *Faith and Philosophy* 12 (1995): 223-36; and "A New Anti-Molinist Argument," *Religious Studies* 35 (1999): 291-97. Responses to some of these arguments can be found in Freddoso's introduction to Molina's *On Divine Foreknowledge*, and in Flint's *Divine Providence*. A number of additional papers can be found in William Hasker, David Basinger and Eef Dekker, eds., *Middle Knowledge: Theory and Applications* (Frankfurt: Peter Lang, 2000).

either true counterfactuals of freedom necessarily exist or they necessarily fail to exist.)[22] And if these propositions are not possibly true this means that contrary to what we assumed earlier they are *not* logically compatible with the existence of God, and they cannot play the role assigned to them in the free-will defense.

Fortunately, that is not the end of the story. On the contrary, it is entirely possible to formulate versions of the free-will defense that do not presuppose the truth of middle knowledge. Plantinga himself, in a later writing, provides such a version, one that does not assume that God knows the truth values of counterfactuals of freedom, or indeed that any such counterfactuals are true.[23] Plantinga's argument, however, involves complex logical machinery that I have been trying to avoid, so I offer here a simpler formulation for the reader's consideration. As before, we begin with

(1) God exists and is omnipotent, omniscient and perfectly good.

The crucial second proposition will be fairly complex:

(2#) God wished to create a world with the possibility of moral good; in order to do this he created free and rational creatures and allowed them to exercise their freedom in choosing between right and wrong; it is impossible for God to allow creatures to choose freely between right and wrong and yet guarantee that they will always choose right; and some of these creatures on some occasions chose to do wrong.

These together entail once again

(3) Evil exists.

The course of action indicated in (2#) is consistent with God's perfect goodness, because of the great value of a world containing moral good. Interestingly, this version does not assume either the truth or the falsity of the theory of divine middle knowledge. However, a different account will be given of God's inability to guarantee that free creatures will always do what is right, depending on the existence or nonexistence of true counterfactuals of freedom. If there are such truths, then this inability will be the result of transworld depravity, as in Plantinga's original version. If there are

---

[22]In this respect the theory of middle knowledge is like certain unproved conjectures in mathematics: they are either necessarily true or necessarily false, but we may be quite unable, at a given time, to determine which of these is the case.

[23]Plantinga, "Self-Profile," pp. 50-52.

no such truths, then it is not in general possible for anyone, including God, to permit persons to make free decisions and at the same time guarantee in advance how they will decide. Either way, the free-will defense succeeds, and the challenge posed by the logical problem of evil is turned back. And once again, it does not matter whether or not proposition 2# is true; what is required is only that it be logically possible and consistent with God's existence and perfection.[24]

A CONCRETE LOGICAL PROBLEM OF EVIL?

Not surprisingly, some philosophers are still not satisfied. One additional point at which the reasoning behind the free-will defense has drawn objections has to do with what might be termed the "global" or "generic" character of the evil that is considered. D. Z. Phillips, responding to Stephen Davis's claim that all it takes to solve the logical problem of evil "is simply to point out the possibility (and that is all it takes, a mere possibility) that God has a good moral reason for allowing evil,"[25] replies, "Since we are dealing with logical issues, it is thought that *any* example, however simple, is sufficient to overthrow the general claim that it is never right to allow a bad state to exist. But this is only so if the logic of examples is independent of their content."[26]

Phillips, however, holds that the logic of the examples is *not* independent of content—that the lessons derived by Swinburne (for example) from a parent's willingness to have pain inflicted on a child for the purpose of getting the child's teeth repaired are not applicable to more serious instances of evil. In a somewhat similar vein Marilyn Adams states that her primary concern is with the "concrete" logical problem of evil, which has to do with the compatibility of divine goodness with "evils in the amounts and of the kind and with distributions of the sort found in the actual world."[27] (The abstract problem, in contrast, concerns merely the compat-

---

[24]I may as well admit here, however, that I do believe proposition 2# to be true, on the interpretation that does not assume divine middle knowledge.

[25]From Stephen T. Davis, "Rejoinder," in *Encountering Evil*, ed. Stephen T. Davis, 2nd ed. (Louisville: Westminster John Knox Press, 2001), p. 102.

[26]Phillips, *Problem of Evil and the Problem of God*, p. 35.

[27]Marilyn McCord Adams, *Horrendous Evils and the Goodness of God* (Ithaca, N.Y.: Cornell University Press, 1999), p. 14.

ibility of God with "some evil or other.") In order to bring the concrete problem into sharp focus, Adams singles out the category of "horrendous evils," which she defines as "evils the participation in which (that is, the doing or suffering of which) constitutes prima facie reason to doubt whether the participant's life could (given their inclusion in it) be a great good to him/her on the whole."[28] These horrendous evils then become the central theme around which her book develops.

Certainly there is some point to what Phillips and Adams are saying. But suppose we take their words to heart and attempt to address the concrete logical problem of evil. What is the argument we need to respond to? The answer to this is not immediately clear because neither of them takes the trouble to formulate for us the argument from evil that (according to them) needs to be addressed. This means that we are somewhat at a loss, lacking a clear target for our inquiries.

In the case of Phillips the implied argument may not be too hard to discern. We have already seen, in chapter two, that he takes it as a fundamental moral principle that a morally perfect person will never consent to a grave evil regardless of the greater good that might be gained or the greater evils that might be avoided by so doing. (At least, this is what I take him to be implying; unfortunately, he never formulates the principle for us himself.) But why should we accept this? In particular, why should we accept it as *logically necessary*, which it must be if it is to underwrite a logical problem of evil? Phillips seems to want to say that this is a matter of "logic" or "grammar" of our moral concepts, but this seems clearly wrong. It simply is not the case that competent language users identify as ill-formed, or as otherwise linguistically inappropriate, statements embodying the kind of consequentialist reasoning he objects to. (His argument has the peculiar consequence that his philosophical opponents—theists and atheists alike—must be considered as being not only morally misguided but linguistically incompetent!) Nor are his appeals to "our moral community" any more convincing. I am not myself aware of the existence of any actual community within which it is taken as axiomatic that consequentialist justifications for the permission of evils are ruled out from the beginning as

---

[28]Ibid., p. 26.

unacceptable, as Phillips insists they must be.[29] I am left to wonder whether the phrase "moral community" is anything more than a tendentious way of referring to just those individuals who agree with Phillips about the moral claims under discussion.

With Adams it is even more difficult to determine what is the "concrete logical argument from evil" we need to respond to. I believe, however, that an important clue can be found in the following passage:

> My contention is that God can be shown to be good to created persons if and only if God guarantees to each a life that is a great good to him/her on the whole and one in which any participation in horrors (whether as victim or perpetrator) is not merely balanced off but defeated within the context of the individual horror participant's life. . . . [T]o say that horrors are defeated . . . means that their negative value has been overcome by weaving them into a larger meaning-making framework of positive significance for the individual in question.[30]

With some trepidation, I take Adams to be asserting the following: For God to be perfectly good, God must be *good to* created (human) persons. God can be good to created persons only if each such person is guaranteed a life that is a great good to him or her on the whole, *and* any person who has participated in horrendous evil finds that this participation is not merely balanced off or compensated but is instead "defeated" in the sense indicated.

What shall we make of this? Adams has indeed identified a way in which God might conceivably be "good to" created persons, one that deserves serious consideration. But is it a *truth of logic* that God can be perfectly good only if he is good to persons in precisely the way she describes?

---

[29]If there is such a community, I would think its members would have to be very strict pacifists, so perhaps that is where we should look for the community referred to by Phillips. But then for many of us this would scarcely qualify as "our" moral community.

[30]Adams, "Afterword," in Davis, *Encountering Evil*, p. 197. Adams further elucidates the notion of the "defeat" of evils by appealing to "Roderick Chisholm's contrast between balancing off (in which value-parts bear a merely additive relation to each other and to the value of their resultant whole) and defeat (in which the negative or positive value of the part contributes to a greater positive or negative value in the whole by virtue of a relation of organic unity that the former bears to the latter)" (ibid., pp. 196-97). She requires, then, that the person's life shall be *more valuable* in consequence of the horrendous evil than it would have been without it—an extremely (and perhaps excessively) strong requirement.

I see no reason to think that it is, and so far as I can see Adams does not provide us with any reasons. As things stand, this seems to be simply an expression of her own moral opinion. (I do not imply that her moral opinions should not be taken seriously.) Furthermore, it is an opinion that will be rejected by the majority of her fellow Christians; in particular, by all those who do not share her belief in universal salvation. So if we are told that the logical problem of evil has not been adequately addressed until it is shown that God is good to all persons in the way described by Adams, I think there is just no good reason to accept this. I want to emphasize, however, that what I say here is not meant to disparage the merits of her truly remarkable book, which has breathed a lot of invigorating fresh air into the debates over the problem of evil. But I believe the cause of clarity would have been better served if she had not billed her work as a contribution to the logical problem of evil.

For all that I have said, it is impossible not to feel some sympathy for the sorts of concerns expressed by Phillips and Adams. We simply miss too much if we limit ourselves to speaking of evil in a global and generic sense. Not only do we fail to see the trees for the forest; even the forest is visible only as a dark smudge on the horizon. We need to deal with more particular evils, and kinds of evils, if we are to address some of the concerns that motivated the problem of evil in the first place. But I doubt that it will be feasible or profitable to do this under the rubric of the logical problem of evil. Alleged moral principles implying that a good God could never permit certain sorts of evil (as claimed by Phillips) or could permit them only if very special conditions are satisfied (as asserted by Adams) are very strong and are correspondingly controversial. Simply to assert that one's moral principles are true as a matter of logic and that the denial of them leads to contradiction has a strong tendency to be question-begging; such a procedure offers little hope of philosophical progress.[31] And on the other hand, the premises necessary for a positive proof of consistency, after the manner of Plantinga, will also be very strong and very controversial. (Arguments that evils of a certain sort may be part of the best creatable world

---

[31]One can of course stipulate meanings for *morally good* and *morally perfect* such that the desired conclusions follow. But this merely changes the subject: the question of interest is not what follows from such stipulated meanings of moral terms, but which moral principles are actually true.

will be ineffective against positions that reject such a consequentialist justification for the permission of evils.) We need then to find other ways to approach these topics, and doing this will be a primary goal in the remaining chapters of this book.

4

Can We Understand Creation?

Now, as there is an infinity of possible universes in the ideas of God, and as only one of them can exist, there must be a sufficient reason for the choice of God, which determines him to select one rather than another. And this reason can only be found in the fitness, in the degrees of perfection, which these worlds contain, each possible world having a right to claim existence according to the measure of perfection which it possesses. And this is the cause of the existence of the Best; namely that his wisdom makes it known to God, his goodness makes him choose it, and his power makes him produce it.

GOTTFRIED WILHELM VON LEIBNIZ, *MONADOLOGY*

In a sense, everything said up to this point is preliminary. The first chapter set out the "ground rules," so to speak, for the discussion of the problem of evil, and sketched the version of Christian theism to be defended here. The second chapter addressed the claim that in view of horrible evils such as the Holocaust any theistic response to the problem is doomed from the outset. The third chapter reviewed the debate over the claim that the existence of evil is logically incompatible with that of the theistic God and concluded that the claim is unfounded. Mere logical compatibility, however, falls far short of what theists wish to affirm and of what is demanded of them by their critics. If the world's evil, while logically consistent with the existence of God, nevertheless renders God's existence extremely *improbable* or *implausible*, then theistic belief has been defeated or at best severely damaged by the problem of evil. So a great deal of work remains to be done.

Now, however, I want to suggest that a book about the problem of evil should not be focused too exclusively on evil. This is particularly the case if in the end we wish to speak of a "triumph of God over evil." No plausible theistic view countenances evil as an entity self-existent in its own right. Rather, evil is seen as "privation of good," as the absence of some good state of affairs that would reasonably be expected to obtain. (Blindness is the absence of the power of sight in a being that would normally be able to see.) In many cases, furthermore, evil is a matter of something that is in itself good being *turned against* good, resulting in a diminution or destruction of good that would otherwise exist. (An example would be a person's using her physical strength, in itself good, to harm another person, or to destroy a beautiful and intrinsically valuable work of art.) Furthermore, theism sees evil in the context of *divine creation*, a creation which is affirmed to be "very good" (Genesis 1:31) even though there is found in that creation a great amount of evil that needs to be accounted for. Surely then some account of the goodness of creation needs to precede the enumeration of evils and the efforts at understanding them. For these reasons the present chapter is focused on the question, Can we understand creation? More precisely, can we understand the *reasons* God created, and created as he has done?

A very little reflection should convince us of the need for modesty and caution in answering this question. In asking ourselves what someone would have done or ought to have done in a certain situation, the normal procedure is to place ourselves imaginatively within that situation and to see what course of action seems to us to be called for. Obviously, though, the more remote the situation is from our actual experience, the less reliance we can place on our imagined responses to it. And yet some otherwise careful and thoughtful philosophers seem to find little or no difficulty in drawing conclusions about what would and should be done by a divine creator. William Rowe, for instance, invites us to "Suppose, for the moment, that you are an omnipotent, omniscient being" who is considering what sort of world to create.[1] Let's stop for a moment and think about what Rowe is asking us to do. Franz Kafka, in a famous story, in effect invites the reader to consider what it would be like to be transformed into a gigantic insect.[2] And it may be that, aided by Kafka's literary genius, we can just manage to imagine this. But the task of imagination set for us by Kafka pales in comparison with the one Rowe wants us to perform—to imagine oneself the majestic Creator of all things! "If *I* were the Creator God, *I* would . . ." It is to be hoped that a sense of humor (if nothing else) will come to our rescue before the end of the sentence is reached!

But if presumption and overconfidence are to be avoided, sheer agnosticism is not an acceptable alternative. If we have no idea whatever what sort of world an all-perfect God could be expected to create, then presumably we have little or no idea what is to be expected from such a God in any other circumstances—and if this is so, reflection on our topic, the problem of evil, comes abruptly to an end. On this supposition, as has often been remarked, the idea that God is *good* lacks any intelligible content. What seems to be required then is an approach that combines due caution with a willingness to make assertions, when the assertions can be warranted by clear principles and not merely by our overstretched imaginations. Even conjectures are not ruled out, but they should be clearly labeled as such and not dignified as self-evident truths.

We shall proceed by considering first the proposal of Gottfried Leibniz, set out in the epigraph for this chapter: God of necessity creates the best possible world. We then consider several ways in which this claim can be challenged, considerations which suggest that God need not, perhaps could not, create the best possible world. In particular, attention is given to an argument of William Rowe, who has argued that if God does not create the best world it is possible for him to create, God cannot be morally perfect. All of this leads to a proposal concerning the rationale of creation, a proposal that allows for divine freedom in creation and also for the real possibility that God might have decided to create nothing at all.

---

[1]William Rowe, "Can God Be Free?" *Faith and Philosophy* 19, no. 4 (October 2002): 419.

[2]Franz Kafka, "The Metamorphosis," in *Franz Kafka: The Complete Stories*, ed. Nahum M. Glatzer (New York: Schocken, 1946), pp. 89-139. Note, however, that Gregor Samsa's *mind* seems to have remained largely unaltered, at least in the earlier stages.

GOTTFRIED LEIBNIZ: GOD CREATES THE BEST POSSIBLE WORLD

One proposal that has commanded a certain amount of assent is remarkable for its simplicity: God creates the *best*—in Leibniz's terms, the "best possible world." This proposal has been extensively criticized, but before looking at the criticisms we need to consider its merits. It is based on a simple, apparently clear principle, one that has commended itself to many minds. At the same time, it embodies a prudent modesty with respect to details; the particulars concerning the best possible world need not be determined in advance. And it seems (at least it seemed to Leibniz) to offer a promising framework for theodicy: the various evils in the world are justified because they are necessary components of the world that is best overall.

There are numerous objections to this proposal. First of all, it seems to many of us simply incredible that this world, the world we actually inhabit, with all the sordid details of its history, is the best that any world could possibly be.[3] Ever since Voltaire, in the aftermath of the hugely destructive Lisbon earthquake, satirized the Leibnizian theodicy in the person of Dr. Pangloss, such a claim has been widely recognized as a liability rather than a strength for those views that affirm it. This objection seems obvious, and we need not tarry over it. There are, however, objections that are philosophically more subtle and that require further discussion. We may state them briefly as follows: (1) Is there such a thing as a single world that is the best possible? It certainly seems conceivable that there might be a number of world scenarios that would be "equal best," so that no one of them would be *the* best possible world—and there are other possibilities, as we shall see. (2) If there is a best possible world, is it within God's power to create it? On the face of it, this might seem obvious, since God is said to be all-powerful. But suppose, as Plantinga and many others (including open theists) believe, God has chosen to create persons with libertarian free will and to allow them to exercise that freedom. Then it may well be the case that in important respects how things go in the world, and many

---

[3] It is important to keep in mind that a "world," in the sense relevant here, is not a collection of objects but a comprehensive *way things could be*, a "world scenario." To say that this world is the best possible is to say that *nothing could be changed in any way* to make things better than they in fact are. As Alexander Pope said, "Whatever is, is right."

things that affect the world's goodness, will depend on the way those free creatures decide. In this situation, which world is actual will depend not only on God but also on those creatures. And if bringing about the best possible world requires the cooperation of the creatures, but in significant respects they fail to cooperate, then the best possible world will not in fact exist, in spite of God's best efforts. (3) If God is perfectly good, does this mean that he must, of necessity, create the best possible world? To many this has seemed to be an obvious implication of perfect goodness, but once again there are complications. For one thing, many theists have wanted to affirm the *freedom* of God in creating: God was free, they say, to create a world very different than this one, or indeed to create no world at all. But how can that be if God's goodness obliges him to create the one world that is best overall?

IS THERE A BEST WORLD?

All of these objections are interrelated, and sorting them out will enable us to make substantial progress in understanding our topic. We begin with the objection that there may be no single world scenario that is the best possible. That there could be multiple worlds that are equally good overall is hard to deny, especially if we consider differences between them that are relatively trivial. Suppose, for instance, a world exactly like this one, except that a single neutrino, lost in the depths of intergalactic space, is traveling on a slightly different trajectory than is the case in our world. On neither trajectory will the neutrino interact with any other particle of matter during the entire future history of the universe. (Neutrinos in any case interact only weakly with ordinary matter.) Here we have a "possible world" that is distinct from the actual world. (Remember, a possible world is a *complete* scenario, comprising everything that takes place; any change, however trivial, means that we have a different possible world.) But can we make any sense at all of the notion that one of these worlds is *better*, of greater value overall, than the other? Nevertheless, Leibniz would reject this possibility: he insists that, were there no best possible world, God would have refrained from creating at all, for there would be no "sufficient reason" for God to create in one way rather than in another. But this is a consequence of Leibniz's overly rationalistic conception of the will, a conception that we have no good reason to accept. (When you are at the grocery store and pick out one can from a row of apparently identical, equally reachable cans of Campbell's tomato soup, it makes no sense to suppose that you do so because you think taking one of those cans is *better* than taking another one.)

There are other, more interesting ways in which there might fail to be a world that is the best possible. Many theists have found the following reasoning to be plausible: Since God is infinite in majesty, power and goodness, any being created by God, indeed any universe created by God, necessarily falls short of God in these respects. There is always, so to speak, metaphysical "room" between even the most excellent of creatures and God—which is to say that, for any world God could create, there is another, better world he could create; the goodness of possible worlds (like the series of prime numbers) has no upper bound. One relatively simple way to cash this out is in terms of the sheer number of good things the universe contains. Consider a universe in which there are, say, ten billion free and rational creatures who enjoy lives that are excellent in every respect—physically, mentally, socially, morally, spiritually and so on. Wouldn't a universe containing twenty billion such creatures, all with equally good lives and with no significant increase in disvalue and evil, be even better? If not, why not? Still another possibility is suggested by Thomas Morris, who writes, "Some world *A* might be better than rival world *B* in some respect, but with *B* surpassing *A* in others, and the relevant values not such that they could be summed over and compared overall."[4] In other words, the different values that can be realized in a possible world may be *incommensurable* in the sense that there is no common measure, no fixed "ratio" as it were, by which they can be measured against one another. I believe this is a very important suggestion, one which has been underappreciated, and we shall return to it shortly.

GOD'S ABILITY TO CREATE A WORLD

Next, we consider God's ability to create the best possible world—or leaving aside for the moment the question as to whether there *is* a best world,

---

[4]Thomas V. Morris, "Perfection and Creation," in *Reasoned Faith,* ed. Eleonore Stump (Ithaca, N.Y.: Cornell University Press, 1993), pp. 236-37.

God's ability to create any particular world he might select. Here it is crucial what assumptions we make concerning freedom, indeterminacy and contingency in the world. Consider, first of all, theological determinism, the view according to which everything that transpires is necessarily determined by a unilateral, efficacious divine decree. On this assumption, it is quite true that God is able to bring about any world scenario he might choose to make actual. (God's goodness might prevent him from choosing certain otherwise possible worlds, but that is a different matter.) Leibniz, a theological determinist through and through, was not wrong in reaching this conclusion.

Many of us, however, subscribe to libertarian free will, which means that in certain situations persons are really able, and have it entirely in their power, to perform any of two or more possible actions. Either of these outcomes is *really possible;* which actually occurs depends entirely on the decision freely made by the person at that time. If God creates a world with this kind of freedom, then he voluntarily *gives up* part of his own power to determine how things go in that world. This of course is the central idea of the free-will defense, and it means that there may be very desirable world scenarios that God is unable to realize because the free creatures simply will not respond as they would need to for those scenarios to become actual.

If we do subscribe to libertarian freedom, there is yet another "branching point" that we must take note of. Suppose, on the one hand, that God possesses middle knowledge, as assumed in the standard version of the free-will defense. In that case God knows, prior to his decision to create a particular sort of world, exactly how all the free creatures in that world would react to each of the situations in which they would find themselves.[5] These reactions may not, in many cases, be what God would most desire, but he knows exactly what the reactions would be and is able to plan the rest of the world history accordingly. On this supposition God may not get everything he wants, but he can count on getting exactly the world he plans for.

---

[5]The priority referred to here is logical priority, priority in the order of explanation; it may or may not involve also temporal priority.

Suppose, on the other hand, that the doctrine of middle knowledge is false and that there are no true counterfactuals of freedom. On this supposition, the future is "open" in a much more radical way. On this assumption it is impossible for God to know, prior to a decision to create certain persons and place them in certain situations, exactly how those persons will respond to the choices they will have to make. Because of this, it is not possible for God to select a particular possible world and guarantee that just that world will become actual. Rather, God selects what we might term a *broad world type;* he decides what sort of world environment to create, and what sorts of creatures there will be in that environment, but the rest of the history is brought about jointly by God and the free persons he has created. To be sure, God's subsequent actions may play a very important role in shaping the direction of events, but the particular way things will go cannot be known in detail even by God prior to his decision about what sort of world type he will create.

At this point I anticipate an objection: *Of course* God will know the outcome of his creative decisions; after all, he is omniscient, is he not? Actually, this implication drawn from divine omniscience is controversial. Open theists, and some others, hold that the contingent future, being as yet indeterminate, is intrinsically unknowable; failure to know the future in detail is no more a defect in divine omniscience than inability to create a square circle is a defect in omnipotence. But suppose this is wrong and God does know the future in full detail. Still, it must be kept in mind that we are assuming that there are no true counterfactuals of freedom and no divine middle knowledge. What God knows, then, is not that *if he were to create* the universe in such-and-such a way, these are the free decisions that the creatures *would make* under those circumstances. Knowing that would require middle knowledge, which by supposition God does not have. What God knows, rather, are the *actual* decisions that will be made by the *actual* persons he will create, in the actual situations they will find themselves in. But this in turn means that in the order of logical dependence (though not in the order of temporal succession) God's knowledge of the outcome of his creative decision comes *after* the decision has been made; it is not available beforehand to guide that decision. God cannot, then, select a particular possible world and make the creative decisions necessary to actualize that world. On the contrary, it is only *as a consequence of* the creative decisions God *actually makes* that he comes to know which possible world will become actual as a result of those decisions. Furthermore, this same limitation applies to divine timeless knowledge so long as this is not supplemented with either theological determinism or middle knowledge. In the order of logical dependence, it will still be the case that God's timeless knowledge of the consequences of his creative acts is subsequent to and dependent upon his logically prior decision to create in a certain way.

To summarize, then, we have three possibilities: If theological determinism is necessarily true then God can indeed make actual any logically possible world he may choose.[6] And given divine goodness, if there is a best possible world we might assume that this is the one that will be chosen. If there is both libertarian free will and divine middle knowledge, God cannot choose to create just any possible world but he can select for actualization any of the possible worlds that are "feasible," that is, that are permitted by those counterfactuals of freedom that are actually true. If there is libertarian freedom and no middle knowledge, then God will choose a "world type" for creation—presumably, a world type containing rich possibilities for the realization of important values—but God cannot guarantee in advance which total world scenario will result from his choice.

ROBERT ADAMS AND WILLIAM ROWE: MUST GOD CREATE THE BEST?

It has seemed evident to many that if God creates any world at all, then in virtue of his perfect goodness he will create the best world it is possible for him to create. Robert Adams, however, has challenged this conclusion. In an important article,[7] he argues that the Judeo-Christian theist "must hold that the actual world is a good world. But he need not maintain that it is

---

[6]Note that, to obtain this result, divine determinism must be *necessarily* true. If it is only contingently true (if, for example, God has simply chosen not to create a world containing free creatures), then there will be possible (but nonactual) worlds containing free creatures, and God's ability to make these worlds actual will be limited in the ways discussed earlier.

[7]Robert Adams, "Must God Create the Best?" *Philosophical Review* 81 (July 1972): 317-32; reprinted in Robert Adams, *The Virtue of Faith* (New York: Oxford University Press, 1987), pp. 51-64 (page references are to this volume). For a critique of Adams's argument, see Mark L. Thomas, "Robert Adams and the Best Possible World," *Faith and Philosophy* 13, no. 2 (April 1996): 252-59.

the best of all possible worlds, or the best world that God could have made."[8] (Adams does not himself believe that there is a best possible world, but he accepts that possibility in conducting the present argument.) In arguing for this, Adams urges the importance of the divine attribute of *grace*, which he defines as "a disposition to love which is not dependent on the merit of the person loved." Grace, he observes is portrayed in the Judeo-Christian tradition as "a virtue which God does have and men ought to have."[9] But if God is required by his goodness to create the best world he can, then God is constrained in his decision to create by the goodness of the potential creatures, and his exercise of grace in choosing which persons to create is excluded.

Adams's argument deserves careful consideration, but I do not believe he has fully established his conclusion. Unlike Adams, I believe that if we grant the existence of a best world, we will be hard pressed to make sense of the notion that God might create some other world instead. The problem is not that God is *obligated* to create the best world; Adams has made a strong case that no such obligation obtains. Nor is it that God would be deficient in goodness or in love were he to refrain from creating the best world. But I think it will be very difficult to make such a choice on God's part rationally intelligible: what possible *reason* could God have for creating an inferior world instead of the best? According to Adams, the graciousness of God in creation "implies that there is nothing in God's nature or character which would require him to act on the principle of choosing the best possible creatures to be the object of his creative powers."[10] Nevertheless, the concept of grace provides no *reason* why God would choose to create less than the best. As Mark Thomas has pointed out, the notion of grace is neutral with regard to which world God creates; it does not provide a reason for which God might create some world other than the best possible.[11] Adams has suggested that "the desire to create and love all of a certain group of possible creatures . . . might be an adequate ground for a perfectly good God to create them. . . . And they need not be the best of

---

[8]Adams, "Must God Create the Best?" p. 51.

[9]Ibid., p. 56.

[10]Ibid., p. 57.

[11]Thomas, "Robert Adams and the Best Possible World," p. 255.

all possible creatures, or included in the best of all possible worlds."[12] Now, no doubt if God were to create a group of creatures that were neither the best possible creatures nor included in the best possible world, God would love them without regret for the better creatures and better world he might have created instead. But his loving those creatures *presupposes* his having chosen to create them; it can't be used to *explain* that choice. (Prior to his making the decision, there *are no* creatures for God to love; there is only a set of abstract possibilities.) A possible explanation for such a choice is precisely what we need but have so far failed to discover.

It might be suggested that God might make such a choice in view of the *properties* of the world created or of the creatures comprised in it, properties God especially desires to see exemplified. Without question, human beings are sometimes attached to particular qualitative features of an envisioned situation and may without irrationality desire that situation to become actual because of those features even though they acknowledge that some alternative situation might be objectively better. ("I know Beethoven is a greater composer than Rachmaninov, but I just *prefer* listening to Rachmaninov's music.") But this sort of partiality and idiosyncratic preference, while understandable in a human being, is very difficult to attribute to the Lord and Creator of all things. God will not have a nonrational attachment to some one value in preference to other objectively superior values. Nor will it be the case for him, as it sometimes is for us, that the greater values are either beyond his grasp or make excessive demands on his energy and attention in order to be properly appreciated. Why then would he not choose them?

It begins to look, therefore, as though in creating a world that was not the best possible, God would be acting in a way that is not only unmotivated but also flies in the face of a motivation that everyone is bound to acknowledge. For surely, that a world is the best possible gives God at least *some* reason to choose it in preference to others. If the concept of grace really does imply that it is possible for God to ignore this reason and create an inferior world without any countervailing reason to do so, that might be a good reason to reconsider our affirmation of divine grace in creation.

---

[12]Adams, "Must God Create the Best?" p. 55.

But the implication follows only if there is in fact a best possible world. So it seems that in order to make room for the exercise of divine grace in creation we need to consider the possibility that there is no best possible world.[13]

Of the various reasons why there might be no best possible world, I believe the notion that there might be "equal best" worlds is relatively unpromising. For one thing, if God's choice is limited to a set of equal best worlds, it is still strongly constrained by the merits of the worlds he might choose, which runs counter to the rationale given by Adams for the importance of grace in creation. It is doubtful, furthermore, that considering only equal best worlds will provide a very broad scope for the exercise of divine choice. If we think of worlds that differ only in the most trivial respects (as with the world containing a single neutrino on a different path), then a choice between such worlds will also be trivial. But if we think of worlds that differ in more significant ways, it seems likely that divine wisdom would after all be able to discern differences in value between them, even if we in our ignorance are unable to do so. At best, the choices afforded to God on this assumption would seem to be quite limited.

Partly for these reasons, there has been considerable interest in the idea that possible worlds form an ascending series in terms of value, with no upper bound. In this case each world would be recommended by its superiority over the worlds lower on the scale of value, but each world would also suffer by comparison with worlds higher on the scale, so no world stands out as the uniquely appropriate world to be chosen. Arguably, then, any one of them, above some minimum acceptable level, would be available as an object of divine choice, thus affording great scope for divine freedom and for the exercise of grace. (Contrary to Leibniz, a wise agent who has reason to choose one from a group of alternatives, but no reason to choose one in preference to the others, will choose arbitrarily and be none the less rational for doing so. It is not a mark of superior rationality to imitate Buridan's ass, who starved to death equidistant between two equally appealing piles of hay, unable to choose between them!)

---

[13]I believe that the considerations developed here are very much in the spirit of Adams's work, even though he believes he does not need to appeal to them to establish his own conclusions.

An interesting objection to this scenario has been raised by William Rowe, who argues that rather than an infinite series of better and better worlds offering wide scope for the exercise of divine freedom, such a series is logically incompatible with the existence of the theistic God.[14] Rowe maintains: "There is an impossibility in the idea both that there exists an infinite series of increasingly better creatable worlds and that there also exists an unsurpassably good, omnipotent, omniscient being who creates one of these worlds."[15] In support of this claim, Rowe articulates a general principle:

> (B) If an omniscient being creates a world when there is a better world it could have created, then it is possible that there exist a being morally better than it.[16]

A little reflection shows that if principle (B) is accepted, Rowe's conclusion is inescapable: no matter which world God creates, there will always be a better world he could have created, so under such circumstances no creator can be unsurpassably good, as God is claimed to be. It also follows from principle (B) ("slightly extended," as Rowe says) that God cannot fail to create any world at all. For, given that there are good worlds God could create, by creating no world at all (we might term this the "null world"), God would be doing less good than he could do. In short, "if the actual world is not the best world that an omnipotent, omniscient being could create, God does not exist."[17]

It has been objected by Norman Kretzmann and Thomas Morris that given the no-best-world scenario the requirement imposed by principle (B)

---

[14]See William Rowe, "The Problem of Divine Perfection and Freedom," in *Reasoned Faith*, ed. Eleonore Stump (Ithaca, N.Y.: Cornell University Press, 1993), pp. 223-33; "The Problem of No Best World," *Faith and Philosophy* 11, no. 2 (1994): 269-71; "Can God Be Free?" *Faith and Philosophy* 19, no. 4 (2002): 405-24; and his book, *Can God Be Free?* (Oxford: Clarendon, 2004) (page references in the text of this section refer to this volume). For responses see Thomas V. Morris, "Perfection and Creation," in Stump, *Reasoned Faith*, pp. 234-47; Daniel Howard-Snyder and Frances Howard-Snyder, "How an Unsurpassable Being Can Create a Surpassable World," *Faith and Philosophy* 11, no. 2 (1994): 260-68; and Daniel Howard-Snyder and Frances Howard-Snyder, "The *Real* Problem of No Best World," *Faith and Philosophy* 13, no. 3 (1996): 422-25. My own previous responses may be found in "*Can God Be Free?* Rowe's Dilemma for Theology," *Religious Studies* 41 (2005): 453-62; and *Providence, Evil, and the Openness of God* (London: Routledge, 2004), chap. 11 and pp. 202-6.
[15]Rowe, *Can God Be Free?* p. 103.
[16]Ibid., p. 97.
[17]Ibid., p. 89.

is unreasonable, since it amounts to requiring God to do something logically impossible. Thus Morris says:

> But failing to do the best you can is a flaw or manifests an incompleteness in moral character . . . only if doing the best you can is at least a logical possibility. If doing the best he can in creating a world is for God an impossibility, given the range of omnipotence and the nature of those considerations making the notion of a best of all possible worlds an incoherence, then not doing his best in creating cannot be seen as a flaw or as manifesting an incompleteness in the character of God.[18]

Rowe forcefully rejects this reasoning. He writes:

> Morris's basic mistake, I believe, is his view, shared by Kretzmann, that to hold, as I do, that if there is no best world for a being to create then no being can create a world and be a being than which a better creator is impossible, just is to hold God accountable for not doing what is logically impossible to be done—creating the best world.

After quoting the passage from Morris previously cited, he continues:

> Of course, if it is logically impossible for there to be a best world, then God's not creating the best possible world does not count against his perfect goodness. Nowhere do I suggest that it does. What counts against God's perfect goodness (specifically, his moral perfection) is his creating a world when he could have created a world better than it.[19]

This point needs to be carefully examined. In addition to (B), Rowe has embraced the following principle:

> (A) If S is a logically impossible state of affairs, then the fact that a being does not bring about S does not entail that the being in question lacks power or perfect goodness.[20]

Principle (A) is unassailable. Any view that finds a person deficient in power or goodness because of a failure to bring about a logically impossible state of affairs can be dismissed out of hand. But now we must ask, what exactly is the state of affairs that, according to principle (B), God must bring

---

[18]Morris, "Perfection and Creation," p. 244.
[19]Rowe, *Can God Be Free?* p. 101.
[20]Ibid., p. 91.

about in order that God may not show himself lacking in perfect goodness? One might suppose, from some of the things Rowe says, that the answer is, *God must "do better than he did" in creating, that is, he must create a
world better than the world that actually exists.* This, however, would be a
mistake. To see why, consider the following scenario: There exists an endless series of better and better possible worlds, and our world, the world
that actually exists, is number 3,001 in the series. Now, what world should
God have created in order to show himself free from moral defect? Well,
to start with, he must have created some world better than this one—for
instance, world 5,023. But suppose God had in fact created world 5,023:
could God then, according to principle (B), be judged free of moral defect?
The answer, of course, is no, because *it would still be the case that God failed
to create a better world than he did.* That is to say, there is another world God
could have created, but did not, that would have been better than the world
he actually created. Merely creating a world better than this one would be
entirely insufficient, according to Rowe's principle (B), to clear God from
the charge that he is morally deficient.

What is it then that God would have to do in order to show himself free
from moral defect? The answer is quite clear: God must *prevent it being the
case that he created a world such that there is a better world that he could have
created instead.* Or, to revert to principle (A), the state of affairs God must
bring about is, *it not being the case that God created a world such that there is
a better world he could have created.* If God were to bring *this* state of affairs
into existence, he would be morally in the clear, at least so far as principle
(B) is concerned.

But now let's ask, Is it in fact logically possible for God to bring about
*it not being the case that God created a world such that there is a better world he
could have created?* The answer, as Rowe clearly sees, is no. No matter
which world God chose to create—3,001 or 5,023 or 1,713,221—it would
still be the case that there is another, better world he could have created instead. But this means that the task assigned to God by principle (B) is logically impossible, and according to principle (A) God's failure to bring this
about does *not* show that he lacks power or goodness. But principle (B) entails that God for that very reason is *not* perfectly good. It follows that if
principle (A) is true, and there is an endless series of better and better pos-

sible worlds, principle (B) is false. And with the abandonment of principle (B), Rowe's argument collapses.

Over and above the difficulty already noted, principle (B) is problematic as an ethical principle. It asserts a connection between a person's moral goodness and the sorts of actions the person will perform, and in general such a connection seems plausible. ("The good person out of the good treasure of the heart produces good, and the evil person out of evil treasure produces evil" [Luke 6:45].) But principle (B) goes well beyond this commonsense notion, in that the amount of good produced is taken, other things being equal, to be an *accurate quantitative measure* of moral goodness, so that a truly good person will of necessity produce as much good as she or he possibly can. This way of thinking has its home in the ethical theory of utilitarianism, the theory that says that the morally right action is always what brings about "the greatest good of the greatest number" and measures moral goodness, other things being equal, in terms of the amount of good produced. Most theists, however, reject utilitarianism as a moral theory, and this means they have good reason to reject a principle such as (B), even apart from the problem already discussed. Thomas Morris offers a plausible counterexample to this tight connection between the production of good and moral virtue:

> Suppose that I give you five dollars. I could have given you ten, but I give you five. Suppose you do not particularly need the gift . . . it's a pure supererogation on my part. . . . If someone else instead had given you ten dollars, would it have been the case that she did a better deed than I? Would she therefore, all else equal, have been a better person than I? I'm not convinced that this follows at all. And it's not just because it's my generosity and stature we're discussing.[21]

Additional counterexamples will emerge in our subsequent discussion.

In view of the failure of Rowe's objection, the idea of God's choosing a world to create from an endless series of better and better worlds remains a viable option. Yet I think an even more promising line emerges from the remaining option for the no-best-world hypothesis: the idea that different possible worlds contain values that are *incommensurable*, so that there is no

---

[21]Morris, "Perfection and Creation," p. 241.

absolute ranking of their respective merits. In order to prepare the way for considering this, I digress briefly on the importance of this idea for the understanding of human choice and action. An important role has been played in discussions of free will by *psychological determinism*, the view that "we always act on the strongest motive." (Recently among philosophers psychological determinism has tended to be displaced by physical determinism, but I believe it still plays a significant role in popular thinking about the topic.) A common rejoinder to this is that we do not in general have any way to ascertain, before the fact, what the "strongest motive" in a given situation may be. (If we take the strongest motive to be the strongest *felt inclination*, then experience shows that we do not, in fact, always act on this.) What is done in practice is to see which action actually results and then declare the motive or combination of motives leading in that direction to be the strongest. But this means that the claim that we act on the strongest motive is empirically vacuous and provides no evidential support at all for determinism.

This rejoinder succeeds in depriving psychological determinism of empirical support. But to support a robust doctrine of free will, I believe something stronger is required. It is not enough that the claim that we act on the strongest motive is empirically unsupported; what is needed is that, at least on certain occasions, there shall *be* no such thing as the "strongest motive." For suppose, on the contrary, that in any given situation all of our motivations do exist in a determinate rank order, from the weakest to the strongest (perhaps with occasional ties). An advocate of libertarian freedom will want to say that we need not, and in fact do not, always act on the strongest motive. But it is hard to make sense of this; what could explain our failure so to act, given that the motives do have a determinate rank ordering to begin with? Caprice, perhaps—but caprice is a poor foundation for a doctrine of free will, and in any case the wish to be capricious could easily be reckoned as just another motive, counterpoised against whatever motive or combination of motives would otherwise be the strongest.

Fortunately, there is no need to assume that motives possess determinate levels of strength in advance of the decision process. Sometimes, to be sure, there is an obvious imbalance in the strength of our motivation for different courses of action; considered briefly, it becomes clear to us that what we "really" want to do is so-and-so, and that the impulse to do such-and-such instead is weak and should be disregarded. But in many of our most significant decisions, what happens is that *we ourselves determine* the degree of importance given to various motives; it is we who "give weight" to the motives, and in doing so we "make up our minds" what to do. One way we do this is simply by directing our attention one way or another; by focusing on a particular motive we impart to it a vividness and forcefulness it would not otherwise possess. And on the other hand we sometimes make a considerable effort to "block out of our minds" a motive we perceive as a temptation to do something other than what we recognize as best. A full description of this process is beyond my ability, but the reader is challenged to consider for him- or herself whether this is not the sort of thing that actually occurs. Is this not, in fact, a more realistic description of the decision process than is given by the assumption that motives have definite weights in advance, and that actually reaching a decision is merely a matter of seeing how the motives, with their predetermined weights and rankings, balance out against each other?

If this is a reasonably realistic picture of human decision making, we can go on to ask, *why shouldn't this be true of God as well?* Why may it not be that, for God as for us humans, certain choices are antecedently indeterminate, in that there *does not exist*, prior to the actual making of the decision, a fully determinate ranking of the values to be realized? Why may it not be that, as Morris has proposed, "Some world *A* might be better than rival world *B* in some respect, but with *B* surpassing *A* in others, and the relevant values not such that they could be summed over and compared overall"? We might be tempted to think that even if we humans are unable to discern which value or set of values is the best attainable in a given situation, surely God in his wisdom must be able to discern this. But to say this is to beg precisely the point at issue, which is *whether there is in fact any such determinate ranking to be discerned.* If the ranking does not exist, then what will be discerned by divine wisdom is precisely that—that the ranking does not exist. But this opens up a wide field for the exercise of divine freedom, in which God *chooses* which values shall be realized and which shall predominate when competing values are in conflict, and brings about the sort of world in which the desired fulfillment can occur.

This should not be thought to imply that there is no objective truth concerning values. Some things really are good, some things really are bad, and no one's decisions—not even God's—will ever make it otherwise. It is better that persons flourish and grow to maturity than that they waste their lives in pursuit of meaningless pleasures. Love and compassion are objectively better than hatred and cruelty. It is not the case, however, that there exists an "axiological exchange rate," a set of quasi-monetary equivalences, that states (for example) exactly how much pain is worth being endured for some particular achievement. We do encounter situations where it is extremely plausible that there is no objectively correct answer to questions of comparative value. Consider, for example, the competing personality traits of venturesomeness and caution. We can say, to be sure, that a person would miss too much by always "playing it safe"; there is much to be gained by taking some risks, and the willingness to do so is rightly considered a valuable and admirable quality. And on the other hand, a person who takes very serious risks for negligible rewards is unwise. But in between the two extremes there is a large territory in which we would be bold indeed to assert that there is a definite "right answer." And so it is, I want to say, with a great many situations in which different sorts of values are compared and choices made between them.

UNDERSTANDING CREATION

Can we understand the divine act of creation? In one sense, clearly not. The notion of our being able to think in the same way the Creator of the universe would think is ludicrous or terrifying or both at once. Once lost in those depths, supposing we could ever get there, we might never emerge with sanity intact. But can we arrive at some very limited understanding, however thin and abstract, of the conceptual structure of a decision to create a world? Perhaps we can; that at least has been our aim in this chapter. We began with Leibniz's notion of God as creating the best of all possible worlds and explored the multiple objections to this notion. If God is to be free and gracious in his creative acts, it cannot be the case that he is tied by necessity to a single creatable world. If human beings are to be free and responsible, their freedom will constitute a limitation, self-imposed by God, on God's ability to bring about any possible world he might desire. (It is part of God's greatness and generosity that he both wishes and is able to create other beings who along with him determine the outcome of his creation.) We also explored three distinct reasons why there may be no such thing as a single best world for God to create. Now the time has come to fit these considerations together as best we can—but still, I trust, with a measure of the humility and intellectual modesty demanded by the topic.

My commitment to open theism as a way of understanding the God-world relationship has already been stated. Theological determinism is emphatically rejected, not least because of the difficulty—the insuperable difficulty, as I believe—it creates for any attempt to deal constructively with the problem of evil. If theological determinism is true, then everything whatsoever that takes place, including all the evil, suffering, degradation and injustice the world contains, is exactly as God wants it to be in every respect. This contradicts a great deal of what is said in the Bible, which repeatedly and emphatically insists that many things are *not* as God wishes them to be. It also, in my estimation, creates a terminally intractable problem for anyone who wishes to give some rationally intelligible account of the world's evil that is consistent with the power, wisdom and goodness of God. No doubt this is a topic in which mystery is unavoidable, but on a deterministic view mystery takes over right from the beginning and no light of reason can be thrown into the resulting darkness.

Molinism, the theory of divine middle knowledge, is also rejected. This view also makes the problem of evil considerably more difficult than it would otherwise be, though not by any means as difficult as it is for theological determinism. (This point will be argued in later chapters.) But there are also serious metaphysical problems for the theory of middle knowledge, including but not limited to the "grounding problem" referred to in chapter three (see pp. 66-67). These points have been argued in detail elsewhere, and the arguments will not be repeated here.[22]

From these assumptions it follows that God's creative choice is not a choice of a particular possible world (or world scenario) but rather of a world type: God puts in place the initial "furniture of the world" (perhaps

---

[22]See the references in the previous chapter.

the starting point for a process of cosmic evolution), and the resulting scenario is determined jointly by God and the creatures. But how can we
think about the selection of a world type? It would seem that all three of
the sorts of considerations that rule out the existence of a single best possible world also apply to world types as well: world types also could conceivably be tied as "equal best" or could form a never-ending ascending series with respect to the value they contain, or they could contain
incommensurable values and combinations of values. So we need to see
how these ingredients fit into our picture.

Here again it seems that the possibility of ties between world types in
their overall evaluation exists but is of relatively minor importance. If the
world types differ only in trivial respects, then the choices between them
will be trivial and may well be entirely arbitrary, whereas in cases where
there is a significant difference between world types it seems unlikely that,
for supreme wisdom, there will be exact parity in overall value. If we wish
to find significant scope for the exercise of divine freedom in creation, we
need to look elsewhere.

The possibility of world types forming an ascending series of value, with
no upper bound, also seems a genuine one. Here the straightforward quantitative argument seems compelling: a world with twenty billion very happy
inhabitants contains more happiness and (other things being equal) more
value overall than a world with only ten billion. And for infinite creative
power, no limitation is imposed by overcrowding or the exhaustion of resources, since more room and more resources can be called into being by divine fiat. In such cases, I want to say, an arbitrary or random choice of the
quantity of good things to be created is entirely acceptable; mere quantitative
increase does not mean that the creative act is a better act or the creative
agent a better agent. To support this claim I offer two hypothetical cases
drawn from human experience (which is the only resource we have available); one is taken from Robert Adams, and one is of my own devising.

First my own example, drawn from the field of art history. As we know,
among the great artists there are some (such as Leonardo) who produced relatively few works, whereas others have been astonishingly prolific. Notable
among the latter is the English painter and watercolorist J. M. W. Turner,
who during his lifetime turned out huge numbers of paintings, mostly wa-

tercolors. Indeed, in his later years he had virtually saturated the market for his work, though some collectors still welcomed his latest creations.[23] These works are almost all of very high quality and give great pleasure today to art lovers who contemplate them. Now, suppose that, over his lifetime, Turner had produced at a slower rate and had turned out, say, 15 percent fewer paintings than he actually produced. Would Turner have been "less good" had he done so? Would he have been a less good artist or a less good human being? Would he have been *morally* a less good person than in fact he was? I can see no basis whatever for any of these judgments. By the same token, I think there is no reason to suppose that God would be less good a Creator or morally deficient in any way were he to create the world type containing "only" ten billion rather than twenty billion very happy people.

And now Adams's example:

> Grace and Patience . . . are (fictitious) sisters. They are extremely similar in their good qualities. In particular, they both have many fine friendships. But Patience spends a certain portion of her spare time lying on the beach, idly and alone, not thinking deep thoughts but just relaxing, which she enjoys very much. Grace, not having this taste for sunbathing, has time for a few more friendships than Patience.
>
> Fine friendships are excellent; and I think Patience's sunbathing is much less excellent. The excellence of fine friendship is exemplified more frequently in Grace's life than in Patience's, without any counterbalancing excellence in Patience's life that is absent from Grace's. Nonetheless, I think it would be an unreasonable excess of ethical earnestness to judge that for this reason Grace's life is more excellent on the whole, or better for the one who is living it, than Patience's, let alone that the total state of affairs would be better if Patience were more like Grace. This is not to deny that Patience's life would be poorer if she had no friendships. It is also not to deny that each of Grace's additional friendships is individually excellent. Trouble begins when we assume that things that are individually excellent must have quantities of excellence that can be added together to produce a greater excellence.[24]

---

[23]Evelyn Joll, "The Market for Turner's Finished Watercolours in His Lifetime," in *Turner: The Great Watercolours,* Eric Shanes with essays by Evelyn Joll, Ian Warrell and Andrew Wilton (London: Royal Academy of Arts, 2000), pp. 26-31.
[24]Robert M. Adams, *Finite and Infinite Goods: A Framework for Ethics* (Oxford: Oxford University Press, 1999), p. 119.

Here Adams eloquently and, I think, persuasively rejects the "book-keeping" perspective on the quantitative addition of values that is implicit in the "more is better" evaluation of possible worlds God could create. If we wish to properly appreciate the divine act of creation, we should leave our green eyeshades at home!

When we are comparing quantities of essentially the same good, an arbitrary or random choice of the amount of good to be produced (given certain very broad constraints) seems entirely acceptable. When on the other hand we are considering diverse sorts of value, it is preferable to go with Morris's suggestion that such values are incommensurable. This should not be taken to mean that no comparison at all is possible between such diverse values; we have noted Adams's acknowledgment that the excellence of friendship exceeds that of sunbathing. But there is no fixed ratio, no formula, which determines in advance how much of value A should be traded off for a certain amount of value B. It seems evident that this perspective, in addition to being necessary for a robust doctrine of free will for human beings, offers wide scope for the exercise of freedom in God's creative choices concerning the world. Once we have thoroughly assimilated this perspective, we find ourselves much closer than before to the traditional understanding of God's freedom in creation; the Leibnizian notion of God's choices being predetermined by a fixed scale of values recedes from view.

It would, however, be presumptuous in the extreme for me to set out at this point a list of the values between which God chooses, together with illustrations of the choices and tradeoffs between them. I do not think we are wholly in the dark as to what God values in his creation, and in coming chapters we will be talking about some of these values so far as they are apprehensible by us. But it is more than likely that some of the excellences perceived by God are beyond our grasp, at least in our present state and perhaps permanently so. And even in the case of those forms of excellence we do have some grasp of, it would be rash to assume that we understand them fully enough to assess their place in the ultimate scheme of things. (Consider the changes in our understanding of natural processes over the last few centuries—and our conceptions of the nature and ordering of human societies have undergone large changes as well.)

Finally, what of the possibility that God might not create at all? No doubt this is the most difficult point at which to defend divine freedom. We can't be expected to feel great enthusiasm for the possibility that we might never have been created, any more than children can be expected to respond positively to the reasons that might have led their parents to remain single and childless. Nevertheless, I believe a plausible case can be made on this point also. The task is to represent the precreation situation in such a way as to make it plausible that God might very well have chosen not to alter it, so that the "actual world" would have consisted of God and nothing else. We are hindered in this not only by a bias in favor of our own existence but by the extreme poverty of our grasp of such a situation. Even our ideas about God, in Scripture and religious practice, are overwhelmingly ideas of God in relation to us and to the rest of the creation. What we must assert, however, is that this is a poverty in *our understanding* of the precreation situation and not a lack in God's own life.[25] We are, in fact, more than a little like small children in school, who often have great difficulty in grasping the fact that their teacher has a life of her own, separate from what she does in teaching them.

Nevertheless, the Christian revelation offers important help precisely on this point. I am referring, of course, to the doctrine of the Trinity, a doctrine rooted in the historical revelation that affords us an important (though extremely limited) insight into the life of God apart from creation. The understanding that there exists, from all eternity, a relationship of love and communion between the persons of the Trinity, Father, Son and Holy Spirit, offers at least a hint of an understanding of the richness of the divine life within itself and apart from creation. Thus Karl Barth writes:

> In order not be to alone, single, enclosed within Himself, God did not need co-existence with the creature. He does not will and posit the creature necessarily, but in freedom, as the basic act of His grace. . . . For everything that the creature seems to offer Him—its otherness, its being in antithesis to Himself and therefore His own existence in co-existence—He has also in Himself as God.[26]

---

[25]This is in contrast with process theism, which holds that apart from creation God's life would be greatly impoverished.

[26]Karl Barth, *Church Dogmatics* 4/1, trans. G. W. Bromiley (Edinburgh: T & T Clark, 1956), p. 201.

In a similar vein, Emil Brunner writes, "Only if, in Himself, from all eternity, God *is* the Loving One, no world is needed for Him to be the Loving One. . . . From all Eternity He loves His Son, and therefore through His Son He creates the world."[27] It seems especially appropriate to cite Barth and Brunner on this point because both of them are emphatically opposed to a "natural theology," a speculative, rational knowledge of God that is independent of revelation. Yet both of them affirm the intratrinitarian love of God, as Father, Son and Holy Spirit, wholly apart from God's involvement with the world in creation and redemption.

We may affirm then that the life of God is completely rich, fulfilling and satisfying without reference to creation, and therefore that God has no need whatever for a created world in order for the divine life to be complete and perfect. Insofar as it makes sense to quantify such matters, we may say that God's life is infinitely satisfying, and the satisfaction cannot be increased by anything that might be added by a created order. Creation, we insist, is a free and gracious act on God's part. It may seem, however, that open theism is at a disadvantage on this point in comparison with more traditional theology. The traditional doctrine of divine impassibility, strictly understood, entails that God cannot be affected by creatures in any way; thus it is self-evident that a creation cannot be "needed" for the fulfillment of God's life. But in rejecting impassibility, open theism affirms that God *is* affected—that he is pleased or displeased, rejoices or suffers, as a result of what happens in the creation. And so it would seem (assuming the value of creation is positive overall) that the creation does make possible an enrichment of God's life—that God's existence is, we might say, qualitatively enhanced even if, considered quantitatively, it is already infinitely satisfying. And if this is so, how can it be intelligible that God might have failed to create?

It must be admitted that the doctrine of divine impassibility does make things easier at this point, though the advantage is one for which a heavy price must be paid. Since we reject impassibility, we have to pose the question, If it is true that God had something to gain by creating a world, what

---

[27]Emil Brunner, *The Christian Doctrine of God*, trans. Olive Wyon (Philadelphia: Westminster Press, 1950), p. 228.

possibilities of *loss for God* are entailed by the decision to create? Once we have decided to ask this question, answers are not too difficult to come by. There is, first, the simple point that in deciding to create, God brings about the existence of a realm of *imperfection*, whereas without creation there is only the perfection of the divine life itself. And surely it isn't self-evident that "perfection plus imperfection" is better than perfection all by itself. It's true, of course, that *for us* perfection is fully appreciated only by way of contrast with that which is imperfect. But God doesn't need imperfection in order to appreciate his own perfection—and without creation, there is no one else who needs this either. Furthermore, it is rather plausible that the more valuable sorts of worlds God might have created all involve free and rational creatures—creatures capable of voluntary friendship with God, but also capable of opposing God, and in the process causing grievous harm to others as well as themselves, bringing grief and suffering into God's own life. The risk of this happening was far from negligible (as is all too obvious), and surely it is far from self-evident that a rational deity would undertake the risk. On this point, we can learn something from the friends of divine middle knowledge, such as Thomas Flint:

> If God knows only probabilities, then he takes enormous risks in creating significantly free beings: he risks creating a world in which many, or most, or even all of his free creatures consistently reject him, a world in which they use their freedom to degrade others and themselves. It seems to me that one can reasonably argue that a good and loving God would not take such a risk.[28]

Open theists, to be sure, will not agree with everything Flint says here; in particular, they will dissent from his conclusion. Since we believe God has in fact created a world of free creatures in which the outcome is not wholly predictable (as it would be if there were such a thing as middle knowledge), we cannot agree that God "would not take such a risk." That much said, the risk surely is far from trivial; that God has actually chosen to take the risk of creating persons such as we are, and has bestowed his love and grace upon us, is a matter of wonder and amazement.

---

[28]Thomas P. Flint, *Divine Providence: The Molinist Account* (Ithaca, N.Y.: Cornell University Press, 1998), p. 107.

These thoughts about the possibility of God's not creating are of necessity highly tentative, since our grasp on the precreation situation is tenuous in the extreme. I don't claim that the considerations I've advanced are clearly decisive, but I do think they show that arguments that God must of necessity create a world are less than compelling. And given the plausibility and inherent appeal of the doctrine of grace in creation, I believe we should affirm this doctrine unless and until clear evidence is produced for the contrary view.

I have argued that we should not conceive of God's moral goodness in terms of his producing the best possible world; rather, his creating a universe should be seen as a manifestation of divine grace and generosity. There is no single best creatable world, but rather many different worlds displaying different kinds of excellence in various degrees, among which God was entirely free to choose. God was also free to create no universe at all; he is not in need of a creation to fulfill his own life, nor is he obligated to create, and his love for the creatures presupposes his decision to create them; it can't be used to explain that decision. It is therefore completely coherent to assert both that God is morally excellent in the highest degree and that he was free to choose among creatable worlds and also free to create no world at all.

If the account of the nature of God and of God's decision to create given here is at least in the neighborhood of the truth, this brings us face to face with the central question of this book: How can it be that a world created in such a way and by such a Creator is afflicted with the numerous and grievous evils found in this our world? To this question we turn in the following chapters.

5

Is the World Cruel?

Look round this universe. What an immense profusion of beings, animated and organized, sensible and active! You admire this prodigious variety and fecundity. But inspect a little more narrowly these living existences, the only beings worth regarding. How hostile and destructive to each other! How insufficient all of them for their own happiness! How contemptible or odious to the spectator! The whole presents nothing but the idea of a blind nature, impregnated by a great vivifying principle, and pouring forth from her lap, without discernment or parental care, her maimed and abortive children!

DAVID HUME, *DIALOGUES CONCERNING NATURAL RELIGION*

Natural evil is evil that comes about through natural processes and is not directly the result of moral fault on the part of human beings. There is some vagueness here, to be sure. A fatal automobile crash resulting from deliberate sabotage clearly qualifies as moral rather than natural evil; a crash resulting from culpable but nonintentional negligence on the part of a mechanic may be a borderline case.[1] Even with the ambiguities, the dis-

---

[1]Consider a case that is prominent at the time of this writing: New Orleans was ravaged in 2005 by Hurricane Katrina, a natural force which at this juncture is beyond human control. But the damage and suffering would have been vastly less had there not been many decades in which flood protection was neglected and delicate coastal areas were developed in reckless disregard of the known danger.

tinction is a useful one. Many have felt that natural evil presents a greater difficulty for belief in God than moral evil, since it cannot be put down to the misuse of free will by the creatures.[2] That is what we must now address.

One aspect of the problem of natural evil is put vividly by Hume's Philo, as seen in the epigraph to this chapter. We should make due allowance for the bathos of Philo's rhetoric, but we are forced to admit an element of truth in his claims. He recognizes the richness, order, variety and immense productiveness of nature. He points out, however, that this richness is bought at the cost of a vast amount of suffering, death and general failure to flourish on the part of individual creatures. Nature, we might say, is overwhelmingly successful on the whole but shows no concern whatever for the wastage of individual lives along the way. This picture serves perfectly Philo's overall goal, which is to argue that if indeed the source of nature "bears some remote analogy" to human intelligence, nevertheless it "has no more regard to good above ill than to heat above cold, or to drought above moisture, or to light above heavy."[3]

So the issue is well and truly joined. Is nature cruel? Or if not actually malevolent, is it at best massively indifferent to the welfare of sentient creatures? And if it is, what does this tell us about the Author of such a nature, if Author there be? This is the problem of natural evil to be addressed in this chapter, which is the longest and most complex in the entire book. In view of this, it may help to have roadmap at the outset. We shall begin by considering two theistic answers to the problem that will be judged inadequate. We then go on to set out several "structural features" of a universe that are desirable in a divine creation, and it is pointed out that these features, while productive of great good, also create the possibility, indeed the inevitability, of a great deal of suffering. This leads to the explicit formulation of a theodicy of natural evil, which is then compared with several

---

[2]There is a semantic issue here that needs to be addressed. Often the word *evil* is used with a strong moral connotation, so that it is taken for granted the evil implies moral wrongdoing. Given this connotation, the notion of "nonmoral evil" becomes an oxymoron. This is *not* the meaning of *evil* as used here; rather evil can include a large range of harmful and destructive phenomena, whether or not they stem from moral fault on anyone's part. In view of this connotation it might be better to avoid the term *natural evil* entirely, but no better replacement seems to be available.

[3]David Hume, *Dialogues Concerning Natural Religion* (New York: Hafner, 1948), chap. 12 (p. 86); chap 11 (p. 79).

other approaches to this problem that have been proposed. Finally, some objections are considered: it will be argued that the objections reveal limitations in the theodicy but do not succeed in refuting it.

HENRY MORRIS AND WILLIAM DEMBSKI: NATURAL EVIL IS THE RESULT OF SIN

The first response to be considered is one that is not greatly favored by philosophers but enjoys considerable popular support and is also claimed to be biblical. We read in Romans 5:12 that "sin came into the world through one man, and death came through sin." According to Henry Morris, patriarch of the creation science movement, this applies not just to human death but to all death whatsoever. Morris writes, "The entrance of spiritual disorder into God's perfect creation (Gen. 1:31) led to the imposition of a universal and age-long reign of physical and biological decay and death as well."[4] The disruption due to sin led to changes even in the fundamental physical laws; in particular, it is the explanation for the second law of thermodynamics:

> This universal tendency toward disintegration and death seems strangely out of place in an orderly, purposeful universe, but is beyond question firmly established as the Second Law of science. Its origin can only reasonably be understood in terms of the great Curse placed on all man's dominion because of his rebellion against God's Word (Gen. 3: 17).[5]

This indeed is one of the important reasons for insisting on a "young earth" that is only a few thousand years old. Over and above the desire to maintain a literal interpretation of the early chapters of Genesis, it is only by insisting on a young earth that it can be maintained that biological death originated in the world as a consequence of Adam's sin.[6]

No doubt there are many reasons to object to this, but the main reason is crushingly obvious: the earth *is not* a few thousands of years old but rather several billion. We know this as securely as we know anything at all about the history of our planet, and a supposed theological principle that

---

[4]Henry M. Morris, *Biblical Cosmology and Modern Science* (Grand Rapids: Baker, 1970), p. 132.
[5]Ibid., p. 19n.
[6]What is essential here is that the earth should be at most a very little older than the human race. If the "unfallen creation" had existed for vast stretches of time prior to the coming of sin into the world, we should expect to find evidence of this in the fossil and geological record.

conflicts with this rock-solid fact has to be reexamined or discarded. Anyone who seeks to make a young-earth chronology scientifically credible has taken on a monumental task, and an account of natural evil that depends on such a chronology is in deep trouble even apart from other objections that may be raised against it. It is perfectly clear, furthermore, that death, suffering and disease were not absent from the earth during all those ages: *Tyrannosaurus rex* was not a vegetarian!

Still, the principle that death is the result of sin may not be doomed by these well-known facts. One possibility has been noted already, in Plantinga's notion that natural evil may be the result of the sins of the devil and his cohorts. As I've already indicated, I believe this idea is successful in bringing natural evil under the umbrella of the free-will defense, and thus in establishing the logical possibility that God and natural evil can coexist. This, however, is the *only* merit of the idea; it has no promise whatever as the actual explanation for the natural evils that beset our world. In a great many cases we know in considerable depth and detail the causation of instances of natural evil, in such a way that the insertion of demonic agency into the causal chain is entirely otiose.[7]

A more serious proposal has been made by William Dembski, one of the leaders of the intelligent design movement. Dembski accepts the prevailing scientific chronology for the age of the earth, but in other respects he expresses considerable sympathy with Morris's project. He lays it down as a requirement for Christian theodicy that it must make peace with the claim that "All evil in the world ultimately traces back to human sin."[8] The reason

---

[7]A possible answer to this objection is suggested in a passage Plantinga approvingly cites from Dom Bruno Weil. According to Weil, an earthquake or a thunderstorm "is due to purely natural causes, but these causes are what they now are owing to the deep-set disorder in the heart of nature resulting from this action of fallen spirits, most subtly mingled with the action of good spirits, throughout the long ages of the world's formation." We would certainly like to be told more: which of the laws of physics were in question in this struggle of the good and evil spirits, in which the fallen angels "acted upon the forces of matter, actuating them in false proportions so far as lay in their power"? (Quoted in Alvin Plantinga, "Supralapsarianism, or 'O Felix Culpa,' " in *Christian Faith and the Problem of Evil*, ed. Peter van Inwagen [Grand Rapids: Eerdmans, 2004], p. 16 n. 26.) And since those laws apparently hold uniformly in the world as it now is, who won the battle? Apparently it was the demons who won, and their "false proportions" which prevailed, otherwise we would still have no accounting for the "deep-set disorder in the heart of nature."

[8]William A. Dembski, "Christian Theodicy in Light of Genesis and Modern Science," March 15, 2007, p. 4 <www.designinference.com/documents/2006.05.christian_theodicy.pdf>.

for this insistence is that "if God's power and knowledge were up to the task, God would be both able and morally obligated, as a matter of justice, to prevent evils from afflicting us for which we are not responsible."[9] He severely criticizes a number of scientists, philosophers and theologians for ignoring or minimizing the Fall of humankind in accounting for natural evil.[10]

But how can it be that human sin is the source of natural evil when that evil, in the form of the suffering and death of sentient creatures, antedates the sin by hundreds of millions of years? As Dembski says:

> A world in which natural evils such as death, predation, parasitism, disease, drought, famines, earthquakes, and hurricanes precede humans and thus appear causally disconnected from the Fall seems hard to square with a creation that, from the start, is created good. Without a young earth, . . . how can such natural evils be traced back to human sin?[11]

Dembski's answer to this is complex, and only a brief summary can be offered here. The answer involves a distinctive interpretation of the creation story in Genesis 1—one that, so far as I know, is unique to Dembski himself. In his view the narrative of the six days does not give a chronological ordering of creation events, either in literal, twenty-four-hour days or in geological eras, as in the "day-age" theory. Nor, on the other hand, is the narrative merely a "literary framework" for the creation doctrine. Rather, the account gives a "kairological" ordering of creation events (from Greek *kairos*, "the right, proper, favorable time"), an ordering in terms of divine purposes. The progression of divine creative words "has an inherent logic since for one word to take effect depends on others having taken effect (e.g., the creation of fish presupposes the creation of water)."[12]

So far there is nothing especially unusual about this interpretation; in fact these ideas could readily be combined with a version of the literary framework theory. It is important, however, that "Genesis 1 describes God's *original* design plan for creation." In this original plan, the world "is

---

[9]Ibid., p. 10.
[10]A partial list of those thus criticized includes Edward Oakes, Patricia Williams, John Hick, John Polkinghorne, Austin Farrer, Ian Barbour, Patrick Miller and Jürgen Moltmann; there is also an off-hand swipe at "process and openness theologies" (ibid.).
[11]Ibid., p. 18.
[12]Ibid.

perfect and contains no natural evils." The Fall, however, constitutes a "subversion of that design plan through human rebellion."[13] And this confronts God with a new problem:

> The challenge God faces in controlling the damage resulting from this original sin is how to make humans realize the full extent of their sin so that, in the fullness of time, they can fully embrace the redemption in Christ and thus experience full release from sin. For this reason, God does not merely allow personal evils (the disordering of our souls and the sins we commit as a consequence) to run their course *subsequent to* the Fall. In addition, God also brings about natural evils (e.g., death, predation, parasitism, disease, drought, famines, earthquakes, and hurricanes) *prior to* the Fall. Thus, God himself disorders the creation, *making it defective on purpose.* God disorders the world not merely as a matter of justice (to bring judgment against human sin as required by God's holiness) but even more significantly as a matter of redemption (to bring humanity to its senses by making us realize the gravity of sin).[14]

That God brings about natural evils as a result of human sin is, of course, an important emphasis of the young-earth creationist position already considered. Dembski's contribution, however, is that God brings about these evils *preemptively:* anticipating, through his foreknowledge the coming of human sin into the world, he created the world *from the beginning* in the defective, partially disordered state that was required as a setting for the life of sinful humankind. In this way natural evil occurs *chronologically* prior to the advent of sin but *kairologically,* in the ordering of the divine purposes, it is subsequent to sin and a consequence of sin. The Garden of Eden is then established as a "segregated area," a sort of oasis of perfection in the midst of the imperfect creation, which provided the appropriate setting for the testing of Adam and Eve.[15]

---

[13]Ibid., pp. 42, 44.

[14]Ibid., p. 42.

[15]Interestingly, a similar idea appears in the writings of theologian Emil Brunner: "If then God knew beforehand that the Fall of man would take place, should not His creation of the world have taken *this* sort of man into account? Is it unallowable to think that the Creator has created the world in such a way that it corresponds with sinful man? Is not a world in which, from the very beginning, from the first emergence of living creatures, there has been the struggle for existence, with all its suffering and its 'cruelty,' an arena suitable for sinful man? We cannot assert that this is so; still less have we any reason to say that this is not the case" (*The Christian Doctrine of Creation and Redemption*, trans. Olive Wyon [Philadelphia: Westminster Press, 1952], p. 131).

It must be acknowledge that this is an ingenious construction, one that provides a way (and perhaps the only way) of harmonizing the different considerations that are important to Dembski. It is, however, subject to a number of objections. For one thing, it requires the assumption of divine middle knowledge, though Dembski does not seem to be clearly aware of this fact. As was pointed out in the chapter on the logical problem of evil, only middle knowledge could allow God to know with certainty, logically prior to his decision to create the world in a certain way, that human sin would result from his decision, thus enabling him to preemptively arrange the world in the way most suitable for the life of sinful humankind. (Simple foreknowledge, on the other hand, means that God's knowledge of human sinfulness arises only in consequence of God's actual decision to create the world in a certain way. But it is then "too late" for God to decide on a different mode of creation, so the foreknowledge of sin cannot inform God's decision about what sort of world to create.)[16] Readers will be aware by this time that I would object to this assumption. I will not, however, press this point here, because I believe Dembski's proposal is subject to additional serious objections that do not depend on a particular position on the highly contentious issue of middle knowledge.

One way of approaching the problem is to ask, what is the benefit of this proposal? Or to turn the question around, what harm would result if we assumed instead that suffering and death in nature were part of God's original design and not the result of God's prevision of human sin? We might be inclined to suppose that the problem lies in the suffering thus inflicted on myriads of sentient creatures without there being any correspondingly grave reason such as would be provided by sin. In fact, however, this is not Dembski's concern. Rather, as seen in the quotation cited, the problem concerns the treatment of *us humans* by God, who is "morally obligated, as a matter of justice, to prevent evils from afflicting us for which we are not responsible."[17] And from this we obtain the result that, *in order to avoid injustice toward humans living today,* the pain and death of sentient creatures during the Paleozoic era *hundreds of millions of years ago* must be the con-

---

[16]The "ordering" here is logical rather than chronological, since it will be held that God's decision about creation is not temporal, but this does not affect the point being made.
[17]Dembski, "Christian Theodicy," p. 10.

sequence of human sin. Readers are encouraged to consider whether their sense of justice really supports this tortuous reasoning.

An even more serious difficulty concerns the nature of the ideal, perfect creation intended in God's original design plan. Dembski deserves full credit for seeing this point and facing it squarely. He writes:

> The worry here is that unlike our fallen world, which is dynamic, such a [perfect] world would be static and insufferably boring (with the evil of this boredom perhaps outweighing the evil of human rebellion). Without death, life increases in a geometric progression. Even if we set aside the dissolution of plants and microbes as not real death (their consumption being necessary for the life of organisms whose life and immortality are in question), we find at least some living forms will quickly overrun the planet unless their reproduction is curbed, at which point we reach a stable boring, equilibrium.

At this point, however, Dembski bails out, and writes:

> I frankly doubt that a static, dull, monotonously perfect world is what God originally had in mind in creating our world. The world God originally had in mind is the world we in fact inhabit, a dynamic messy world filled with tragedy, comedy, romance, and adventure. There never was any other world.[18]

Well said! But Dembski seems not to realize that this admission dooms his overall project. The real problem does not, however, lie in the surface contradiction between the claims that, on the one hand, the perfect creation was the *original* design plan, and yet "the world God *originally* had in mind is the world we in fact inhabit." That contradiction can be avoided by distinguishing two senses of "original": taking "original" in a temporal sense, we can say that *at no time* did God ever intend to create a world different than the one that actually exists. Nevertheless, in the nontemporal *order of divine decrees* God's "original intent"—his intent logically prior to his foreknowledge of human sin—was to create the perfect world, devoid of natural evil. The real problem, however, lies in the conflicting valuations assigned to the "perfect" world. One simply can't have it both ways: it cannot be true both that the perfect world is the ideal world that, absent the tragedy of human sin, God would have wanted to create, and also that it is

---

[18]Ibid., p. 48.

a "static, dull, monotonously perfect world" that would be far inferior to our own admittedly messy and highly imperfect world! Dembski, however, is firmly committed to both of these conflicting valuations.

This objection is, I believe, fatal to Dembski's proposal. But it also faces a serious exegetical difficulty. At the end of the creation story in Genesis 1, God sees that his creation is "very good." According to Dembski, this evaluation must apply to the "perfect" creation, free from natural evil, which was God's original intention and is the subject of the entire creation narrative to that point. God would hardly have said of a world that he himself had deliberately disordered and made defective that it was "very good"! (Perhaps such a world could be "good enough" or "the best that could be done under the circumstances"!) But surely, this interpretation is exegetically untenable. There is absolutely nothing in the text, in this chapter or elsewhere, to suggest that what God is praising is not the actual creation but a different, ideal world that he would have liked to create under different circumstances. Furthermore, there seems to be conclusive evidence in the text that the world thus praised is *not* the ideal world, free from suffering and death, proposed by Dembski. We read that on the fifth day "God created the great sea monsters, and every living creature that moves, with which the waters swarm." A large proportion of these sea creatures are predators, and the Hebrews certainly did not think of the "great sea monsters" as inoffensive or harmless! On the same day God created "every winged bird according to its kind"—once again, many of them either predators or scavengers. It is *these* creatures that are pronounced to be "good" and to be part of God's "very good" creation. At this point, it is hard to see how Dembski's claim to be presenting a biblical view can be sustained.

DIOGENES ALLEN AND EPICTETUS: NATURAL EVIL AND THE HARMONY OF THE WHOLE

A perspective on natural evil almost diametrically opposed to Dembski's has been proposed by theologian Diogenes Allen. For Dembski, the phenomena of natural evil constitute a disorder and a defect in the creation, and because of this they need to be explained in terms of human sin. For Allen, on the other hand, these phenomena are an integral and proper part of the created order; they require no special explanation and, when rightly understood, create no particular intellectual difficulty for Christian theism. Allen introduces his view as follows:

> There is some important data which has not as yet found its way into philosophic discussions on the problem of evil. Some religious people report that suffering, instead of being contrary to the love of God, is actually a medium in and through which his love can be experienced. . . . My procedure will be to deal primarily with the suffering caused by the natural world. I will argue that when a person performs certain specific *actions*, it becomes possible for that person to conceive of God's love and to experience it in and through suffering.[19]

In our discussion of Allen's view we shall first follow his exposition of the three actions in question and then consider their implications for the problem of natural evil.

Allen begins his exposition of the first action by considering the claim of the Stoic Epictetus that "from everything that happens in the universe it is easy for a man to find occasion to praise providence."[20] The difficulty, of course, is finding occasion to praise when the things that happen are seriously harmful to us and to others about whom we care. In order to capture the force and flavor of the reply of Epictetus (and Allen) to this difficulty, it is necessary to quote somewhat extensively:

> But all does not go well for human beings. Epictetus responds to this fact by asserting that we can make use of whatever befalls us. . . . The goodness of the cosmos is not that everything goes according to our will, with each of our desires catered for; but if we take a comprehensive view of the entire order of the universe, we will see that we are but one item among many in a vast interconnected whole. Many pleasant and unpleasant things occur to individuals because of the interconnections, but in every instance we have the ability to bear whatever happens to us "without being degraded or crushed thereby.". . . We can wipe our noses because we have hands; we can accept being lame as a small sacrifice toward the rest of the universe; we can even endure an unavoidable death from the hands of either nature or the social order without degradation.

---

[19]Diogenes Allen, "Natural Evil and the Love of God," *Religious Studies* 16 (1980): 439-56; reprinted in *The Problem of Evil*, ed. Marilyn McCord Adams and Robert Merrihew Adams (New York: Oxford University Press, 1990), pp. 189-208; quotation is from p. 189.
[20]Ibid.

This is achieved by recognizing "necessity" and by exercising the only real freedom we have. Our position in the physical and the social world is that of but one reality among many in a system of interconnected events, most of which are utterly beyond our control. What is beyond an individual's control can sometimes injure his or her wealth, social position, body and even bring utter destruction. In such circumstances an individual's only real freedom is the manner in which he or she responds to untoward events beyond control. The individual can complain about this misfortune or bear whatever comes, even death, without degradation by seeing its necessity and yielding to it courageously and magnanimously.

One thus makes *use* of whatever befalls, by using it to bring out these qualities of character.[21]

We do not, to be sure, find it easy or natural to respond to suffering in this way. Our inclination, rather, is to feel that things ought to have been arranged differently, so as to spare us the need to undergo suffering. The question as to whether the universe could have been better arranged is however one that, due to our cognitive limitations, we are unable to answer with any degree of confidence. And if we insist on pressing that question, we will be unable to learn from suffering as we ought to do:

> Suffering can teach us that we are a very small part of the universe and that we are not to expect as much as we do from its workings. When this is learned, we can then see more soberly and accurately what it does provide for us. What it does provide gives us ample reason to be grateful, in spite of the tragedies its workings produce, whether for us or for others. Indeed in our humbled and more realistic condition we can see the glory of the entire world-order and be grateful for our capacity to yield ourselves to it courageously and magnanimously.[22]

What often prevents us from taking this enlightened viewpoint is our natural egoism, in which we see everything from the standpoint of how it affects us personally. But it is precisely suffering that can "melt the illusion that we are immensely significant, and to show us that we are dust and ashes, formed of the clay of the earth."[23]

---

[21]Ibid., p. 190.
[22]Ibid., pp. 192-93.
[23]Ibid., p. 194.

Epictetus stressed the attainment of this kind of humility. He regarded people, and himself especially, as part of the cosmos with no special privileges beyond the ability to perceive its order, to give thanks for its positive benefits, and for the ability to endure whatever happens to us without being crushed or degraded thereby. Only with such humility—a humility that is achieved by one's response to adversity—is it possible for a person to look at this world and to find it gloriously ordered and praiseworthy.[24]

We can say by way of summary that the first of the actions recommended by Allen is the act of renouncing the overvaluation of self that measures the worth of the universe by its efficiency in meeting our desires; this renunciation in turn brings with it a grateful appreciation of the glorious richness and beauty of the universe considered as a whole.

At this point Allen confronts an obvious objection: "the world-order may be good enough for a stoic, but a stoic is not a theist." In Christianity, people are said to be the objects of a perfect love, and "their vulnerability to accident, disease, and tragic death from natural forces does not seem to cohere with the picture of a loving Father who cares for people more than he does for the birds of the air and the lilies of the field."[25] Allen responds:

Actually, *belief* in a loving Father is precisely what enables a person to perform, in the face of adversity, a second act. It is that action which enables a person to *experience* God's love in the midst of suffering. It can be performed only by a person who believes in a loving God and who also has the humility of the stoic. . . . Those who have found themselves not to be encompassed completely by the principles that operate in all matter, by yielding to nature's might, can yield themselves to its might *as a reality that obeys God*. We have been told that when we do this, we find ourselves experiencing God's love. . . . Through this act it is claimed that the gracious presence of God is known; it flows into one and gives a felicity that is beyond the calculation of the pluses and minuses of the pleasant and unpleasant things of this life.[26]

Allen cites Sister Basilea Schink, Edith Barfoot and Simone Weil as offering testimony to the blessedness thus received through suffering. Nevertheless he acknowledges:

---

[24]Ibid., pp. 194-95.
[25]Ibid., p. 195.
[26]Ibid., pp. 195-96.

Of course we cannot accept at face value the claim of these women that *God* is experienced by yielding to the workings of nature as forces obedient to God. . . . But there is no reason to doubt that a felicity is experienced which transcends the normal pluses and minuses of life. That data does exist.[27]

The third action in Allen's series comes into play because one of the assumptions made to this point turns out not to be universally applicable. This is Epictetus's assumption that, however severe the evils that befall us, we have it in our power to endure them with dignity and without degradation. The exception to this is what Simone Weil calls *malheur*, usually translated as "affliction," which is "a type of suffering that does crush or degrade us." "For there to be affliction, there must be some event or events that uproot a life and affect it physically, socially, and psychologically. . . . An afflicted person feels self-contempt and disgust, and even guilt and defilement in proportion to his innocence!"[28] Allen states:

Weil's account of how we may find the love of God in affliction enables us to relate physical suffering brought on by nature to the love of God in a new way. So far we have only claimed that we can experience God's love *through* suffering; now we will see how we may experience the love of God *in* suffering itself.[29]

It is necessary here to skip over much of Allen's summary of Weil's thought about affliction—and he emphasizes that even his own account is only "an approximate sketch of her brilliant and complex analysis."[30] The central idea, however, is that "Weil claims that in affliction we have the most perfect contact with the love of God that is possible for a human being in this life." According to her, "it is possible for a person to be in distress and to recognize the very distress to be itself a contact with the love of God. This is not simply to recognize a gracious presence *through* yielding to suffering; it is to find the distress itself as the touch of his love." To illustrate this claim she says that "We should think of a friend who has been away for a long time and who, upon returning, grips us very hard. It hurts, but that grip is his love. It feels just as painful as when it is the grip of someone who wants to hurt

---

[27]Ibid., p. 197.
[28]Ibid., pp. 198, 199.
[29]Ibid., p. 199.
[30]Ibid., p. 198.

us, but in this case it is an effect of one who loves us and wants contact with us. Sometimes through the universe of matter God grips us very hard."[31] The paradigm case of affliction is the suffering of Christ on the cross, when he cried out, "My God, why have you forsaken me?" In this supreme instance, the Father and the Son "are united over the great span of distance since there is love at both ends. Their distance from one another thus becomes a measure of the extent of their love." And so too for the afflicted one today: "The pressure of the world on us is an indirect contact with God, its ruler. . . . However horrible the pressure may be, one can have faith that it is still contact with a loving Father because his Son went the greatest distance possible and was not by that very distance separated from the Father's love." And so, "For those who regard nature as subject to God's providence and rule, their own unavoidable suffering that arises from nature's workings can thus be a way to participate in the suffering of Christ."[32]

We now have before us, in however inadequate a form, the three actions that form the substance of Allen's proposal. We might be inclined to think, on the basis of this material, that he is really addressing what we earlier (in chap. 1) termed the "pastoral" or "existential" problem of evil—that he is providing counsel about how we ought to respond, in the face of natural evil and physical suffering. To think this would not be a mistake,[33] but Allen wishes to claim more than this; he considers that these actions are relevant also to the philosophical problem of evil, the problem of whether the evil in the world provides rationally compelling reason to disbelieve in God. Since this is the topic of the present book, we need to see what conclusions can legitimately be drawn.

The most general conclusion drawn by Allen is that "from the viewpoint of those who have learned from suffering, answers to all the philosophic questions raised by the problem of evil are not necessary in order for belief in the goodness of God to be reasonable."[34] This is because they have come

---

[31]Ibid., p. 201.

[32]Ibid., pp. 202, 203.

[33]Allen is at pains to point out that these actions may require long preparation; they are not decisions that can be taken in a moment. "In no case is the act whereby one yields to nature's might *as something which obeys God* simply a matter of reading an article such as this and then saying on the next occasion of an illness, 'Yes, Father'" (ibid., p. 197).

[34]Ibid., p. 208.

to experience the love of God in and through their suffering, which for them is no longer a barrier to believing in God's goodness. I am happy to agree with this, and I will go even farther: answers to all those philosophic questions may not be essential to a rational belief in God even for those who have *not* performed the actions described by Allen. The notion that a person must have compelling answers to all of the objections that may be raised against belief in order to be rationally entitled to believe as he or she does is fundamentally unsound, and if pursued consistently would reduce virtually everyone to a state of perpetual agnosticism. In practice, this requirement is only insisted on when it seems an opportune way to put pressure on a belief system one dislikes; in the meantime, one conveniently forgets or ignores unanswered questions that may be lurking in the vicinity of one's own preferred way of understanding things.[35]

It is unfortunate, however, when Allen states, "For a person to reflect on the problem of evil without having performed even the first action we have described, means that he is trying to deal with the logic of certain concepts (such as unlimited power, goodness, and evil) without some of the relevant data."[36] For a person to perform that first action, the person must in effect adopt a large part of the attitude toward natural evil recommended by Allen; so what Allen is saying is, in effect, "Unless you agree with me you aren't qualified to discuss this topic." This is not, frankly, a very helpful way to proceed in a philosophical discussion of any kind, and I hope that, on reflection, Allen would not insist on it. What he is entitled to ask is that his opponents in the discussion acknowledge that the experiences he cites do in fact occur; whether the attitudes implicit in these actions are the right ones for a person to have is what is up for discussion.[37]

Allen considers briefly discussions by three philosophers of the problem of evil and claims that his approach resolves problems that they present.

---

[35]This is not of course to deny that in particular cases difficulties with one's beliefs may become so severe that unless they are resolved one can no longer hold those beliefs with integrity. But when this occurs, it is because of the circumstances of the particular case, not because of a general principle of the sort objected to.

[36]Allen, "Natural Evil," p. 207.

[37]Allen takes a better line in the passage already quoted: "Of course we cannot accept at face value the claim of these women that *God* is experienced by yielding to the workings of nature as forces obedient to God" (ibid., p. 197). Here the "data" is simply the occurrence of the experiences, not that they are veridical experiences of God.

For a variety of reasons I do not think his answers or objections to the approaches of these philosophers are particularly successful.[38] Rather than working through all that we may best proceed by striking out on our own and assessing for ourselves the relevance of Allen's three actions to the philosophical problem of evil. We begin with the third action, the response to affliction as described by Simone Weil. Allen writes approvingly of Weil that in her justification she takes the most severe suffering and the greatest evil—affliction, and indeed Christ's affliction—and relates this to the love of God. Then all other forms of suffering, from human affliction on down, are described as ways we can participate in Christ's affliction and thereby love God with as near a perfect love as human beings in this life are capable of. Thus we can in any adversity have contact with the love of God, although we must prepare ourselves for this opportunity if we are to make use of it.[39]

Now, I do not doubt that there are some, such as Weil, who experience affliction as the direct touch of a loving God and as a participation in the sufferings of Christ, and who find this an immensely valuable experience. Nor will I contest the validity of such an experience.[40] But there are problems that stand in the way of our drawing sweeping conclusions from the experience. First of all, I note that the number of persons who have actually had such an experience is probably rather small. (So far as I can see, Allen does not claim this experience for himself but relies heavily on Weil's account.) And on the other hand, the prevalence of "affliction"—of suffering that crushes and degrades the sufferer—is far from being small. (Epictetus and the other great Stoics were grossly overoptimistic in their claim that it is always possible for us to "endure whatever happens to us without being crushed or degraded thereby.") Is it feasible to present a theodicy that justifies affliction in general by claiming that, if the sufferers had properly prepared themselves for the opportunity, they could have experienced their affliction as a participation in the sufferings of Christ? Would

---

[38]The philosophers considered (on ibid., pp. 204-7) are Anthony Flew, John Hick and J. L. Mackie.
[39]Ibid., p. 207.
[40]Weil's analogy, however, is unconvincing. Isn't our long-absent friend supposed to be someone who knows us very well? And if so, shouldn't he know how much we can take and refrain from gripping us so hard that it causes excruciating pain? Does our friend not know his own strength?

Allen say this, for instance, about the sufferings of Jankiel Wiernick, the Holocaust survivor referred to in chapter two (see pp. 34-35)? And what about young children who are crushed and degraded by sexual child abuse? I sincerely doubt that either Allen or Weil would upon reflection attempt to justify these instances of affliction in this way. Furthermore, the attempt to justify all lesser instances of adversity on this same principle is wholly unconvincing. I conclude that Allen's third action, however valuable and important it may be from the standpoint of the sufferer, contributes rather little to the general task of theodicy.

The second of the three actions, in which persons accept suffering as God's will and find comfort in God's loving presence, is probably considerably more common than the third. Without doubt such an experience can be of great value to the sufferers and is likely to negate any tendency they might have to see the suffering as a reason to question God's love. Once again, however, there is a problem in universalizing and in finding here a justification for suffering in general. By Allen's own account, the action is not one to be performed by a simple act of will; it requires serious preparation, and the needed preparations may not be within the power of many sufferers. (Again, one thinks of small children.) So the contribution to a general justification for suffering is rather small.

This brings us back to the first action, the renunciation of egoism exemplified by the Stoicism of Epictetus. Here at least there is the advantage that the action does not depend on specific prior beliefs, such as a belief in a loving God or in the Christian doctrine of the Trinity. (As indicated in chapter one, appeals to Christian doctrine are not out of place in a Christian approach to theodicy. But insofar as an experience depends on specific doctrinal beliefs, it is unavailable to those who do not share those beliefs.) The marvelously intricate ordering of the natural world and our relatively insignificant place as individuals therein are available to reflection regardless of one's prior religious or philosophical beliefs. The downside of this is that the perspective implicit in this action is not specifically Christian and indeed may appear deficient from a Christian point of view. Actually, there are a fair number of philosophical naturalists whose views on these matters are not too different from those recommended by Epictetus. They marvel and delight in the intricate and beautiful ordering of the cosmos, made evident to us not only through daily experience but through the ever-increasing evidence of the natural sciences, from astronomy and cosmology to ecology, molecular genetics and nuclear physics. And on the other hand, they recognize our comparatively minute place in the universe, and do not expect the universe to have any particular care for us or for our interests. They may not be especially grateful when adversity strikes as a result of natural forces, but—*pace* Epictetus—why should they be?[41]

But here is the point: these same individuals may perfectly well be proponents of an argument from natural evil against the existence of God. They may think that while the world order is about as good as can reasonably be expected from either a Stoic or a naturalistic perspective, it is not good enough to square with the existence of the all-loving God of Christian belief. And they have a point, insofar as our faith in God implies that he has a *particular* concern for individual human beings, going beyond a generalized benevolence directed at the world order as a whole. But to vindicate this particular concern, Allen has only his second and third "actions" and their results, a resource we have seen to be of very limited value in this context.

There are additional features of Allen's thought that seem to reflect the Stoic background in Epictetus, and that may be dubious from a Christian standpoint. The Stoics were determinists, which led them to say that everything that occurs is a necessary part of the destiny of the universe as a whole. If we are not determinists (as Allen is not), then this thought becomes highly questionable.[42] This has a bearing on the sense in which the natural processes that lead to suffering are "obeying God" in so doing. They obey God, to be sure, in fulfilling their own natures and operating

---

[41]I hope I may be forgiven for inserting at this point a bit of comic relief. In P. G. Wodehouse's novel *The Mating Season* the ever-astute and learned Jeeves is attempting to console his employer, the narrator Bertie Wooster:

"I wonder if I might call your attention to an observation of the Emperor Marcus Aurelius? He said: 'Does aught befall you? It is good. It is part of the destiny of the Universe ordered for you from the beginning. All that befalls you is part of the great web'."

I breathed a bit stertoriously.

"He said that, did he?"

"Yes, sir."

"Well, you can tell him from me he's an ass."

[42]See Diogenes Allen, *Christian Belief in a Postmodern World: The Full Wealth of Conviction* (Louisville: Westminster/John Knox Press, 1989), pp. 167-71.

according to their inherent laws. But if natural processes are affected by the undetermined actions of human beings, and if, as I shall argue, nature itself has been granted a degree of freedom and autonomy by God, we cannot immediately conclude that, in causing someone pain and suffering, the natural processes are fulfilling a specific divine intention. This may be so in a particular case, of course, but one would need a specific reason to think so; it doesn't fall out of the general scheme of things, as it does on a deterministic assumption. (A terrorist's bullet is "obeying God" by conforming its trajectory to the laws of ballistics, but only the terrorist thinks it is fulfilling God's purpose by so doing.)

In spite of these criticisms I want to say that the fundamental line of thought about natural evil adopted by Allen has a great deal of merit. That nature operates according to its intrinsic, God-created laws, which are impersonal in form and do not have regard to the lives and welfare of particular individuals, is a fact that is highly relevant to our understanding of natural evil. This evil results, in many cases, from the operation of impersonal natural laws in ways that unavoidably impinge from time to time on the well-being of sentient beings such as ourselves. As such, "natural evil" need not imply wrongdoing on anyone's part—certainly not that of the Creator—but this does leave us with the question about how to understand the relationship between the impersonal, and in the end indifferent, order of nature, and the purposes of a loving Father. This question remains to be addressed.

REQUIREMENTS FOR THEODICY

What is required for a theodicy of natural evil? For we do need such a theodicy. Unlike Diogenes Allen, I believe that extreme pain, suffering, disease and death are genuinely bad things, and that their presence in God's good creation needs to be accounted for. But what should such a theodicy consist of? The purpose of theodicy is not, or need not be, to show that evil is merely apparent—that, viewed properly, what seems to us to be evil is really good. Rather, the purpose of theodicy is to show that *God is not morally at fault* for permitting the evil in question—that God's permission of the evil is *morally justified*, even if the events in question really are evil in themselves. As understood here, a theodicy essentially involves two elements: there is a *justifying principle,* a moral principle stating that under certain conditions God is morally justified in permitting evils of a certain sort to occur. In addition, there is a *justifying circumstance,* a state of affairs which is claimed to obtain and which is such that, were it to obtain, the conditions for God to be justified in permitting the evil in question would be satisfied. Anyone, then, who accepts both the justifying principle and the justifying circumstance must acknowledge that God is not at fault for permitting the evils in question; these evils provide no basis for an argument from evil against God's existence. Here as elsewhere, however, the truth does not arrive on our doorstep neatly labeled, so in practice what is required of a theodicy is that it be plausible, and judgments of plausibility will themselves be contested. It is obviously desirable that a proposed theodicy be widely perceived as plausible; most crucial, however, is plausibility as perceived from the standpoint of the theistic worldview that is being defended.

There are a couple of additional points that need to be addressed here in order to remove potential objections from religious believers to the enterprise of theodicy. Talk of the "justification of God" may well make us uncomfortable; it may suggest that God, having been indicted based on probable cause, is sitting nervously in the dock hoping that we, his attorneys, will be able to get him off from the charges. Such a thought is of course wholly inappropriate, but this is not what is going on when we set about constructing a theodicy. God is the holy and righteous One, the One before whom we ourselves will be judged, not someone subject to our judgment. The fact remains, however, that the proponents of arguments from evil have indeed "put God in the dock"; they have alleged that the phenomena of evil in the world are in conflict with the presumed existence of such a good, wise and powerful being, so that faith in such a being's existence can be maintained only in defiance of reason. Once this has been said, the believer has a choice: withdraw from the discussion or attempt to answer the charges. The theodicist chooses the latter option, but does so with the realization that it is not God who needs to be defended. Rather it is we ourselves who need a defense; we need to defend the coherence of our religious worldview in the face of charges that it cannot rationally be believed. God does not need a theodicy, but we do—at least, some of us do.

Another reason some believers are suspicious about theodicy is that it seems to express an unbecoming overconfidence about our ability to discern God's purposes. Alvin Plantinga asks, "given that God *does* have a reason for permitting these evils, why think we would be the first to know? Given that he is omniscient and given our very substantial epistemic limitations, it isn't at all surprising that his reasons for some of what he does or permits completely escape us."[43] Certainly there is a point to this. Already in chapter four we have noted the lack of wisdom implied in our presuming to know with confidence what God would or should do in various circumstances. I pointed out, however, that complete agnosticism would also be a mistake. (Even Plantinga speaks only about *some* of what God does or permits.) As pointed out there, if we have no idea whatever of the sorts of things God can and cannot be expected to do, the notion that God is good in some intelligible moral sense lacks all content. And the Bible itself has quite a bit to say about God's reasons for doing one thing or another. Our task, then, is to steer a prudent middle course between overconfidence and agnosticism. Now a successful theodicy, with respect to a particular evil, does provide a "justifying reason" for God to have permitted that evil. There is absolutely no need, however, for the theodicist to insist that this is God's *actual* reason for permitting the evil, much less that it is God's *only* reason for doing so. So the theodicist can and should make full allowance for the fact that God may have reasons for what he does that are other and better than any that may have occurred to us. The theodicist need not, and if wise will not, pretend to have sounded the depths of the divine counsels.

Before leaving this topic, it will be helpful to say a bit more concerning the general dialectical situation. A successful theodicy, with respect to a particular evil or class of evils, has the consequence that no successful argument from evil can be mounted based on the evil in question. But the converse does not hold; the failure of a theodicy does not imply the success of an argument from evil against God's existence. For there to be a successful argument from evil, *all possible* theodicies must fail, and showing that this is the case is a formidable undertaking. So as we go about

---

[43]Alvin Plantinga, *Warranted Christian Belief* (New York: Oxford University Press, 2000), p. 67.

the business of constructing theodicies, it should not be supposed that the rational defensibility of theism hangs on the success or failure of a particular theodicy. That will be so only if the theodicy in question is the *only possible* justification for the evils in question, but that will not in general be the case.

THE STRUCTURE OF A WORLD

Now at last we are ready to begin the task of theodicy—specifically, the task of setting out a constructive theodicy of natural evil. I will proceed in three main stages. First, I will set out some very general structural features of a world. These features are, of course, abstracted from the world we live in, but they are general enough to apply across a wide variety of possible universes. I claim that we can see that it is *good* that a world with these features should exist. I will then go on to point out that the various forms of natural evil arise as a consequence of these structural features. If it is good that a world should exist with these structural features, it is also justifiable that the natural evils should be allowed to exist; they are, so to speak, the price of admission for the existence of such a world. Finally, I will consider some limitations of and objections to my theodicy.

First, *it is good that there should be a world.* By "world" here I mean the sum total of concrete things that exist, other than God (if there is a God). And saying that it is good that there should be a world means that it would *not* be better if, instead of any world's existing, there should be absolutely nothing at all—again, apart from God (if there is a God). To say that it is good that there should be a world is an extremely minimal affirmation of the value of existence. The denial of this affirmation, while conceivable in the abstract, would be an expression of utter nihilism; for most of us, I hope, such a denial is not merely implausible but virtually inconceivable, and is not in any sense a live option. That it is good that there should be a world is of course compatible with the view that it would be far better if a world vastly different from this one should exist, so this is only a small first step toward our goal of theodicy.

Is this claim, however, inconsistent with the point argued for in chapter four, that God might well have decided to create nothing at all? I think there is no inconsistency here. In that chapter the attempt was made, even as we recognized its virtual impossibility, to place ourselves in the situation of a perfect being deciding whether or not to exercise his creative powers in bringing about the existence of a universe. From that standpoint I argued that creation might involve for the Creator both advantages and disadvantages, so that it was not a foregone conclusion that an actual creation would occur. At present, on the other hand, I take the view from within the world and affirm that it is better that a world should exist than that it should not. The costs that creation might impose on the Creator are not in our purview.[44]

Here is my second claim: *It is good that there should be a complex, multileveled natural world.* This proposition is itself quite complex, but the various ingredients do not readily lend themselves to separate consideration. To say that a world is *complex* is to say that it contains many different entities and kinds of entities, interacting with each other and doing many different sorts of things. To say that it is *multileveled* is to say that the entities exhibit different degrees of complexity, both in their internal structure and, more importantly, in their causal powers; those that are more complex in their structure and powers are thereby "higher" than those that are less complex. To say that the world is *natural* is to say that the entities act and interact in accordance with their inherent causal powers, as opposed to being manipulated by some other, presumably "higher," being. (Think of the difference between a puppet show and a group of human beings and animals interacting naturally. The charm of the puppet show, of course, consists in the fact that the puppets, if skillfully handled, are able to simulate many aspects of such natural interaction.)

Of the features mentioned, perhaps the idea that a world should be *multileveled* especially invites further exploration. A world that did not exhibit this feature would consist of entities all on the same level in terms of complexity of structure and causal powers. At one extreme, this might be a world simply of "atoms," the simplest, most elementary objects there can

---

[44]There is a parallel in the decision parents make when considering whether or not to have a child. They may be confident that were they to bring a child into the world, the child's life would be good for it on the whole. But they are not bound to take that as the overriding consideration; they may very well consider the effect of a child on their own lives and decide against adding to the family.

be.[45] (This is not the same, by the way, as a world *composed* of atoms and nothing else; such a world might well contain structures of extraordinary complexity. Nothing is said here against that possibility.) I do not suppose there will be much objection to the judgment that a world consisting only of separate atoms would be uninteresting, even boring, if there were anyone around to be interested or bored. The other extreme would be a world such as Berkeley's, consisting of rational spirits and nothing else. Notably, however, Berkeley's world contains the *systematic illusion* of a myriad of less complex entities, providing for those rational spirits an arena in which to act and interact with each other. Berkeley himself, to be sure, did not admit that his "world" was illusory, but that was because of his (clearly mistaken) claim that his view of sensible objects is that of the ordinary person. In a positive way the notion that a world should be multileveled captures something of the sense of the "great chain of being" that was thought to connect God and all of creation; it was important for the completeness of the whole that all the levels of metaphysical excellence—all the "links in the chain"—should be occupied.

Consideration of the atoms-only and the spirits-only worlds suggests yet another desideratum: *It is good that a world contain living beings that are sentient and rational.* In thinking about the atoms-only world, we were forced to imagine at least one rational being (perhaps the Creator) in order to make sense of the notion that the world could be assigned any valuation. But if the world is good, then it is desirable that it be found to be so by its inhabitants, and surely their appreciation of it will require extensive sensory capacities as well as reason, which is needed to enable the evaluation. Conceivably this desideratum taken by itself could be supplied by a single sort of beings that are both sentient and rational. But a multileveled world will contain beings with graduated arrays of sensory and rational capacities, allowing for a rich variety of ways that the world can be apprehended and appreciated.

Beyond this, I maintain that *it is good that the creatures in the world should enjoy a considerable degree of autonomy. Autonomy* suffers from a poor reputation in some religious circles, and not without reason. To be autonomous is

---

[45]The atoms of modern science, of course, are not elementary objects but have a complex internal structure. The word *atoms* is used here simply to represent the simplest elementary components of physical reality, whatever those components may in fact be.

to be self-ruled, and often this has been taken to imply freedom from all rule by another, even by the Creator. This is *not* the kind of autonomy advocated here. First of all, each creature is totally dependent on the Creator for its very existence; not only for its original coming into being but for sustaining its existence from moment to moment. Surely, however, it is conceivable that a being that depends on a superior power, and lies properly within that power's scope of control, should nevertheless in many situations be allowed the freedom to operate according to its inherent capabilities, without direct control or interference by that power. And to the extent that this is done, the intrinsic worth of the being is more clearly exhibited than it would be were this degree of independence not allowed. This is most evident, I believe, in the case of persons endowed with free will; that after all is the key insight on which the free-will defense relies for its credibility. But there is a good measure of plausibility in applying it to nonpersonal agents as well; much of the fascination of computers and robots, for example, stems from the impression they can give of acting spontaneously without direction and producing novel and surprising results. This autonomy acquires an added dimension if, as seems most likely to be the case in our world, there is an element of "chanciness," of indeterminacy, in the fundamental processes of the natural world. (Without this, an all-knowing Creator exercises a very high degree of control even without direct interference, by his control of the initial conditions and his knowledge of the outcomes that flow from them according to the laws of nature.) It is important, however, to stress that the autonomy praised here is a relative, not an absolute autonomy; the self-activity of the creature is not valued so highly that any special action by the Creator, above and beyond sustaining the creatures in existence with their inherent causal powers, is ruled out as unacceptable.

Finally, I claim that *it is good that there should be an evolving world, a world in which the universe as a whole as well as its component systems develop from within, utilizing their inherent powers and potentialities.* This judgment is obviously dependent on contemporary science; until recently the judgment could not easily have been made because we knew too little about the developmental history of the world to envision an evolving world as a realistic possibility. (Here as elsewhere, reality has far outrun our imagination.) But now we do have that history available—enough of it, at least, to perceive its inherent wonder. The majesty of the Grand Canyon, for instance, is greatly enhanced by the recognition of the hundreds of millions of years of geological history recorded in its successive strata. In this "golden age of cosmology" who can help but marvel at the story of the unfolding, since the big bang, of the astronomical structures of which our universe is composed? And ever since Darwin there has been the story, still far from complete but continually enriched with new discoveries, of the development of life on this our earth.[46] That this is so cannot be seriously contested. But is it *good* that it should be so? Is a world that has unfolded in this way *better* than if, as our fathers believed until very recently, the major features of the universe, and each separate kind of living creature, had been "hand-crafted," as it were, by the Creator? Not all will agree on this, to be sure—but I believe that it *is* good, and in support of this I cite earlier thinkers who reached a similar conclusion. Consider, then, these words of Henry Ward Beecher:

> If single acts would evince design, how much more a vast universe, that by inherent laws gradually builded itself and then created its own plants and animals, a universe so adjusted that it left by the way the poorest things, and steadily wrought toward more complex, ingenious, and beautiful results! Who designed this mighty machine, created matter, gave it its laws, and impressed upon it that tendency which has brought forth almost infinite results on the globe, and wrought them into a perfect system? Design by wholesale is grander than design by retail.[47]

Beecher, of course, wrote when Darwinism was in the ascendancy, and he might be suspected of tailoring his theology to the mood of the times. But similar themes appear in much earlier Christian writers; Gregory of Nyssa, in the fourth century, wrote

> The sources, causes, and potencies of all things were collectively set forth in an instant. . . . Then there followed a certain necessary series, according to

---

[46]To avoid possible misunderstanding, let me state emphatically that I am *not* endorsing a conception of "moral and spiritual evolution" in which the need for redemption is obviated by the evolutionary progress of humankind. Human sin and degradation are not part of the divine intent in creation, and they cannot and will not be remedied by the self-perfecting of that creation.

[47]Henry Ward Beecher, *Evolution and Religion* (New York: Fords, Howard and Hulbert, 1885), p. 114. I am indebted to Michael Murray for this quotation.

a certain order, as the nature of the Maker required, appearing not by chance but because the necessary arrangements of nature required succession and the things that would come to be.[48]

It would be difficult to find a clearer expression of the excellence of a world produced by evolutionary development, yet this was written by one wholly innocent of evolutionary science. Finally, I cite the words with which Darwin concluded *The Origin of Species:*

> There is grandeur in this view of life, with its several powers, having been originally breathed into a few forms or into one; and that, whilst this planet has gone cycling on according to the fixed law of gravity, from so simple a beginning endless forms most beautiful and most wonderful have been, and are being evolved.[49]

THE CAUSES OF NATURAL EVIL

We have before us the conception of a natural world that is complex and multileveled, containing creatures some of which are sentient and even intelligent. This is an evolving world, one that enjoys a considerable degree of autonomy in its operations. The task now is to show how, in our actual universe, these features lead inevitably to the sorts of occurrences we describe as "natural evil." There is however an inherent limitation in this enterprise, marked in the previous sentence by the words, "in our actual universe." It will not be possible, in general, to show that these same features must lead to similar results in a universe quite different from this one, made up of different fundamental constituents and operating according to different natural laws. For the truth of the matter is that we have very little grasp of the nature, or even the real possibility, of such alternative universes. This fact, which will come to our attention repeatedly in this sec-

---

[48] Gregory of Nyssa, *Apologetic Treatise on the Hexaemeron*, in *Patrologia Graeca* 44.72., ed. J. P. Migne (Petit-Montrouge: J. P. Migne, 1863). My thanks to Ernan McMullin for supplying this reference.

[49] Charles Darwin, *The Origin of Species: A Facsimile of the First Edition* (Cambridge, Mass.: Harvard University Press, 1954 [originally published 1859]), p. 490. I believe the point made by Beecher, Gregory and Darwin can stand on its own merits, but there is an interesting *ad hominem* aspect to this situation. Theistic believers, whatever their initial predispositions, will find it hard to contest the point once they are convinced by the evidence that God *has in fact* created the world through an evolutionary process. And nontheists are likely to find it awkward to insist that it would be much better for the world to have been created by a complex series of specific divine actions rather than allowed to evolve naturally!

tion, constitutes a fundamental limitation on the enterprise of theodicy: we are unable to compare the actual universe with possible universes that differ radically from it in order to show that the actual universe is better than those others, or at least as good as any of them. However, the limitation is much more serious for the enterprise of constructing arguments from evil in that someone who wants to claim that some very different sort of universe would be better than this one is quite unable to flesh out the alternative possibility or even to show clearly that there *are* alternative possibilities. (Of course it is comparatively easy to show that there are possible universes that differ from ours in minor details, but this will turn out to be much less significant than alternatives that are radically different.)

Sometimes, however, it is supposed that there is no need to envision alternatives in concrete detail; it suffices for us barely to imagine a universe different from and in some way better than the present one, and we then can ask, "Why didn't God create *that* kind of universe instead?" And in support of this it is pointed out that God, who is supposed to be omnipotent, is capable of creating any universe we can imagine. This, however, is a serious mistake. What is true is that God is capable of creating any universe we can *coherently* imagine. But we are quite able to imagine things that are really incoherent, without realizing that this is so. Think, for instance, of all the energy that has been spent in attempting to devise a Euclidean method for trisecting an angle, even though the task is demonstrably impossible. In other cases, our grasp of the internal details of an imagined project is so slight that we have no real basis for deciding whether the project is coherent (logically possible) or not. We have no difficulty in imagining robots made of metal and silicon that can duplicate or exceed any human behavior, but the actual creation of such an entity is so far beyond us that we have only the faintest grasp of the difficulties or perhaps impossibilities that would be involved. So in envisioning a world without natural evils, it isn't enough to point to idyllic nineteenth-century paintings of the Peaceable Kingdom![50] Some account of the relevant de-

---

[50]A teacher of mine once confessed that he had seriously considered writing a master's thesis on the zoology of the millennium, when "the lion shall lie down with the lamb" and presumably peace and harmony will prevail throughout the animal kingdom. Needless to say, the project was soon abandoned!

tails (such as what a noncarnivorous lion would eat) is essential.

Or am I asking for too much here? One reader of the manuscript thinks so, pointing out that I affirm my own belief in a heavenly state without being able to supply any details as to its nature. The cases, however, are not parallel. My belief in heaven is a matter of faith, based on what I take to be divine revelation. I am not asking or expecting the nontheist reader to accept this belief, nor do I make it the basis for an argument against her position. But the proponent of an argument from natural evil must presuppose that it is really possible for there to be a natural world that includes most of the benefits we receive from the actual world order and yet is without the negative features comprised under the rubric of natural evil. This is a presupposition that can fairly be challenged; so far as I can see there is no reason to accept it, though it cannot be disproved absolutely. (But might heaven itself be the "other world" God should have created instead of this one? I don't think so, but we shall return to this question shortly.)

But it is time to proceed with the main agenda: How is it that the realization of the features we have enumerated leads to the phenomena of natural evil? Let's begin with some of the largest and most impressive natural disasters: volcanic eruptions, earthquakes, tsunamis. All of these events can have truly catastrophic consequences; they are often enormously destructive of life forms within the affected areas. These events result from the fact that much of the interior of the earth is in a molten or semimolten state; the earth's crust to which we cling is only a thin skin over the inferno beneath. It is also true, however, that the availability of the earth as a site for life depends heavily on these same facts: a planet that was geologically "dead" would have little prospect of harboring life forms like ourselves.[51] To cite one factor among many, a molten interior is a requirement for the earth to have a strong magnetic field, which shields life forms from the otherwise damaging effects of the "solar wind" and cosmic rays. Furthermore, key transition points in the evolution of living creatures came about as a result of enormous volcanic eruptions, eruptions that were catastrophic in their immediate results but immensely creative in the longer term.

---

[51]For further elaboration, see chap. 3 of Guillermo Gonzalez and Jay W. Richards, *The Privileged Planet: How Our Place in the Cosmos Is Designed for Discovery* (Washington, D.C.: Regnery, 2004).

These transition points are an integral part of the history that has resulted in the appearance of our own species. As a result of the earth's molten interior we have plate tectonics, resulting in mountains and earthquakes, volcanism and tsunamis—and also in the presence on earth of Homo sapiens.

Similar considerations apply to the phenomena of weather and climate, which can often have seriously harmful consequences: hurricanes, tornadoes and drought. These phenomena result from the circulation of the atmosphere in its interaction with earth and oceans, all governed by the fundamental laws of physics. Some of the phenomena thus produced are astonishingly complex and even now defy accurate prediction for more than a few days in advance. They do cause harm and destruction on occasion, but they also provide good conditions for the life and growth of living creatures much of the time and over much of the earth's surface. If we are inclined to complain about this arrangement, the complaints will undoubtedly be centered on the destructive events: why can't we have just "normal" weather, without the occasional catastrophe? (Never mind that a certain approximate number of hurricanes and tornadoes each year *is* normal; a whole different pattern of normality would be required to exclude them.) Or to put it more bluntly: why isn't the weather more responsive to human wants and needs? Raising this question leads us to an important observation: the fundamental laws of nature are *impersonal:* they specify the behavior of the fundamental constituents of nature in ways that may be mathematically complex but that make no reference to purposes that are meaningful in the context of human life. The stones in an avalanche do not go where they go because it would be a good thing for them to go there; the physical and chemical properties of water do not suddenly change when air-breathing creatures are in danger of drowning. The laws of nature, it seems, are not respecters of persons.

Would it not, however, be *better* if things were different in this respect? Actually, whether this would in fact be better is very much open to question. But there is another, prior question to be asked: is a situation in which the subpersonal forces of nature adapt their operations with special regard to human concerns even *possible* in a *natural* world—one in which the entities act and interact in accordance with their inherent causal powers? Suppose, for instance, the desired goal is that lightning should avoid striking where it would endanger human lives. To accomplish this the lightning, or the meteorological conditions that produce the lightning, would have to be able to recognize the presence of human beings and the fact that a lightning strike in the area would endanger them, and then to select an alternative, nonthreatening target area, and finally to redirect the strike to that alternative area. It is wholly implausible that there is anything in the natural situation capable of this kind of discernment; what really is required is a "spirit of the lightning" that deliberately (and intelligently) selects targets according to some previously determined protocol. But then, of course, we would no longer have a *natural* world in this respect—nor, I would think, in very many other respects if similar "human-friendly" behavior is to be expected from other forces of nature. These scenarios simply can't be taken seriously.[52]

Turn now to consider living organisms, the centerpiece of the story. It is immediately evident that organisms are subject to the various kinds of natural disasters previously enumerated; indeed the events would not be termed disasters at all were it not for their devastating effects on life forms. We must also consider the need of organisms for sustenance, the energy and nutrients required in order to live, function and reproduce. Plants and some microorganisms can derive sufficient energy from sunlight and obtain needed inorganic nutrients directly from the soil. But sustaining life in this way is a slow business and is not conducive to a way of life involving the higher functions characteristic of the more complex animals. Some highly evolved animals are vegetarian, but many are not; there are significant advantages to be derived from ingesting the highly concentrated nutrients that are available from the bodies of other animals. The general theme of evolution, of course, is that organisms evolve to occupy an available ecological niche, and some of these niches are open to predators and to parasites; disease organisms also have developed so as to exploit opportunities that are available in the ecosystem.

All this is to say that the death of living creatures is a pervasive and in-

---

[52]Austin Farrer states it well: "The atomic world is run by the atomic energies. And it is a manifest absurdity to suppose that they can consider the whole, or even consider one another. They cannot consider anything; the principle of their action is simply that it should go on discharging itself" (*Love Almighty and Ills Unlimited* [London: Collins, 1966], p. 56).

escapable feature of any world remotely resembling our own. Dembski does well to highlight the boringly static and stagnant character of a death-free world, but he does not adequately bring out how very different—I am inclined to say, how unimaginably different—such a world would have to be in order to be viable at all. And once we have complex creatures suscep-tible to death and harm, pain and suffering are likewise inevitable. Many potential sources of harm can be avoided, and some harms can be allevi-ated, but only if the organism is sufficiently motivated. Pain is nature's way of "getting our attention," and it is remarkably effective in doing so. Ad-mittedly, great pain is sometimes suffered when the harm is already beyond the point where anything can be done about it. But to insist that pain ought to be present only when it is possible for the harm it signals to be alleviated is to make a demand that surpasses the engineering limitations of the organism.

All of this becomes especially evident, to be sure, when we consider the world in an evolutionary aspect. Whatever else may be involved, evolution as we know it depends on natural selection, and this in turn involves the winnowing process brought about by the death of less fit organisms. This is one reason some Christians object to evolution; if God has deliberately chosen to create the world through an evolutionary process, this makes it impossible to see death and suffering as interlopers brought about as a re-sult of human sin. (Dembski's proposal might evade this difficulty, though not, as I have argued, with a great deal of plausibility.) But most of the rea-sons given why death is inevitable in a complex natural world hold with or without evolution. If anything, the idea of evolution should be the more welcome because it points to a constructive result from the vast amounts of death and suffering that are inevitable in the natural world in any case.

At this point it may occur to some readers to object, But what about heaven? Heaven is supposed to be a world, or at least a state of existence, in which there is no harm, no death, no suffering. So if that is possible, death and suffering must not be inevitable, as you have been arguing. My answer to that is that I don't know all that much about heaven! I *believe* in heaven; I *have faith* that there will be such a state, but as for filling in the details, I am at a loss—and I think all of us are at a loss. Clearly the biblical descriptions of heaven (as, for instance, in the Apocalypse) are highly poetical and symbolic; they provide nourishment for faith and for hope, but surely not the materials for a literal description. Heaven is not, I want to say, available as a logical counter to be used in our calculations. (Here is a question to ponder: Will there be wilderness areas in heaven? If not, why not?)

Or am I being too quick with this objection? The objector might respond, Even if you don't know the details concerning heaven, you do believe that it is a very happy state in which embodied human beings will live without death or suffering. So why wouldn't a good Creator have created that instead of the world of suffering we now inhabit? If taken as a real (rather than merely rhetorical) question, this is obviously unanswerable. Since we lack not merely detailed knowledge of the heavenly state but also knowledge of the more particular purposes it is designed to serve, we are in no position to evaluate it as a candidate for the original creation. One thought that comes to mind is that it may be suitable for the lives of redeemed persons with some degree of maturity, but not for persons just beginning their life journey. Heaven may be excellent as the final stage in the drama of creation, but wholly unsuitable as the beginning stage. But we really have no resources for answering such questions. Those who believe in heaven will be content to trust that their Creator and Redeemer got it right; for those who don't, it's an idle speculation in any case.

Is the world cruel? Under certain circumstances, it is natural for us to think so. But the world is not cruel, for it lacks the capacity to be cruel. Cruelty is defined as "willfully or knowingly causing pain and distress to others" and as "enjoying the pain and distress of others."[53] Nature does neither of these things, for "nature," conceived as a system of natural laws and forces, neither wills nor knows nor enjoys. The system of nature simply *is there* and operates according to its inherent powers, with no thought for the pain or enjoyment of any creature. One might say, cruelty can exist only where there is the potentiality for kindness, and nature is neither cruel nor kind. Even to call nature "indifferent" is to indulge in the pathetic fallacy, for nature is not the sort of thing to which the pleasures and pains of sentient creatures could ever make a difference. True, some animals are capa-

---

[53]This definition is from the *Random House Dictionary of the English Language.*

ble of understanding to some degree the mental state and the suffering of another creature, but this capacity—what students of animal behavior term a *theory of mind*—probably is less common than we are inclined to think. In all likelihood a cat, playing with a mouse before dispatching it, has no thought or awareness of the pain it is causing the mouse. Subjectively, the cat is playing with an especially amusing toy; in the broader evolutionary picture, the cat is practicing tactics to be used in hunting for prey. (It is considered quite remarkable when, among our hominid ancestors, remains are found of an individual who apparently survived for a number of years with an injury that would have prevented it from foraging effectively for food. The individual must have been maintained by support from members of its group, an early sign of altruism.)

But if nature can be neither kind nor cruel, should we conclude that cruelty is rather to be attributed to the one who planned and created such a system? Not unless, reversing the judgments we have made up to this point, we are prepared to say that existence of the world is a bad thing overall—that it would be better that nothing at all should exist (or nothing other than God) than that such a world as this one should be. Such a nihilistic denial of the goodness of reality, if consistently maintained, cannot be answered by argument; fortunately, however, this is very rare. (More often, it is *inconsistently* maintained; the person who makes such a claim shows through other judgments and through actions that he or she really does value life in spite of its pains and hardships.)

At this point a natural response for some is to say, No I don't say that a good God should not have created any system of nature at all; what I do say is that such a God would have created a *better* system than this one, producing a far more favorable balance of pleasure over pain, of happiness over misery. We need to see, then, why such a "better system of nature" is not a possibility of which we can have any real grasp. Our failure to grasp such a thing is not a matter of mere ignorance, comparable to our lack of information about some as-yet-undiscovered species of insect. This is a *fundamental* ignorance, and one of the reasons it is so can be found in the phenomenon known as "fine tuning." It is a remarkable fact, widely acknowledged in the scientific community, that many of the fundamental constants of nature are balanced as if on a knife's edge, within an extremely narrow range that is essential for the existence of life as we know it. According to Martin Rees, the British Astronomer Royal:

> A few key numbers are crucial to our shared cosmic environment. Six of these numbers . . . determine key features of our universe: how it expands, whether planets, stars and galaxies can form; and whether there can be a "chemistry" propitious for evolution. Moreover, the nature of our universe is remarkably *sensitive* to these numbers. If you imagine setting up a universe by adjusting six dials, then the tuning must be precise in order to yield a universe that could harbour life.[54]

The six numbers Rees refers to are (1) N, the ratio of the strength of the electrical forces to the force of gravity; (2) ε, the fraction of the mass of hydrogen that is converted into energy in the process of hydrogen fusion; (3) Ω, the ratio between the actual density of matter in the universe and the critical density that would lead to a geometrically "flat" universe; (4) λ, the "cosmological constant" which balances gravity and causes the expansion of the universe to accelerate; (5) Q, a measure of the irregularities in the otherwise uniform early universe; and finally (6) D, the number of spatial dimensions of our universe.[55]

These facts, let me say again, are not seriously controversial. What is controversial is what should be made of them. Many have argued that such a remarkable combination of improbabilities points to the existence and activity of Something or Someone that has deliberately selected from all the possible values of these physical constants the precise combination that makes possible the existence of sentient and rational beings.[56] Needless to say, there is great resistance to this suggestion; one of the most popular counters to it lies in the concept of a "multiverse"—essentially, a vast ensemble of universes, exhibiting tremendous variety in the values of the fun-

---

[54]Martin Rees, *Just Six Numbers: The Deep Forces That Shape the Universe* (New York: Basic Books, 2000), p. 22.

[55]For further explanation of these "six numbers," and of why it is so crucial that they are as they are, consult Rees's book; other authorities on the subject add a number of other "fine-tuned" constants to Rees's six.

[56]In addition to Rees's book, important sources for this discussion are John D. Barrow and Frank J. Tipler, *The Anthropic Cosmological Principle* (Oxford: Clarendon Press, 1986); John Leslie, *Universes* (London: Routledge, 1989); and Neil A. Manson, ed., *God and Design: The Teleological Argument and Modern Science* (London: Routledge, 2003).

damental constants.[57] It is no surprise, in this case, that we are the "lucky" ones to inhabit a universe that permits the existence of carbon-based life: in those other universes, in which life is impossible, there is no one there to wonder why they missed out! There is, to be sure, the small problem that we have no basis, aside from some extremely speculative hypotheses unsupported by evidence, for supposing that those other universes actually exist.

For the present, however, we have no need to take sides in this controversy. What is important is that, so far as we can tell, there very likely *could not be* a universe with significantly different natural constants than this in which intelligent observers could live and raise philosophical questions about its existence. True, we cannot absolutely rule out that some combination of values very different from those in our own universe would make possible some form of life that we are at present unable to imagine. Nor can we rule out absolutely the possibility of a universe even more radically different from our own in which the fundamental constituents and forces, and the laws of nature, are completely unlike anything presently within our ken. But anyone who would base an argument on such possibilities as these is whistling in a darkness so profound that no light is likely ever to shine into it.

It is worth pointing out here that these considerations are relevant to the comparison between traditional, orthodox theism (including open theism) and process theism. Process theism is noteworthy for the limitations it places on divine power. God as viewed by process thinkers cannot unilaterally or coercively bring about particular worldly events; God can only "lure" or "persuade" the creatures, but how they respond to this lure is beyond God's control. Process theists uniformly claim that this gives their view a great advantage in addressing the problem of evil: if there is less that God can do than others have supposed, there is also less reason to fault God when things go badly. With regard to the problem of natural evil, it is postulated that God does not control the laws of nature and is thus not responsible for their untoward consequences. The God of traditional theism, on the other hand, is so responsible, for he has chosen this system of

---

[57]This is Rees's preferred view; see chap. 11, "Coincidence, Providence—or Multiverse," in his *Just Six Numbers*.

nature, with all the pain and suffering it entails, in preference to others that presumably were open to him.

The topics we have been discussing reveal to us a far different picture of the situation. For all the reasons that have been given, we have no basis for supposing that there is some other system of nature open to God that would have been superior to the one we presently inhabit. The bare possibility that such a superior alternative system exists cannot be disproved—but such a bare possibility affords little purchase for an effective argument. Furthermore, the fine-tuning phenomenon has led at least one leading process theist to reconsider the claim that the process deity has no control over the laws of nature. Process theists, like everyone else, have need for an explanation of the extraordinary combination of improbabilities that seems to be essential for the existence of life in the universe. This need has led David Ray Griffin to postulate that, in the chaos preceding the present cosmic epoch, "the divine influence, in seeking to implant a set of contingent principles in the universe, would have no competition from any other contingent principles," and would thus be able to "produce quasi-coercive effects."[58] And what this means is that the fundamental laws of nature, established in the first moments of this cosmic epoch, will be exactly as God desires them to be. Later on the "saltations," or major advances in the evolutionary process, are brought about by "a specific form of divine creative-providential activity."[59] Since it is these evolutionary "jumps" that determine the new types of creatures that appear, and these jumps are the direct result of special divine activity, it seems likely that the new forms are very much as God wanted them to be. And it is, of course, these new forms that determine the future lines of evolutionary development and thus, ultimately, the overall shape of the natural world God is luring into existence. It would seem then that God as conceived by process theism bears very nearly the same responsibility for the general ordering of nature as does God more traditionally conceived; the supposed advantage for process theism on this topic has disappeared.

---

[58]David Ray Griffin, "Process Philosophy and the Christian Good News: A Response to Classical Free Will Theism," in *Searching for an Adequate God,* ed. John B. Cobb and Clark H. Pinnock (Grand Rapids: Eerdmans, 2000), p. 30.

[59]Ibid., p. 29.

A NATURAL-ORDER THEODICY

It is time to draw the threads together and to present formally the theodicy of natural evil that emerges from our deliberations. This theodicy will be termed the "natural-order theodicy" in virtue of its central theme; it can be stated in four propositions.

1. The actual universe is a complex, multileveled natural world containing creatures that are sentient as well as some that are intelligent. The world has developed to its present state through a complex evolutionary process and enjoys a considerable amount of autonomy in its functioning.

2. The universe so constituted makes possible a large amount of good, both in the order and beauty of the physical universe and in the development and flourishing of a myriad of living creatures. It also unavoidably contains a great deal of suffering and death.

3. There is no reason for us to suppose that some alternative order of nature, capable of being created by an all-powerful God, would surpass the present universe in its potentiality for good or in its balance of good versus evil.[60]

4. In virtue of propositions 1-3, it is good that God has created this universe; there is no basis for holding God morally at fault for doing so or for supposing that a perfectly good Creator would have acted differently.[61]

It is hardly to be expected, of course, that the bare statement of these propositions should by itself be sufficient to produce conviction. But taken together with the considerations in the preceding pages, along with additional supporting information drawn from the reader's background knowledge, I submit that this constitutes a plausible and satisfying theodicy with respect to God's permission of the kinds of natural evil that are inherent in the existence of a universe such as this one. In order more fully to appreciate the character of this theodicy, it will be helpful to compare it with some views put forward by others.

This theodicy differs from that of Henry Morris and William Dembski

---

[60]It is not assumed that if a better kind of universe were possible God would of necessity have created it. Conceivably, there might be an endless series of better and better kinds of universe, and in that case the considerations discussed in chap. 4 become relevant. It simplifies things, however, if there is not such an infinite series.

[61]It will be noted that in terms of the structure for theodicy discussed earlier, propositions 1-3 together constitute the "justifying circumstance" while proposition 4 is the "justifying principle."

in that it does not assume that suffering and death in nature are consequences of human sin. In this, I believe the natural-order theodicy has
Scripture on its side, specifically the Old Testament, which has a great deal
more to say about the natural world than does the New Testament. The
first chapter of Genesis already has been cited, with God's creation of the
"great sea monsters" as well as an abundance of carnivorous creatures of
sea, land and air. In the concluding chapters of Job God's creation of the
monsters Behemoth and Leviathan is especially celebrated; Job also is
asked:

> Is it at your command that the eagle mounts up
>   and makes its nest on high?
> It lives on the rock and makes its home
>   in the fastness of the rocky crag.
> From there it spies the prey;
>   its eyes see it from far away.
> Its young ones suck up blood;
>   and where the slain are, there it is. (Job 39:27-30)

And in the Psalms we read,

> The young lions roar for their prey,
>   seeking their food from God.
> When the sun rises, they withdraw
>   and lie down in their dens. (Psalm 104:21-22)

There is no trace here of any embarrassment at finding such creatures in
God's good creation: this is the way the world is because God has made it
so. Emil Brunner states well the Old Testament's perspective on these
matters:

> Apart from the evil in men's hearts, and in their actions, everything in the
> world is God's creation: the course of the stars, the changing seasons, the
> form and the life of plants and animals—even of wild animals—the human
> body in its relation to the soul, the series of human generations, birth and
> death—all this is, as it is, and takes place in this way, because, and as, God
> has appointed it, from the standpoint of His creation.[62]

---

[62]Brunner, *Christian Doctrine of Creation and Redemption,* p. 18. There seems to be a certain tension
between these thoughts and the view referenced earlier in the section on Dembski (see p. 106 n. 15.)

The natural-order theodicy has some obvious affinities with the view of Diogenes Allen discussed previously (see pp. 109-19). Natural evil, in the form of suffering, pain and death, is the result of the overall order of the cosmos, an order which, taken as a whole, is good and admirable. Since we are part of this order—individually, each a *very small* part of it—we must expect that these things will affect us also; we are granted no exemption from suffering. Insofar as natural harms are unavoidable they are best accepted in an attitude of humble dependence on God. Nevertheless there are important differences, representing points at which we dissent from the Stoicism of Epictetus. This theodicy does not deny, as the Stoics did and as Allen very nearly does, that severe pain, suffering, and death really are evil. Nor does it teach us that in every instance natural forces that harm and oppress us are fulfilling God's specific purposes by doing so. They are "obedient to God" in conforming to the natural laws built into creation, but whether they are carrying out God's purposes in some more specific sense is an open question. We are free to affirm this if it seems to be the case in a particular instance, but there is no general theorem to the effect that this is so everywhere and always. I do not expect unanimous agreement on this point, but I believe this difference represents a significant advantage for the natural-order theodicy. If every instance of harm arising from natural causes is said to be intended by God for a specific purpose, it is inevitable that the question will be asked: What *is* the purpose of this terrible suffering that I, or my child, or my community is being forced to endure? Available answers include such standard options as: the suffering is a punishment for sin, it is a means to bring us closer to God, it is to make us better people, and the like. In some cases these answers may seem apt, but in others they leave almost everyone completely unsatisfied. We are then left with the sense that God has "some purpose or other," which may however be completely incomprehensible to us; the assurance that God's purpose is fulfilled in our suffering becomes not a comfort to faith but a burden. Let me illustrate the point with a small story. A number of years ago I had in class a student in his late twenties, who had recently suffered the loss of his father. What made this especially poignant was that his father had recently become a Christian, and the student had looked forward to establishing a better relationship with him than had been possible for a number of years past. Before this could occur, the father died of a heart attack, and the student naturally wondered what the reason was for this. His conclusion: "His heart wore out." I thought at the time, and I still think, that this was a mature and spiritually sound way to understand the event—and it is wholly in keeping with the natural-order theodicy.

A number of writers have articulated themes that resonate with the natural-order theodicy. Physicist-theologian John Polkinghorne advocates a "free-process defense," paralleling the free-will defense for moral evil, according to which

> In his great act of creation . . . God allows the physical world to be itself, not in Manichaean opposition to him, but in that independence which is Love's gift of freedom to the one beloved. . . . It is inevitably a world with ragged edges, where order and disorder interlace each other and where the exploration of possibility by chance will lead not only to the evolution of systems of increasing complexity, but also to the evolution of systems imperfectly formed and malfunctioning. . . . God no more expressly wills the growth of a cancer than he expressly wills the act of a murderer, but he allows both to happen. He is not the puppetmaster of either men or matter.[63]

Another example is found in Peter Geach who, quoting William Makepeace Thackeray, spoke of God as "The Ordainer of the Lottery,"[64] and wrote:

> Our freedom is our supreme dignity; that makes us children of the Most High; we can enjoy it only by living in a partly chancy world—and that means a world in which there will be goods and evils of fortune distributed according to the laws of chance. . . . We cannot opt out of the lottery nor alter its terms; and it is vain to look *here* for distributive or retributive justice; it is only that the Ordainer of the lottery plays fair.[65]

One of the most striking parallels with the natural-order theodicy is found in the medieval Jewish doctrine of *Tzimzum*. First put forward by the kabbalist Rabbi Isaac Luria, *Tzimzum* (best translated as "withdrawal"

---

[63]John Polkinghorne, *Science and Providence: God's Interaction with the World* (London: SPCK, 1989), pp. 66-67.
[64]This is the title of chap. 6 in Peter Geach, *Providence and Evil* (Cambridge: Cambridge University Press, 1977).
[65]Ibid., p. 120.

or "retreat") means, according to Gershom Scholem, that "the existence of the universe is made possible by a process of shrinkage in God."[66] The idea is initially motivated by what Scholem terms a "somewhat crude" question: "How can there be a world if God is everywhere? If God is 'all in all,' how can there be things which are not God?"[67] The answer, according to Luria, is that "God was compelled to make room for the world by, as it were, abandoning a region within Himself, a kind of mystical primordial space from which He withdrew in order to return to it in the act of creation and revelation."[68] Robert Oakes suggests that we picture this anthropomorphically by imagining God " 'inhaling deeply' or 'sucking in his chest' and just holding it there in order to allow for His Creation of a distinct domain of contingent being."[69]

Now of course this concept cannot be taken literally, as the rabbis were well aware. God's universal presence, in all metaphysically possible spaces, is an essential property of which he cannot divest himself. What is needed, in order for creation to be possible, is not strictly speaking the *absence* of God but rather restraint in the *manifestation* of the divine presence. The analogy is suggested of a teacher who is attempting to explain to students a concept that is far above their level of comprehension. "Since the class could not begin to grasp the relevant idea at the teacher's plane of comprehension, she needs to 'reduce' the concept to a level at which it *can* be properly grasped by her students without sacrificing any of its core content."[70] Similarly, it is held, "there is just so much of the Divine Holiness that human persons have the capacity to sustain. Anything stronger than this would ensure their annihilation or nullification as individuals metaphysically distinct from God."[71] Thus in Exodus 33 God puts Moses in a cleft of the rock while he passes by, permitting him to see only God's back, because "you cannot see my face; for man shall not see me and live." Because of this, "the Jewish mystical tradition has insisted that some 'veiling' of the Divine Countenance—

---

[66]Gershom G. Scholem, *Major Trends in Jewish Mysticism* (New York: Schocken, 1961), p. 260.
[67]Ibid., pp. 260-61.
[68]Ibid., p. 261.
[69]Robert Oakes, "Creation as Theodicy: In Defense of a Kabbalistic Approach to Evil," *Faith and Philosophy* 14, no. 4 (1997): 512.
[70]Ibid., p. 514.
[71]Ibid., p. 515.

some 'hiding of the face' (as it were), i.e., *Hester Panim*—is required so that the Divine Light '. . . *shall not manifest itself in a greater radiance than the lower worlds are capable of receiving.*'"[72] And this, according to Oakes, provides the "proper or authoritative interpretation" of the divine *Tzimzum*.

The relevance of this doctrine for theodicy is stated by Oakes as follows:

> The divine Tzimzum requisite for Divine Creation comes at a serious meta-physical price; namely, an unavoidable by-product of the "veiling" of the Di-vine Countenance (Radiance, Holiness) to the extent required for finite being to survive intact—for it not to be absorbed or consumed by the Infi-nite—is a serious potential for unmerited suffering. For the revelatory depth of Divine Radiance or Holiness necessary to cure the world of such evil could not but result in the eradication of the finite as a distinct domain of being. Here is an analogy: the intensity of gamma radiation that it would take to cure patient S of his pathology would clearly result in his death. . . . [S]ince finite persons (along with finite being in general) . . . are constitu-tionally unable to withstand anything close to a full scale revelation of God's Infinite Radiance, Divine Creation requires divine *Tzimzum* (or *Hester Panim*), i.e., some serious concealment of that Radiance. This, in turn, pro-vides "metaphysical room" (as it were) for unmerited suffering.[73]

And now at last we are able to see the parallel between the *Tzimzum* doctrine and the natural-order theodicy. God's "withdrawal" can be seen as the other side of the "autonomy" granted by God to created agents ac-cording to the theodicy. In order to allow created agents to be themselves, to have a distinctive range and mode of operation of their own, God gra-ciously refrains from doing what he is fully able to do, namely, exercising direct and immediate control over everything that occurs within his cre-ation. And from the self-activity of the creatures, whether natural forces or created intelligences, evil sometimes comes.

Perhaps I should say that I am not certain how fully the doctrine of *Tzimzum* can be incorporated into the natural-order theodicy. Certainly the Neo-Platonic, and indeed quasi-Gnostic, aspects of Rabbi Luria's doc-trine of creation will be problematic for many mainstream theists.[74] The

---

[72]Ibid. The imbedded quotation is from Rabbi Joseph Schocet.
[73]Ibid., p. 516-17.
[74]See Scholem, *Major Trends in Jewish Mysticism*, pp. 265-68.

doctrine is presented here as a striking and highly suggestive development of some themes that resonate with the theodicy that has been developed in this chapter.

OBJECTIONS AND LIMITATIONS

We now consider briefly three objections to the natural-order theodicy; two of the three, however, can be rephrased rather as limitations of the theodicy. The first objection can be stated like this: You have a great deal to say about the order of nature, the beauty of the whole, the grandeur of evolutionary history and all that. But that ignores the real problem. People who are concerned about Hurricane Katrina or the AIDS virus don't want to hear about all those vague abstractions; what they are asking is whether there is any justification for those particular evils that are ruining their lives. That is a fair observation, and the truth is that this theodicy does not have any answer to that question—at least, not the sort of answer the people referred to are looking for. Consider, for instance, the remark made by Austin Farrer about the hugely destructive Lisbon earthquake of 1755: "The will of God in the event is his will for the elements of the earth's crust or under it: his will that they should go on being themselves and acting in accordance with their natures."[75] Clearly, this is not an answer to the sort of question people in such situations want to ask; equally clearly, nothing that would be perceived as a satisfactory answer to *their* question can be derived from the natural-order theodicy. That theodicy, insofar as it is successful, vindicates God's wisdom in instituting the general course of nature; it cannot offer special reasons, in terms of divine purposes, for particular events whether beneficial or tragic. Insofar as answers of the latter sort are needed, they must be sought elsewhere.[76]

A similar objection—or perhaps it is another version of the same objection—is found in the point raised previously against Allen's appropriation of Epictetus: the grandeur of the world order as a whole may be a fine thing, but that says little or nothing about the love of God for particular persons. This is quite true, and it marks an inherent limitation of the

---

[75] Austin Farrer, quoted in Polkinghorne, *Science and Providence*, p. 67.
[76] For further discussion of this point, see chap. 7.

natural-order theodicy. That theodicy, if accepted, vindicates God's wisdom and goodness as seen in the general order of creation; it does not speak of God's particular concern for individual human beings. But God's love for individuals is absolutely crucial for Christian faith; it is not something that could conceivably be given up. Earlier I argued that Allen's second and third "actions" are not sufficient by themselves to provide answers on this point; the reader will have to judge whether adequate answers are to be found in the subsequent chapters of this book.

A third objection to the natural-order theodicy can't be accommodated, as the first two were, by turning it into an acknowledged limitation of the theodicy. This third objection amounts to outright rejection: the world, whether "cruel" in human terms or not, is just too full of death, suffering and waste to be morally tolerable; it would be better if no such place had ever existed, and a good God would never have created it. Such a rejection is suggested in some words of Annie Dillard:

> Any three-year-old can see how unsatisfactory and clumsy is this whole business of reproducing and dying by the billions. We have not yet encountered any god who is as merciful as a man who flicks a beetle over on its feet. There is not a people in the world who behaves as badly as praying mantises. . . . The universe that suckled us is a monster that does not care if we live or die.[77]

When I first read this, I wanted to ask, "Do you really hate your life that much?" Dillard's words seem to be saying that it is a *bad thing* that a world such as this should exist; it would have been far better that the Creator (if any) should have had second thoughts and refrained from creating it. But assuredly Dillard herself, and the other human beings she cares about, and for that matter all of us, are the products of precisely the world system and the evolutionary process she deplores. To wish that none of this had existed is to wish that neither you yourself nor other people whom you love had ever existed—and that is not an easy thing to wish for, unless you are already desperately unhappy. Rejecting the world in this way may not be impossible, but there is a steep price to be paid for the rejection, a price few of us (I hope) will be willing to pay.

---

[77]Annie Dillard, *Pilgrim at Tinker Creek* (New York: Bantam Books, 1975), p. 180. I am indebted to Michael Murray for this quotation.

Taken in context, though, this is not really what Dillard means to say. In the words quoted she is expressing her shock that the world of nature, produced by an evolutionary process, is so often sharply at odds with human values and emotions. But this is not, in the end, a reason to reject such a world; more likely it is the emotions that are misdirected, when applied to natural occurrences such as predation. She writes, "Although it is true that we are moral creatures in an amoral world, the world's amorality does not make it a monster. Rather, I am the freak. Perhaps I don't need a lobotomy, but I could use some calming down, and the creek is just the place for it. I must go down to the creek again."[78]

As a matter of fact, the nonmoral character of the evolutionary process, so vividly portrayed by Annie Dillard, can actually be of help to the natural-order theodicy. It does so by removing the impression that each specific arrangement in nature, including the ones we find gross and repellent, represents a particular divine intention. The point is well captured in a poem by Robert Frost. He begins by describing a grisly little scene in which a white spider sits on a white flower holding up a white moth it has trapped and killed. He then asks:

> What brought the kindred spider to that height,
> Then steered the white moth thither in the night?
> What but design of darkness to appall?—
> If design govern in a thing so small.[79]

If design govern—but suppose it doesn't? Suppose, that is to say, that (as we have good reason to believe) the endless contest of spider and moth, of predator and prey, is the product of an evolutionary process that is unintelligent and without intrinsic purpose, even though purposed by divine wisdom to perform the function of engendering a rich array of biological life? We may sometimes be appalled, but there is no "design of darkness" and no reason in all this to question the wisdom or the goodness of the Creator. But he is not a *tame* God, and he has not given us a tame world.

---

[78]Ibid., p. 182.
[79]Robert Frost, "Design," in *The Poetry of Robert Frost,* ed. Edward Connery Lathem (New York: Holt, Rinehart and Winston, 1969), p. 302.

6

Why Is Life So Hard?

I must have had faith then. I certainly had something. How had I lost it?
When had I stopped believing the god thing? I didn't need to worry it to
death, I knew when it was: the night I looked down into the bloodless face
of the little girl who had been raped and strangled by her father.

JOHN DUNNING, *THE BOOKMAN'S PROMISE*

In *The Bookman's Promise* John Dunning's hero, Cliff Janeway, recounts his loss of belief (probably it had best not be called "faith") in "the god thing." The words are compelling; we can readily understand that confrontation with such a horror might lead to a person's giving up belief in God. Yet further reflection may lead to puzzlement. It was the little girl's father, not God, who did these horrible things to her, so why is it belief in God that is targeted in the response? (Janeway does not, so far as we can tell, lose his belief in "the father thing.") What is making the connection here?

Part of the answer may lie in the assumption, implicit in some religious outlooks and lurking deep in the thoughts of many who might not consciously affirm it, that God is ultimately the cause of absolutely everything that happens. If that is what Janeway is thinking—or rather what he is feeling—then his response is understandable, whether or not it is justified.

But this is not the only possibility. I believe that in the minds of a good many people there is the thought of something like a deal made between God and humans, a deal that runs like this: God says, in effect, "Keep your nose clean. At any rate don't do anything too horribly bad, and I will make sure nothing really terrible happens to you." Think of this as a sort of scaled-down version of the biblical covenant: it doesn't ask too much of us, only that we lead minimally decent lives, and it doesn't expect too much of God—no promise here of transcendent happiness, just a sort of insurance policy that the very worst, at any rate, won't happen to us. But in the case of the little girl, the deal has been violated; what has happened to her is just about as bad as anything we can imagine, and she certainly has done nothing to deserve *that*. But if God doesn't come through on the terms of the deal he has made with us, what point is there in believing in him?

Of course the deal isn't on, as was learned long ago by Job and his friends. Just try for a moment to see the affair from Job's friends' perspective. If the calamities that befell Job had been less extreme—say, just the raids that decimated his cattle holdings, without all the rest of what happened to him—then Eliphaz, Bildad and Zophar would have been all over sympathy. They might well have offered help from their own resources to get Job on the road to rebuilding his fortunes. But with disaster piled upon disaster, their assumptions about the normal course of life—in particular, their assumptions about the deal—were shaken to the core. If Job is really as innocent as he proclaims himself, and as his life hitherto has seemed to show, then God is seriously remiss in allowing these terrible things to happen to him. But that is unthinkable, so the friends were forced to the conclusion that Job was guilty of hidden sins that justified the terrible treatment he had received. The friends were not unmerciful; they repeatedly insisted that, once Job repented of his faults, forgiveness and restoration would follow. But the more fiercely Job refused to acknowledge a guilt he did not feel, the more the friends' deepest beliefs were threatened, and the more strident their denunciations of him became. They were wrong, terribly wrong, but their responses were all too human.

And this, of course, brings us squarely up against the problem of evil in its most troubling form. We may feel concern, even anguish, at the sufferings sometimes endured by animals. But for almost all of us, the most disturbing thing of all is the bad things that happen to people—to good people, as often as not. How, we ask, can God possibly be justified in permitting this? Meeting this challenge is the task of the present chapter. Many of these evils, like the little girl's rape and murder, are perpetrated by other people, but suffering due to natural causes plays a role here too. (Thus, there is some overlap of subject matter with chapter five.)[1] At least in recent years, moral evil has been more thoroughly studied and discussed by philosophers than natural evil, and there is widespread (but not universal) agreement that the concept of free will must play an important role in any answer to the problem; this has already become apparent in our discussion, in chapter three, of the free-will defense.[2] Now, however, we are concerned with much more than a mere defense of the logical compatibility of God with evil, and so a deeper consideration of the concept of free will is required. What exactly is free will? Why is free will essential for an adequate theodicy? What are the implications of free will for God's governance of the world? If, as I shall argue, free will is the explanation for an enormous amount of the evil in the world, what is it about free will that makes it worth the terrible price? Answering these questions will not by itself do the whole job of theodicy, but it is an important part of that job, and without good answers success may not be possible.

THE NATURE OF FREE WILL

What then is free will? There are two main conceptions of free will that are prevalent among philosophers, commonly referred to as *compatibilist* free will and *libertarian* free will. According to compatibilism, an action is free if it is done without constraint or compulsion—that is, if we are free to do whatever it is we most want to do in a given situation. (There are refinements that can't be gone into here; I am trying to convey the main idea as

---

[1]Actually, the overlap goes in both directions; the "affliction" spoken of by Simone Weil and Diogenes Allen has social degradation as a major component and thus involves moral evil as well as natural evil. Natural evil and moral evil are conceptually distinguishable, but they are too closely interwoven in human life to make a clean separation feasible.

[2]Oddly enough, a partial exception to this assertion is found in Alvin Plantinga, who, while himself a libertarian, has recently put forward a theodicy in which free will does not play a major role. See the appendix to this chapter for details.

succinctly as possible.) The view is called *compatibilism* because it is logically compatible with the claim that everything we do is causally determined, either by the "strongest motive" (psychological determinism) or by physical causes. It is also compatible with the theological view according to which everything we do is determined by immutable divine decrees—that is, with what some would describe as absolute divine sovereignty. For compatibilists, the age-old problem of predestination and free will is not a problem at all; we "freely" choose to do exactly what God has predestined us to do.

The contrasting libertarian view insists that for an action to be free in the most important sense it is not enough that a person be able to do what he most desires to do. The further question arises, was it really possible for the person to desire and to do anything other than what he in fact desired and did? If this was not possible, libertarians say, that person is not really free; he may not be subject to external constraint or compulsion but is all the same controlled by his desires and ultimately by whatever it is that determined that his desires should be as they are. In order for the person to be really free, it must be *really possible* for him either to perform the act in question or to refrain from it; it must be *entirely within the person's power* to do one or the other.[3] But this "two-way ability" is not at all guaranteed by free will in the compatibilist sense.

The compatibilist view of free will has considerable currency among contemporary philosophers; it is also attractive to those theologians who wish to maintain the strong view of divine sovereignty, according to which God's decrees determine everything that takes place. The majority of Christian philosophers, on the other hand, reject this view and insist on a libertarian understanding of free will. One reason for this is that free will in the compatibilist sense is of *no real help* in answering the problem of evil; it can be argued, in fact, that it makes a rationally intelligible answer to that problem impossible. The reason for this can be seen by comparing the

---

[3]Libertarians will not hold that all of our actions will be free in this sense. Choices are constrained by motives, and when we have compelling reason to act in a certain way and no reason not to the action may be inevitable. In many instances libertarian free choice is best conceived along the lines discussed in chap. 4, as a choice as to which of two motives (or sets of motives) shall prevail, when both make a significant appeal to us.

compatibilist view of free will with the free-will defense. A crucial claim in that defense is that it may be impossible for God both to grant to his creatures the gift of free will and at the same time control their use of that gift in such a way as to guarantee that they will never choose evil; thus the existence of evil (moral evil, to be exact) is not incompatible with the perfect goodness of God. But on the compatibilist view it is entirely possible for God to create free persons and guarantee that they will always freely choose good; he need only create them and, if necessary, influence them in such a way that their predominant desires will never lead to a choice to do something morally wrong. On the assumption of compatibilism, the free-will defense is a failure.

But it is not merely this one formidable weapon in the philosopher's armory that is neutralized by compatibilism. The point that it is imperative to keep in mind is this: On the compatibilist view of free will, combined with the doctrine of absolute divine sovereignty and predestination, *God is entirely pleased with the world exactly as it is; there is no single fact he would wish to alter in any respect.* This may at first seem surprising, but the conclusion is really inescapable. For consider the situation of God prior to creation, as he is deciding what sort of world to bring into existence. God holds before his mind every possible scenario for world history—all the different "possible worlds," as philosophers say—and selects the very one that he finds most satisfying and most in tune with his creative purposes. (Or he selects "one of the best," if there are multiple worlds that are equally good.) Then he proceeds to put that scenario into effect, and of course there is no possibility whatever that the actual result will differ in any respect from that envisioned prior to creation. Since God in his wisdom has selected a world scenario that, out of all those that are logically possible, was most pleasing to him, he cannot fail to be entirely delighted with the course actually taken by his creation.

But when we apply this conclusion to the actual events the world contains, the result is chilling. Why was the little girl in Dunning's story raped and murdered? Because God wanted it that way; this terrible event was part of the world scenario that God, in his unconstrained freedom, decided should become actual. True, it was her father rather than God who performed the actual deed—but for many of us, that will be little consolation. And the same is true of the innumerable instances of rape, murder, infanticide—the list goes on and on—that occur in real life and not merely in fiction; every one of them happened precisely because God desired that they should happen and took whatever steps were necessary to insure that this would be the case.[4] Personally, I find this thought appalling, and I am astounded that fellow Christians are able to persuade themselves that it is acceptable. Without doubt, there is a great deal in the Bible that speaks against this way of thinking—that says that many things that take place in the world are *not* as God wishes them to be but are in fact very much opposed to his wishes. Think of the lament of Jesus over Jerusalem—"How often have I desired to gather your children together as a hen gathers her brood under her wings, and you were not willing!" (Matthew 23:37). Or the anguish of Yahweh, described by Hosea, at the unfaithfulness of Yahweh's wife Israel. An interpretation of these Scriptures that holds these events to be exactly what God has always wanted seems forced indeed. And if we are told that God is good and loving—indeed perfectly good and perfectly loving—in spite of this, we cannot help but wonder what words like *good* and *loving* can mean in such a context.

I shall not belabor this point further, because I am not hopeful that those who are firmly committed to a divine determinism will be persuaded by a direct assault. I can only ask such readers (if any of them have persevered thus far!) to consider the views presented here as a thought experiment, a way of understanding God and his relation to the world which is interestingly different (though in their view misguided) from their own understanding of these matters.[5]

I conclude then that a libertarian view of free will is essential for any adequate solution of the problem of moral evil. It should not be supposed,

---

[4]To be sure, not every such event need be one that God would desire considered simply in itself, apart from its relation to all other events. It remains true, nevertheless, that every event that occurs, however evil or tragic, is exactly what God intended to occur, and God has taken whatever steps are necessary to guarantee its occurrence.

[5]One of the best expositions of theological determinism is Paul Helm, *The Providence of God* (Downers Grove, Ill.: InterVarsity Press, 1994). Helm is both clearer and more candid about the implications of determinism than many other writers. See also William Hasker, "God Takes Risks" and Paul Helm, "God Does Not Take Risks," both in *Contemporary Debates in Philosophy of Religion*, ed. Michael L. Peterson and Raymond J. VanArragon (Malden, Mass.: Blackwell, 2004).

though, that it is only for this reason that libertarianism commends itself. On the contrary, there are strong reasons supporting such a view that have nothing to do directly with the problem of evil. One such reason is found in the fact that all of us naturally view our own decision making in this way, unless we have been talked out of it by philosophical, theological or scientific arguments. And perhaps not even the arguments can change how we really think about the matter. According to John Searle:

> for reasons I don't really understand, evolution has given us a form of experience of voluntary action where the experience of freedom, that is to say, the experience of the sense of alternative possibilities, is built into the very structure of conscious, voluntary, intentional human behaviour. For that reason, I believe, neither this discussion nor any other will ever convince us that our behaviour is unfree.[6]

The irony of this is that Searle is himself a determinist—or was one when he penned these words; more recently he has come to entertain libertarian free will as a serious possibility, precisely because of what seems the ineluctable testimony of experience.[7]

Another classic argument in this debate concerns moral responsibility. According to compatibilism, a person can perfectly well be morally responsible (and, in the case of a morally wrong action, guilty) for an action the occurrence of which is guaranteed by sufficient causes that are entirely outside the person's control. To others this seems incredible, so they maintain that if we are to hold people morally responsible for their actions, we must affirm libertarian free will. It would probably be fair to say that this argument has reached a standoff. Compatibilists have developed complicated counterarguments to show that under certain conditions it is perfectly reasonable to hold people responsible for actions whose sufficient causes existed before they were born and were therefore entirely beyond their control. Libertarians find these arguments uncon-

---

[6]John Searle, *Minds, Brains and Science* (Cambridge, Mass.: Harvard University Press, 1984), p. 98. Searle's point may call for further elucidation. I take him to be saying that while we may believe, on a theoretical level, that our actions are causally determined, we are unable to maintain this perspective when actually performing a voluntary action.

[7]For these more recent views see John R. Searle, *Rationality in Action* (Cambridge, Mass.: MIT Press, 2001), chap. 9.

vincing, but neither side is able to persuade the other.[8]

This argument between libertarians and compatibilists has generally taken place in the context of the assumption that the (alleged) sufficient causes of behavior will be natural causes, whether physical or psychological. The situation changes drastically, however, when we introduce God as the ultimate controller of everything that occurs, including the morally wrong action. In that case we are supposing that God, with full knowledge and deliberation, intentionally creates a situation in which human beings unavoidably act in morally abhorrent ways, and then God punishes those humans for that behavior while remaining beyond reproach himself. I can only say that I find this entirely incredible; further comment on it by me seems pointless.[9]

THE VALUE OF FREE WILL

It has been argued that libertarian free will is both credible in itself and essential for an adequate solution to the problem of moral evil. But here someone may ask: Isn't this really just part of the problem? Should we perhaps conclude with John Roth that free will is both too prolific of evil and suffering and too ineffective in dealing with the harms it creates, and is thus more a problem than a solution (see pp. 33-34)? Or to put the question in a more positive vein, what is there about free will that makes it worth the price it exacts?

By way of answering this, the reader is invited to perform a thought experiment. Imagine yourself as a prospective parent shortly before the birth of your first child. And suppose that someone has offered you the following choice: On the one hand, the child will, without any effort on your

---

[8]For a careful defense of compatibilism, see John Martin Fischer and Mark Ravizza, *Responsibility and Control: A Theory of Moral Responsibility* (Cambridge: Cambridge University Press, 1998). A number of essays relevant to the debate will be found in Robert Kane, ed., *The Oxford Handbook of Free Will* (Oxford: Oxford University Press, 2002). See also Timothy O'Connor, *Persons and Causes: The Metaphysics of Free Will* (New York: Oxford, 2000); and Derk Pereboom, *Living Without Free Will* (Cambridge: Cambridge University Press, 2001).

[9]It must be acknowledged that theological determinists usually do not describe their position as I have done. But what I have written is strictly entailed by the views they espouse, so I do not believe my characterization is unfair. They will also explain that God's actions are for his own good and wise purposes—purposes which, however, are inscrutable to us. I will leave it to the reader to decide how much this mitigates the situation.

part, always and automatically do and be exactly what you want him or her to do and be, no more and no less. The child will have no feeling of being constrained or controlled; nevertheless, she will spontaneously carry out your wishes on any and every occasion. Or on the other hand, you can choose to have a child in the normal fashion, a child who is fully capable of having a will of its own and of resisting your wishes for it, and even of acting against its own best interests. You will have to invest a great deal of effort in her education, with good hopes to be sure, but without any advance guarantee of success. And there is the risk, indeed the near certainty, that the child will inflict on you considerable pain and suffering as you strive to help her become all that she can be and ought to be. Which do you choose?

Such a choice is admittedly deeply subjective, and it may be that some readers will choose the first alternative, to have a child who is always and automatically in compliance with their wishes for it. It is my hope, however, that many readers—perhaps even a strong majority—will agree with me in saying that it is far better to accept the challenge of parenting a child with a will of its own, even at the price of pain and possible heartbreak, than to opt for an arrangement in which the child's choices will all really be my choices made for it, its life a pale reflection of mine lived through the child. If you agree with this, then it should have implications for the choice you think it would be best for God to make in choosing to create a world. In any case, it seems certain that God did *not* choose to create persons who always and automatically do exactly what he wants them to do— not, at any rate, if his wishes for created persons are anything like the teachings attributed to God in the Bible.

Here is another thought experiment: Suppose that at the end of a long and busy day you meet a stranger who says he has something interesting to tell you. The two of you sit down over a cup of coffee, and he explains that, entirely unknown to you, he has been controlling your activities throughout the day. He shows you a few pages of computer printouts, several days old, showing exactly what he has done to make sure that, in each of the decisions you made during that day, you would make that decision in a way that fits in with his own (undisclosed) objectives. Furthermore, he shows you a sealed envelope, to be put in a safe-deposit box to insure against tampering, containing comparable information concerning your activities and decisions for the next few days. (He confides that in calculating for the coming days he has had to make special allowance for what he foresees as your reaction to his revelations.) You are incredulous but agree to meet him again in a few days. When the meeting occurs, the sealed envelope is opened, and you find that he has indeed predicted and controlled your behavior just as he had said.

What is your reaction to this situation? My own prediction (made without benefit of a computer) is that it will be one of frustration, anger and resentment. This will be so, I predict, even if you do not, upon consideration, object strongly to any of the particular decisions the stranger has caused you to make. (If you do object to some of them, your resentment will be all the greater.) This resentment, I submit, is a measure of your attachment to the autonomy you believed yourself to have in making the decisions of your life. It is, in other words, a measure of the value you find in free will.

The value of free will does not end there. All sorts of experiences and relationships acquire a special value because they involve love, trust and affection that are freely bestowed. The love potions that appear in many fairy stories (and in the Harry Potter series) can become a trap; the one who has used the potion finds that he wants to be loved for his own sake and not because of the potion, yet fears the loss of the beloved's affection if the potion is no longer used. For that matter, individuals without free will would not, in the true sense, be human beings at all; at least this is the case if, as seems highly plausible, the capacity for free choice is an essential characteristic of human beings as such. If so, then to say that free will should not exist is to say that *we humans* should not exist. It may be possible to say that, and perhaps even to mean it, but the cost of doing so is very high.

THE STRUCTURE OF A HUMAN WORLD

At this point I will set out certain very general, structural features of a "human world," features that parallel those specified for the natural world in chapter five. Here as before, the features are general enough that they might well apply across a broad range of conceivable worlds containing persons, but it would be idle to pretend that we can imagine such alternative worlds except by selecting or modifying features familiar to us from human society. So I speak here of a "human world," but I mean to speak about its characteristics in as broad and general a way as possible.

First, *it is good that there should be free, rational and responsible persons.* This, of course, is a general claim about the goodness of existence that parallels the similar claim concerning the natural world. Here as before, the denial of the claim would seem to amount to a sweeping nihilism, something that may be possible to entertain in the abstract but is exceedingly difficult to embrace sincerely. One might imagine, to be sure, that there could be an alternative scheme of things that would have comparable or greater value and would not involve the existence of free, rational, and responsible persons. My own view is that it will be extremely difficult, and perhaps outright impossible, to flesh out such an alternative scheme in such a way as to give us reasonable confidence that we are dealing with a real possibility. Still, anyone who sees this as a promising line of thought is welcome to make the attempt.

Second, *it is good that persons should have occasion and opportunity to develop their inherent potentialities.* Given that persons exist, this seems self-evidently true; it would be absurd to claim that it is a good thing that the persons with their potentials exist, but not a good thing that the potentials should be developed and manifested. To be sure, there are in a sense potentialities for evil as well as potentialities for good; the response to this is that the potentialities for evil are merely the perversion of those for good, and they involve no positive excellence of their own that deserves to be cultivated. These potentialities fall into two broad categories, perhaps inseparable in practice: potentialities for cultural development, and potentialities for the development of individual character. Both sorts of potentialities are conditioned by historical circumstances, the former more conspicuously so. Intelligent extraterrestrials observing the earliest members of the species *Homo sapiens* would have had little evidence on which to predict the proficiency of some later members in non-Euclidean geometry or the composition of such works as the Ninth Symphony of Beethoven.

A little reflection suffices to show that both sorts of potential require for their development an objective environment, one in which the reactions of surrounding objects to the actions of persons is generally reliable and predictable. What is required, in short, is precisely the sort of environing natural world that was described in chapter five. Obviously there could be no sciences if the world of nature were not reliable in its reactions, and in view of this understandable and predictable. Music is possible because of the reliable acoustic properties both of voices and of the materials musical instruments are made of; speech itself is possible only because patterns of sound are reliably transmitted through the atmosphere. And as John Hick rightly points out, "The presence of an objective world—within which we have to learn to live on penalty of pain or death—is also basic to the development of our moral nature."[10] This is one of the major themes of Hick's Irenaean or "soul-making" theodicy. In a recent statement Hick elaborates the point as follows:

> We can imagine a paradise in which no one can ever come to any harm. Instead of having its own fixed structure, the world would be plastic to human wishes. Or perhaps the world would have a fixed structure, and hence the possibility of damage and pain, but a structure that is whenever necessary suspended or adjusted by special divine action to avoid human pain. Thus, for example, in such a miraculously pain-free world, one who falls accidentally from a high building would presumably float unharmed to the ground; bullets would become insubstantial when fired at a human body; poison would cease to poison; water to drown, and so on. We can at least begin to imagine such a world. . . . But . . . a world in which there can be no pain or suffering would also be one without moral choices and hence no possibility of moral growth and development. For in a situation in which no one can ever suffer injury or be liable to pain or suffering, no distinction would exist between right and wrong action. No action would be morally wrong, because no actions could ever have harmful consequences; likewise, no action would be morally right in contrast to wrong. Whatever the values of such a world, its structure would not serve the purpose of allowing its inhabitants to develop from self-regarding animality to self-giving love.[11]

---

[10]John Hick, "An Irenaean Theodicy," in *Encountering Evil*, ed. Stephen T. Davis, 2nd ed. (Louisville: Westminster John Knox Press, 2001), p. 46.

[11]Ibid., pp. 46-47. When Hick first developed the soul-making theodicy he was a theist of a rather traditional sort. At present he is a religious pluralist who takes the theodicy to be "mythologically true" though literally false. He still believes, however, that it is the most viable of the various Christian theodicies (see Davis, *Encountering Evil*, pp. 65-66).

It seems to me that Hick is right about this, and that this provides a further reason, above and beyond those cited in the chapter on natural evil, why the existence of a natural environment such as the one in which we exist is a good thing to be celebrated and not an evil to be deplored.

It needs to be said here also that Christian faith contemplates a further goal of personal development, one that lies beyond the cultivation of moral character though that is an essential component of it. Our true end, it is said, is to "glorify God and enjoy him forever"—to become sons and daughters of God, living in loving fellowship with God and with one another in the enjoyment of God's love. Clearly, this aim is less widely recognized in our society than is the importance of moral character, but for Christian faith it is nonnegotiable.

Third, *it is good that persons be joined together in families, communities and larger forms of social organization, within which persons are responsible to and for each other.* These communities are really presupposed in the two desiderata already stated: free and responsible personhood, and the development of the potentialities of persons, are for beings such as ourselves impossible apart from a community of some kind. (Even the hermit has been shaped by the community he has departed from, and his project is largely determined by his wish to separate himself from it, or at least from some of its aspects.) Higher culture is possible only in a society with a considerable division of labor; the very expression, "civilized way of life" refers both to a certain quality of human existence and to the social organization needed to sustain it. But communities and social organization inevitably involve differences of power and status between persons; these may be exaggerated or minimized depending on the proclivities of a particular group, but they can never be eliminated entirely. The "noble savage," noble precisely because of his independence from organized society, is and must always remain a myth.

Finally, *it is good that the structures and processes of human societies develop from within, utilizing the potentials and the ingenuity of the members of those societies rather than being imposed from without by a "higher power."* This is of course the counterpart to the "evolutionary clause" in our account of the natural order; it tells us that the structures of human society are precisely *human* structures, the product of human ingenuity and foresight, and that it is good that this should be so. Or would it be better if the structure and organization of society were an "ideal" structure and organization prescribed from above? It would, however, be the very same, decidedly nonideal individuals who must live in this ideal society and carry out its requirements, and the results could hardly be expected to conform to the perfect ideal. (Consider the uneven success of recent attempts to impose the "democratic ideal" on nations around the globe.) In any case, no single ideal pattern would be feasible; a structure that was the best possible at an early stage of social development would be entirely unsuitable for a more advanced society.

These four features have been described more briefly than the corresponding features of the natural order because they are more familiar and, in a sense, more obvious. It is also all too obvious how evil, specifically moral evil, can and does arise from these features. Free and intelligent persons can use their freedom and intelligence for self-centered purposes rather than for the common good. The opportunities for development can be neglected or, more ominously, perverted to serve evil purposes. The differences of power and status that are inherent in any society or community can be exploited by some to the detriment of others. The fact that the structures of society are humanly devised means that at best they will be imperfect and at worst highly dysfunctional. All this is unfortunately too familiar in practice to need elaboration.

There are, however, a few points that need further emphasis in order to maintain proper perspective. First of all, there is the absolutely crucial role played by sin in the entire process. As we have seen, it is doubtful that sin is an important component in the explanation of natural evil. There is, of course, the ecological harm done by human activities that disregard the needs of the environment. Beyond that, however, it is at best highly speculative to affirm a deep, structural effect of human sinfulness on the system of nature. With the evils that now concern us the situation is much different. Viewed in a theological context, sin and moral evil are very nearly coextensive, and their effect on human lives is pervasive and profound. And this means that whereas there is no compelling reason to suppose that there is something fundamentally amiss with the system of nature, there is every reason to suppose (indeed, it would be foolish to deny) that there is something deeply disordered about the lives of human beings. This disorder was not part of the Creator's intention and is not chargeable against the design plan of creation. As we contemplate the human scene we are not viewing a more-or-less faithful image of the divine intention but a badly marred and distorted version of it. There is, to be sure, the absolutely vital question as to what a loving God would and should do to counter and overcome this distortion of his creative intention; an answer to this question is the central theme of the Christian doctrine of redemption. This topic, however, must be postponed for the time being in order to continue our consideration of the ground plan of creation.

This having been said, it is also important here as elsewhere not to permit ourselves a myopic, one-sided emphasis on the evils in human life at the expense of the good it contains. Family life can be the source of great misery and the occasion for horrendous crimes. But it also provides the nurture that is essential for persons to grow to a healthy maturity, and it is the source of a very large part of the happiness enjoyed by human beings. Communities can be the locus for oppression and discrimination, but they should not be viewed solely in this light; there do exist relatively sound and healthy human communities in which many needs are cared for and in which human flourishing becomes a realistic possibility for many members. Nations can make war and wreak devastation on neighboring peoples as well as their own; they can also be a force, imperfect though it may be, for peace and justice in the world. It serves no good purpose if, when reflecting on the problem of evil, we abandon ourselves to an unrelieved pessimism that would serve us poorly in other facets of our lives.

Here is a further point: as we consider the communal dimension of human life, it is important to reflect on the fact that in communities we are responsible *to and for each other.* It is integral to the nature of any true community that its members establish standards for behavior within the community, work to inculcate the standards in members and potential members, and hold themselves and each other responsible for upholding those standards. (There may or may not be honor among thieves, but even a community of thieves has to have some standards of behavior so that its members know what to expect of each other.) The community standards will also include some common concern for the welfare of members of the community; otherwise communal life might offer too little benefit to be worthwhile. An important implication of this is that it may be destructive rather than beneficial for a community if persons or other entities outside the community take over these functions, thus relieving the members of the responsibility for each other. (This is one source of the aversion to government "interference" in the family among social conservatives. They feel, rightly or wrongly, that by taking over the functions of the family the government will weaken family bonding, something in which they set great store.)

All this evidently has implications for the role that should, and should not, be played by God in relation to human communities. God's parental concern for his children will not be expressed by his taking over the role of the human parents in nurturing and instructing their children. God is concerned for the material needs of people, but he will not take over and preempt the efforts of those who can and should meet these needs by their own labor and ingenuity. God is Judge of all the earth, but he does not preside in the local traffic court, nor is he the omnipresent policeman, patrolling the neighborhood and making sure that nothing improper takes place on his beat. God's concern for human fulfillment and maturity is precisely what rules out certain types of intervention—at least, rules them out as routine and habitual occurrences.

A FREE-WILL THEODICY

Once again, it is time to draw the threads together and state formally the theodicy developed through our reflections. The free-will theodicy comprises five propositions:

1. The world contains persons who are intelligent and free, living in communities within which they are responsible to and for one another. Human societies have developed by actualizing the inherent potentials of persons and utilizing these potentials for the development of progressively more complex social and cultural systems and progressively increasing control over the material environment.

2. The human world so constituted offers great potential for good in the realization and fulfillment of the potential of human persons and the development of human culture; beyond that, persons have the opportunity to

become children of God, enjoying the ultimate fulfillment human beings are capable of. The human world also offers the possibility, and indeed the reality, of great evil, as persons utilize their freedom to choose evil over good, short-term gratification over the common interest, hatred over love.

3. So far as we can see, no alternative world that does not share these general features could offer a potentiality for good comparable to that afforded by the actual world; only free and responsible persons are eligible to become sons and daughters of God.

4. Frequent and routine intervention by God to prevent the misuse of freedom by his creatures or to repair the harm done by this misuse would undermine the structure of human life and community intended in the plan of creation; accordingly, such intervention should not be expected to occur.

5. In virtue of propositions 1-4, it is good that God has created a universe containing human society as described; there is no basis for holding God morally at fault for doing so or for supposing that a perfectly good Creator would have acted differently.

As with the theodicy of natural evil, it is not to be expected that these five propositions by themselves will suffice to produce conviction. They function rather as a summary of a certain way of viewing the human world, a way that makes the evils that it contains understandable (though not acceptable) and counters the inclination we sometimes feel to blame the Creator or doubt his existence on account of these evils. This perspective on the world admits of indefinite elaboration, some of which has been provided by the other remarks in this chapter. There are, however, two additional topics that have been less emphasized here than in many other treatments of the subject and that call for comment at this point. Both of these topics have to do with possible reasons for particular instances of suffering.

A pervasive theme in religious writings concerning suffering, and in some treatments of the problem of evil, is the moral and spiritual value for the individual that can result from such suffering. We saw some of this emphasis in chapter five, in Diogenes Allen's references to the experiences and testimonies of Sister Basilea Schink, Edith Barfoot and Simone Weil. This is an important theme in writing on this subject because it plays an important role in the lives of many religious people. How is one to learn patience, except by dealing with difficulties that persist over a considerable period? (Everyone recognizes the irony in the prayer, "Lord, make me patient, and please do it *right now!*") Love in the deepest sense is sacrificial love, but sacrificial love requires an occasion for sacrifice, and most often this involves suffering of some kind. I will leave the elaboration of these themes to those who are more skilled in them than I am. However, there is a pair of cautions that may be appropriate at this point. The first is that while suffering can be the occasion for moral and spiritual growth, it may be unwise to assume that "the reason" for an instance of suffering is to provide such an occasion. This may sometimes be so, to be sure, but I suspect that we are not usually in a position to be confident that this is the case. This assumption is particularly problematic when the suffering involved affects another person. The sudden and unexpected death of a friend may lead me to reconsider my own careless attitude toward life, with beneficial results, but it would be worse than insensitive to assert on that account that my friend died in order that I might make such a reassessment. Furthermore, we should resist the temptation to claim that all suffering has such beneficial results; there simply are too many apparent counterexamples, instances in which suffering ruins someone's life with no visible benefit. On this topic I agree with Austin Farrer (himself a theodicist of the first order), who wrote, "Good, even animal good, such as physical health or a moderate plenty, is a more fertile breeder of good on the whole—yes, even of moral good—than evil of any kind can be."[12]

The other theme to which I wish to call attention is the perspective that views instances of suffering in the light of punishment for sin. The idea is not merely that sin and moral wrongdoing are prolific causes of the suffering in the world. What we are now considering is the idea that particular instances of suffering are to be seen as punishment precisely for the sins of the sufferer. This idea certainly occurs in the Bible, and not only in such discredited sources as the friends of Job. It is also something that comes readily to the minds of some religious people, and it finds an echo even in our secular culture in the phenomenon of "blaming the victim." (If those who suffer can be viewed as doing so because of some fault of their own,

---

[12]Austin Farrer, *Love Almighty and Ills Unlimited* (London: Collins, 1962), p. 167.

this reduces our anxiety that we may be vulnerable to similar misfortune.) There is no reason to deny that suffering may sometimes be a punishment, but caution is needed here just as it is in extolling the beneficial results of suffering. Most often we simply are not in a position to assert that someone is suffering as a punishment; the role of Job's comforters is always open to us, but we should be leery of stepping forward to occupy it. Even less should we commit to the general proposition that *all* suffering is punishment for the sins of the sufferers. We are warned against this, not only by the example of Job but by the words of Jesus, who denied that a certain man was born blind either because of his own sin or that of his parents (John 9:3). We should not doubt divine justice, but neither should we rush to interpret it.[13]

OBJECTIONS AND LIMITATIONS

It is time to acknowledge that the free-will theodicy faces objections that parallel those raised in chapter five against the natural-order theodicy. Like the natural-order theodicy, the free-will theodicy has relatively little to say that might provide a moral justification for particular evils. Indeed, I have recently criticized two different approaches that sought to provide such a justification—namely, that the evils are a means to moral and spiritual good, and that they are inflicted as punishment for sins. It was argued that while either of these might be true in a particular instance, we should refrain from generalizing and applying them to all cases of evil and suffering. But if these are not the justification for particular evils, what is?

Again, the free-will theodicy resembles the natural-order theodicy in that it does not provide a satisfying account of the love of God for particular men and women. The theodicy explains why God has created a world of free creatures, creatures who on all too many occasions utilize their freedom in doing harm to one another and to themselves. Perhaps we can see in this plan evidence of God's general benevolence toward his creation. But up to this point not much has been said about the love and care of God for individuals, particularly for those who are the losers in the lottery he has

---

[13]On one occasion John Paul II was asked whether the AIDS epidemic was a judgment of God on the sin of homosexuality. His answer was a model of circumspection: "It is difficult to know God's intentions."

ordained. Surely, however, this does need to be accounted for in a Christian theodicy.

The response on behalf of the free-will theodicy to these complaints must be the same as that previously given for the natural-order theodicy: these are limitations inherent in the two theodicies, and effective answers are not available in terms of the arguments developed to this point. The free-will theodicy, like the natural-order theodicy, seeks to give an account of the overall order of creation and to show that it is indeed the sort of creation that might be expected from a just and loving God. But to account for the overall order of creation is not the same as giving a morally satisfying account of the particular evils that trouble us, and vindicating God's overall beneficence falls short of exhibiting his undying love for each one of us. Surely, however, these matters do require our attention. So I must beg your indulgence and ask for a final verdict on our enterprise to be withheld pending the evidence of the final two chapters.

Finally, there may be a response that parallels the final objection in chapter five: in spite of all that has been said, there is simply *too much* evil and suffering in human life for the world to be seen as the creation of a loving God. Even granting the importance of the ends for which moral evil is said to be permitted—chiefly, the growth and maturation of persons— the means are too inefficient and there is far too much wastage. I am inclined to think that such a response is more plausible when moral evil is in question than when we focus primarily on natural evil, because there is an obvious state of moral disorder in human affairs that is different from anything we find in the natural world. The critic's response to this surplus of evil is likely to be not so much that human beings should never have been created but that a beneficent Creator would be *doing more* than apparently is being done to prevent or alleviate the worst results of human wickedness. Once again, this is a highly relevant issue; indeed it is the topic of chapter seven.

Why is life so hard? There are a myriad of reasons, but the main answer is surprisingly simple. The recalcitrance of nature plays its part, but in the main life is hard for human beings because we do this to ourselves. Or more often, we do it to each other.

Appendix

Plantinga's *Felix Culpa* Theodicy

I have not undertaken in this book to survey all the alternative theodicies and defenses that have been offered. However, a recent proposal by Alvin Plantinga deserves special notice.[1] One reason for this is that it constitutes a dramatic reversal of his earlier opposition to theodicy. The ancient Israelites, witnessing some uncharacteristic behavior from the newly anointed King Saul, asked one another, "Is Saul also among the prophets?" In the same way, we may ask ourselves, Is Plantinga also among the theodicists?

The theodicy deserves notice also because of its content. It is built around the ancient idea that Adam's sin was a *felix culpa*—a "fortunate fault"—because it became the occasion for our redemption in Christ. For Plantinga, the key to this is God's desire to create (more accurately, to actualize) a *very good* world. Now of all the worlds that are feasible, there are none (at least, none that we can imagine) that come even close, in their overall goodness, to those that contain "the towering and magnificent good of divine incarnation and atonement."[2] This being the case, God desired to actualize such a world—but in order for incarnation and atonement to be in order, there must be sinners in need of redemption. So we might picture the Lord's deliberative process in deciding which world to actualize as going something like the following. (The anthropomorphic description is my own, but the logic of the deliberations closely tracks Plantinga's exposition.)

> I want to actualize a very good world. No other worlds are anywhere near as good as those in which the Son is incarnated and suffers and dies as an atonement for sin. But in order for that to happen, there have to be sinners in need of atonement. Furthermore, there need to be *a lot* of sinners, committing some really terrible sins; otherwise I might seem to be overreacting. And just sin by itself, without suffering, won't do either; to make the world as good as it can be, and for the greater good of the creatures themselves,

---

[1]See Alvin Plantinga, "Supralapsarianism, or 'O Felix Culpa,'" in *Christian Faith and the Problem of Evil*, ed. Peter van Inwagen (Grand Rapids: Eerdmans, 2004), pp. 1-25.
[2]Ibid., p. 9.

they need to undergo a lot of suffering. Now, let me see which feasible world offers these features . . .

And as the saying goes, "the rest is (our) history." It should be evident that, while Plantinga himself remains a Molinist and a libertarian, free will does not play a prominent role in this proposal. The reason there is sin and evil in the world is not, as the free-will defense would have it, that they are the byproducts, which God cannot prevent, of a world containing free will. The reason, rather, is that they are among the necessary conditions of a world containing incarnation and atonement. God doesn't just put up with sin and suffering in his world; he positively seeks them out by selecting a world to actualize that contains plenty of both. The free-will defense is not, perhaps, invalidated by this; it may still perform its function of show-ing that God and evil are logically compatible with each other. But the "real reason" for sin and evil (and Plantinga does seem to think he has found the real reason; that is, he thinks his theodicy is *true*) is something else entirely.

There are serious problems with this theodicy. It is true, of course, that Christ's gift of himself and his life in sacrificial love is an enormously great and wonderful thing. It's a different matter, however, to suppose that this was the *only* way God could actualize a very good world. Plantinga does consider briefly the possibility that there may be other worlds in which God does something else comparable in its greatness to incarnation and atonement. But he says it is hard to imagine a world such as this, so he pro-poses that we ignore those possible worlds! One sort of possibility he ig-nores is the possibility of sin-free worlds that nevertheless do contain di-vine incarnation. If suffering is as good as Plantinga thinks it is (which is certainly open to doubt), then those sin-free worlds might contain ex-tremely difficult tasks, set both for the incarnate Son and for his followers (i.e., in such worlds, for everyone)—tasks that would involve serious suf-fering, though not of course separation from God and his love.

By far the most serious objection, however, is one that Plantinga con-siders but does not, in my opinion, succeed in defusing: God in this theodicy is *using* his creatures, treating them as means and not as ends in themselves, by placing them in great peril in order to get the glory of saving them. As Plantinga suggests, God seems "too much like a father who throws his children into the river so that he can then heroically rescue them, or a doctor who first spreads a horrifying disease so that he can then display enormous virtue in fighting it in heroic disregard of his own safety and fatigue."[3] In answer, Plantinga invites us to "suppose . . . that the final condition of human beings, in this world, is better than it is in the worlds in which there is no fall into sin but also no incarnation and redemption."[4] As I've noted, this ignores those worlds with incarnation but without sin and redemption. But perhaps it is sin itself that is essential; Plantinga cites Jonathan Edwards to the effect that "by virtue of our fall and subsequent redemption, we can achieve a level of intimacy with God that can't be achieved in any other way."[5] I think this claim is seriously problematic. It would be quite plausible to suppose that the intimacy with God of a redeemed sinner is *qualitatively different* than that of one who has never sinned, but to assert that it is *better* is troublesome. The apostle Paul was quite severe with those who accused him of saying, "Let us do evil that good may come" (Romans 3:8). But now it seems that the *felix culpa* theodicist is saying very much the same thing! (True, the theodicist is not encouraging us to commit *more* sins; presumably those already committed are sufficient to permit the desired intimacy.) Taken at face value, the claim would seem to imply that Jesus, who was sinless, did not enjoy the maximal level of intimacy with God. No doubt the reply will be that Edwards's principle does not apply to Jesus, who was the Son of God incarnate. But it seems odd to "trade off" divine incarnation and human sinfulness in the way presupposed by this answer: Jesus was maximally intimate with God because he was God's Son, but because we are not hypostatically united to the divine Word it is necessary, in order for us to achieve the greatest possible closeness to God, that we should be sinners. That is not contradictory, but I suspect I will not be alone in finding it exceedingly odd.

In any case, not everyone gets to enjoy this intimacy—at least, this is so if we accept the teaching of Scripture and the church that not all people

---

[3]Ibid., pp. 21-22.
[4]Ibid., p. 25.
[5]Ibid., p. 18.

find ultimate salvation. Those that do not, will be quite literally (as Plantinga's Calvinist forebears would have it) "damned for the glory of God." I believe that Plantinga owes it to us to state plainly whether he accepts this apparent consequence of his theodicy or whether he avoids it by embracing universalism.[6]

---

[6]For additional discussion of the *felix culpa* theodicy, see Kevin Diller, "Are Sin and Evil Necessary for a Really Good World? Questions for Alvin Plantinga's Felix Culpa Theodicy," *Faith and Philosophy* 25, no. 1 (2008); and Marilyn McCord Adams, "Plantinga on 'Felix Culpa': Analysis and Critique," *Faith and Philosophy* 25 (2008), forthcoming.

7

Shouldn't God Be Doing More?

We can often be certain that something . . . evil has happened, such as the sadistic murder of a child, and it is equally obvious that we can often be certain that it could have been prevented if there had been someone there who had some modest physical power, an understanding of the situation, and some interest in preventing evil or pain. God, by His nature, must know about and is capable of an interest in preventing the occurrence of a great deal of such evil and pain to those who have not deserved it. It follows that He would, if He existed, prevent such things from occurring, and since they do occur He does not exist; the existence of this kind of evil is the evidence which disproves the existence of God.

MICHAEL SCRIVEN, *PRIMARY PHILOSOPHY*

If your approach to the problem of evil resembles that of Michael Scriven, the theodicies presented in the last two chapters will seem largely irrelevant. Those theodicies were directed mainly at vindicating the general order of creation, both in the world of nature and in the human realm, as the sort of thing that might well have been brought about by a God who is good and wise and powerful. Scriven is not much interested in that; he looks at particular instances of evil that, in his view, could and should have been prevented by such a God, if one exists. Since God obviously does not prevent them, there is no God.

This is not the first time this issue has arisen on these pages. Several times in previous chapters the question has come up of giving some account of particular evils in relation to the goodness of God's creation. Each time, however, the question was deferred. In the chapter on natural evil, this was pointed out as an objection to the quasi-Stoic theodicy proposed by Diogenes Allen. Even if the general ordering of creation is as excellent as the Stoics say it is, this does not yet tell us anything about God's particular love for individual human beings, an essential part of the Christian (though not of the Stoic) idea of God. And God's permitting the sorts of horrors referred to by Scriven does not seem to be evidence of such an overwhelming divine love.

It may be worth pointing out that, historically speaking, this way of putting the issue has things backward. It is not the case that people first came up with the idea of a loving God, and then went on to ask what such a God might be expected to do about instances of terrible evil. On the contrary: the idea of a loving God was first elicited by *what God was believed to have actually done*, first in the history of the Hebrew people but especially in the life, death and resurrection of Jesus. "No one has greater love than this, to lay down one's life for one's friends" (John 15:13). When the apostle wrote "God is love," he immediately followed it by saying, "God's love was revealed among us in this way: God sent his only Son into the world so that we might live through him" (1 John 4:8-9). God's love for human beings is not presented as a self-evident fact but as a stunning revelation, inseparable from the revelation in Jesus Christ.

Still, we have the challenge presented by Scriven and by many, many others. And that challenge will not go away merely because of the facts we have cited about the history of our idea of God. What can we legitimately conclude about what a good and loving God should do about instances of terrible evil? Shouldn't God be doing more—a great deal more, in fact—than is actually being done? I will address this topic by considering a version of the argument from evil put forward by William Rowe. I will then discuss at some length three different kinds of response to this argument; I will argue that the last of these is the most successful. Before doing all this, however, I must ask the reader's indulgence for what may seem at first a digression: a discussion of the relevance for the problem of evil of a particular view of God's foreknowledge and divine providence. Far from being a digression, this will lead us straight to the heart of the issue we need to address.

EVIL AND DIVINE MIDDLE KNOWLEDGE

The theory of divine middle knowledge first made its appearance on these pages in chapter three, in connection with Plantinga's free-will defense. It turned out, however, to be less momentous in that context than at first appeared: there is, as we saw, a version of the defense that does not assume middle knowledge and that is at least equally as effective as the version that does presuppose it. The importance of middle knowledge (or Molinism, as the theory is called in honor of its inventor, Luis de Molina) for our topic is, however, by no means limited to that defense. On the contrary, Molinism provides the key to a far-ranging theory of divine providence, one that has important implications for the problem of evil.[1] That is what we must now consider.

Let's begin by recalling from the previous chapter the account of God's creation of the world according to divine determinism: God holds before his mind every possible scenario for world history—all the different "possible worlds," as philosophers say—and selects the very one that he finds most satisfying and most in tune with his creative purposes. (Or he selects "one of the best" if there are multiple worlds that are equally good.) Then he proceeds to put that scenario into effect, and of course there is no possibility whatever that the actual result will differ in any respect from that envisioned prior to creation. Since God in his wisdom has selected a world scenario that, out of all those that are logically possible, was most pleasing to him, he cannot fail to be entirely delighted with the course actually taken by his creation.

Now, Molinism differs from this view in an important way: it holds that human beings have received from God the gift of free will, understood in

---

[1]The Molinist theory of providence finds its best exposition to date in Thomas P. Flint, *Divine Providence: The Molinist Account* (Ithaca, N.Y.: Cornell University Press, 1998).

the libertarian sense, which means that in certain cases it is *entirely within their power* to determine which of two or more ways the world's future shall go. Rather than keeping all control entirely in his own hands, *God has granted to creatures some power to determine the course of events for themselves.* This is enormously important, and it establishes a fundamental difference between divine determinism and Molinism.

In spite of this difference, however, Molinism has certain implications for divine providence and the problem of evil that are remarkably similar to those of divine determinism. According to Molinism, God knows, logically prior to his decision to create, exactly what would be done by any free persons he might create in any possible situations he might place them. In virtue of this knowledge God is enabled, just as in the case of determinism, to select the world (or one of the worlds) that is most pleasing to him and most in accord with his creative purposes. There is, however, a limitation here that was not present in the deterministic case. The worlds God chooses between are limited to *feasible* worlds, worlds that can become actual *in the light of the decisions that creatures would freely choose to make.* God might prefer a world in which Adam and Eve, given the choice as it was in fact given to them, would have freely chosen to reject the serpent's enticements and to remain faithful to God's command to them. But this world is not a feasible world because the truth known to God through his middle knowledge was that, if placed in those circumstances and allowed to make that choice, Adam and Eve would freely choose to sin against God. Not all possible worlds are feasible, and it is only among the feasible worlds that God can make his choice of which world to make actual.

In spite of this limitation, however, God has available to him a very wide selection of feasible worlds, and he is able, just as with determinism, to ensure the actualization of the one that best suits his purposes. So we can adapt the previous description as follows: God holds before his mind every feasible scenario for world history—all the different "feasible worlds," as philosophers say—and selects the very one that he finds most satisfying and most in tune with his creative purposes. (Or he selects "one of the best" if there are multiple worlds that are equally good.) Then he proceeds to put that scenario into effect, and of course there is no possibility whatever that the actual result will differ in any respect from that envisioned prior to creation.

Now, since God is limited to feasible worlds, it may not be the case that he will be "entirely delighted with the course actually taken by his creation." There may be things about the world that God genuinely regrets—especially, one would think, some of the sins committed by his free creatures. Nevertheless, it remains true that, within the (very large) group of feasible worlds, his control of which one becomes actual is exactly the same as it would be under the assumption of theological determinism. Lest I be accused of misrepresenting Molinism in this respect, I quote here from Alfred J. Freddoso, translator of Molina and one of his leading contemporary interpreters. According to Freddoso, the doctrine of providence implies that

> God, the divine artisan, freely and knowingly plans, orders, and provides for all the effects that constitute His artifact, the created universe with its entire history, and executes His chosen plan by playing an active causal role sufficient to ensure its exact realization. Since God is the perfect artisan, not even the most trivial details escape His providential decrees.[2]

Note especially Freddoso's emphasis on the fact that even the most trivial details of the world scenario are part of God's plan and God's decrees. God *specifically intends* for every event to occur as it actually does.[3] But this is where things become difficult with respect to the problem of evil. For when the event God has "planned, ordered, and provided for" is something horribly evil, the question that unavoidably comes to mind is, Why did God choose to include *that* event in his plan? Now, no one can expect that in all or even in most cases we should be able to give a specific and detailed answer to this question. But the general outlines of the answer that is required do seem clear: if God included in his plan some event that is clearly evil, the reason must be that the scenario lacking the event in question

---

[2]Alfred J. Freddoso's introduction to Luis de Molina, *On Divine Foreknowledge: Concordia* 4, trans. Alfred J. Freddoso (Ithaca, N.Y.: Cornell University Press, 1988), p. 3.

[3]Molinists tend to dispute this and to claim that only some of these events are intended by God. I believe they do this because they think of "intending" as indicating *approval* of the events in question, which will not be the case with (for instance) sinful actions. Nevertheless, the act is part of God's plan and God's decree, and it is *that plan*, in all its details, that God intends to make actual. There may be some elements in the plan that God would prefer to have otherwise—but as the saying goes, you can't make an omelet without breaking eggs.

would be *even worse* than the one that actually occurs. Or, viewing things in a more positive light, there must be some great good, sufficiently great to outweigh the evil in question, that *could not be achieved* without the occurrence either of that evil event or of some other event as bad or even worse. To put things more concisely, *each instance of evil that occurs must be such that it could not be avoided by God without either losing (without equivalent compensation) some greater good or permitting some evil equally bad or worse.*[4] Now, this is a very strong claim about the "need" for the world's evils as a means to a greater good, a claim that some may find inspiring and encouraging. On the other hand, the claim may seem "too good to be true" and too strong to be plausible; it may place a burden on theodicy that theists will be hard put to make good on.

In the interest of clarity, I think it best to state at this point my own view about these matters. As has been intimated several times previously, I am no friend of the doctrine of divine middle knowledge. I consider that the metaphysical difficulties of this theory are severe and forbidding, and are sufficient in themselves to make the theory unacceptable. These issues, however, are extremely difficult and technical, and will not be argued for here. But beyond that, I believe that, on balance, middle knowledge is a hindrance and an obstacle to a viable doctrine of divine providence and an effective solution to the problem of evil. In particular, the claim about the "greater good" for which each instance of evil is necessary, which is italicized in the preceding paragraph, is in my view unsound and creates immense difficulties. The arguments for these views will be given in due course, but I think it is likely to be most helpful if they are stated clearly early on. (In philosophy, I've learned, the suspense created by withholding one's views for a surprise ending is seldom worth the resulting confusion!) At this point we can best proceed by attending to an important contemporary version of the problem of evil.

---

[4]The qualification about compensation is needed for this reason: Sometimes Molinists have attempted to evade the problem by proposing that *the existence of the actual world* is a great good that would be "lost" if the evil did not occur, since *any* change whatsoever would mean that the world scenario that is in fact the actual world would *not* be actual, but some other world scenario would be actual instead. It's evident that this is a trifling evasion—the "replacement" scenario might be every bit as good as or even better than the present actual world—but the "without compensation" clause disposes of it nicely.

ROWE'S EVIDENTIAL ARGUMENT FROM EVIL

Probably no single version of the problem of evil has attracted as much discussion in the last quarter-century as the "evidential argument from evil" championed by William Rowe. His argument is stated concisely:

(1) There exist instances of intense suffering which an omnipotent, omniscient being could have prevented without thereby losing some greater good or permitting some evil equally bad or worse.

(2) An omniscient, wholly good being would prevent the occurrence of any intense suffering it could, unless it could not do so without thereby losing some greater good or permitting some evil equally bad or worse.

(3) There does not exist an omnipotent, omniscient, wholly good being.[5]

As an example of the pointless suffering proposition (1) claims to exist, Rowe asks us to "Suppose in some distant forest lightning strikes a dead tree, resulting in a forest fire. In the fire a fawn is trapped, horribly burned, and lies in terrible agony for several days before death relieves its suffering."[6] If we agree, as Rowe thinks we should, that the fawn's suffering is pointless, the first premise is secured. And if we concur also in the second premise, the conclusion that God does not exist cannot be avoided.

In subsequent discussion Rowe's case of the fawn has been supplemented by an actual case described by Bruce Russell, in which a five-year-old girl was raped, beaten and strangled by her mother's boyfriend. Following William Alston, I will refer to the former case as "Bambi" and the latter as "Sue." Bambi and Sue, then, are representative instances of what seem to be innumerable cases of apparently pointless suffering that seem to show the truth of Rowe's first premise. Rowe's argument is termed an "evidential" argument from evil, to distinguish it from the logical argument from evil discussed in chapter three. That argument, it will be recalled, claimed to show a logical inconsistency between propositions that are in-

---

[5]William Rowe, "The Problem of Evil and Some Varieties of Atheism," *Philosophical Quarterly* 16 (1979), reprinted in *The Evidential Argument from Evil*, ed. Daniel Howard-Snyder (Bloomington: Indiana University Press, 1996), p. 2. This book is devoted entirely to discussion of Rowe's argument and variations thereon and of responses to it, especially the "skeptical theist" response discussed in the next section.

[6]Ibid., p. 4.

trinsic parts of the theological worldview. Rowe's argument, in contrast, employs a premise (1) that is not a necessary part of a theological worldview but that he considers to be abundantly supported by the evidence of the world in which we live. Given this premise, however, Rowe's is a deductive, logical argument just as much as the argument discussed in chapter three. Since the conclusion is unacceptable to theists, it is necessary for them to contest at least one of the two premises.

It may already be evident to the reader that Rowe's second premise (2) is very close to the requirement for theodicy arrived at in the previous section (see "Evil and Divine Middle Knowledge") of this chapter. In fact, if we broaden the class of evils from Rowe's "intense suffering" to include serious evils of any description, and if we assume a "without compensation" clause to be implied, the two principles are essentially identical. (Neither change, I'm confident, is contrary to Rowe's intentions.) For ease of reference, we will speak of Rowe's premise (2), so augmented, as "Rowe's Requirement." And instances of evil that violate this requirement—that are not essential for God's being able to achieve some greater good or to prevent some equal or greater evil—will be termed "gratuitous evil."

Now a strong majority of philosophers, both theists and atheists, who have considered this argument have taken Rowe's Requirement as axiomatic. They have assumed, that is to say, that God and gratuitous evil (in the sense defined) are incompatible—that if God exists, there can be no gratuitous evil and vice versa. Theists, on this assumption, must contest the first premise, which affirms that gratuitous evil does indeed exist. The most important way in which this has been done will be the topic of the next section (see "The Skeptical Theist Defense") of this chapter. There is, however, a relatively simple and direct way to reject gratuitous evil, one that Rowe himself recognized as a possibility. Rowe argued: gratuitous evil exists; God and gratuitous evil are incompatible; so God does not exist. But it is perfectly possible to reverse the argument, as follows: God exists, God and gratuitous evil are incompatible, so gratuitous evil does not exist. This is not a mere trick, as might seem at first glance. It is a perfectly legitimate argumentative strategy, sometimes termed the "G. E. Moore shift" for the twentieth-century English philosopher who called attention to this form of argument. The shift can properly be employed whenever one's reasons for rejecting the conclusion of an argument are stronger than one's reasons for accepting one or more of the premises. In the present case, if you are strongly convinced by the evidence for the existence of gratuitous evil and see only weak evidence, or none at all, for the existence of God, then you will reason as Rowe does. If on the other hand you find yourself having strong support for your belief in God and find the evidence for gratuitous evil to be inconclusive, you will follow the second line of reasoning and conclude that gratuitous evil does not exist. Which argument is more compelling, logically speaking, is a matter of the relative strength of the evidence supporting the premises of the respective arguments.

This approach, then, does provide a relatively straightforward way in which theists can resist Rowe's argument. It needs to be seen, however, that there is a price to be paid for taking this line. The approach in question begins by acknowledging that the evidence that seems to indicate the existence of gratuitous evil *counts against* the existence of God. Now if the evidence in favor of God's existence is very strong and the evidence for gratuitous evil has little or no force, this may not matter very much. But for many of us, this does not seem to be the situation. Many of us will find that the evidence favoring the existence of gratuitous evil is rather compelling. Just ask yourself, what might the "greater good" be, in the cases of Bambi and Sue? It is not easy to come up with candidates that are even moderately plausible. Of course, we might suppose that there are, unknown to us, special circumstances about these particular cases, circumstances which mean that, in these instances, preventing the evils really would have meant having to give up some greater good or permitting some even greater evil. This sort of response might not be implausible *if* the cases of Bambi and Sue were singular and isolated, far removed from the sort of thing that ordinarily goes on in the world. Unfortunately, this is very far from being the case. On the contrary, these cases were selected as *representative* of a very large class of evils from which there is no apparent good result, or none that seems at all comparable in its significance to the evil itself. To suppose that *in every such instance* there is, wholly unknown to us, some greater good that results from the evil *and that God could achieve in no other way* seems far-fetched indeed. But according to Rowe's Requirement, even a single instance of gratuitous evil is sufficient to disprove the existence of God.

If this is so, then it seems that the weight of the evidence for gratuitous evil has quite a lot of force and can't readily be brushed aside even if one's initial faith in God is fairly strong. Such evidence might lead a person to have serious doubts about God's existence—and it actually does have this effect for a good many people. And if a person's initial belief in God is somewhat weak and vacillating, it might be overwhelmed entirely by the evidence of gratuitous evil. It would be idle to deny that this is the actual situation of many people in our society. For these reasons, many theists have felt the need to find a better response to the evidential argument than the one that has been sketched here.

THE SKEPTICAL THEIST DEFENSE

The response to the evidential problem that has attracted the most attention in recent years is what has come to be known as "skeptical theism."[7] The skeptical theist accepts Rowe's Requirement and argues that it is satisfied—or at least, that we have no good reason to suppose that it is not satisfied. This is not done, however, by proposing a hypothesis concerning the actual sorts of good made possible, or worse evils averted, by instances of apparently gratuitous evil. Nor is it done by adducing evidence for God's existence that can outweigh the evidence for gratuitous evil. Rather, the skeptical theist attempts to undermine the force of the evidence for gratuitous evil; he or she argues that, in view of our cognitive limitations, we simply are in no position to conclude that any given instance of evil is gratuitous. This is the "skepticism" of skeptical theism: the skeptical theist denies that we have good reason to believe something that, in the view of many others, we have very good reason to believe. (Skeptical theists need not be, and in typical cases are not, skeptics about philosophical or commonsense claims in general.)

An important early statement of skeptical theism came in Stephen Wykstra's paper "The Humean Obstacle to Evidential Arguments from Suffering: On Avoiding the Evils of 'Appearance.' "[8] Wykstra fastens on

---

[7]For a more extensive discussion of skeptical theism see "The Sceptical Solution to the Problem of Evil," chapter 3 of William Hasker, *Providence, Evil, and the Openness of God* (London: Routledge, 2004).

[8]Stephen Wykstra, "The Humean Obstacle to Evidential Arguments from Suffering: On Avoiding the Evils of 'Appearance,' " *International Journal for the Philosophy of Religion* 16 (1984): 73-94.

Rowe's claim that in the case of the fawn "there does not appear to be any outweighing good."[9] He notes that there are at least two ways in which such an "appears" claim can be disputed:

> One way is to admit that the adduced situation does have the *prima facie* evidential import imputed to it . . . but to argue that there is other evidence that outweighs or defeats this *prima facie* evidence. The other way is to argue that the adduced situation does not even have the *prima facie* evidential import imputed to it by the "appears" claim.[10]

In pursuing this latter strategy, Wykstra articulates the "condition of reasonable epistemic access," or CORNEA:

> On the basis of cognized situation s, human H is entitled to claim "it appears that p" only if it is reasonable for H to believe that, given her cognitive faculties and the use she has made of them, if p were not the case, s would likely be different than it is in some way discernable by her.[11]

In arguing that CORNEA is not satisfied in the case of the fawn's sufferings, Wykstra proposes an example:

> Searching for a table, you look through a doorway. The room is very large—say, the size of a Concorde hangar—and it is filled with bulldozers, dead elephants, Toyotas, and other vision-obstructing objects. Surveying this clutter from the doorway, and seeing no table, should you say: "It does not appear that there is a table in the room"?[12]

Clearly the answer should be no—and Wykstra thinks the same answer is obviously called for in the Bambi case.

It should be noted that there is no suggestion, so far, that the good for which Bambi suffers is of a kind that is radically different from the goods we are ordinarily acquainted with. There is nothing particularly mysterious or

---

[9]Ibid., p. 79.

[10]Ibid., p. 81.

[11]Ibid., p. 85. CORNEA as stated is ambiguous. Richard Swinburne interprets Wykstra to mean that "we can only assert 'it appears that *p*' if we have positive reason to think that if *p* were not so, our experience would be different" (*Providence and the Problem of Evil* [Oxford: Clarendon, 1998], p. 26). Swinburne objects to this on the ground that it generates a demand for an infinite regress of justification. CORNEA can, however, be interpreted to mean merely that we must "have no reason to think that if *p* were not so, our experience would be the same" (ibid.). On this interpretation, CORNEA is acceptable—and is arguably met in the case of gratuitous evil.

[12]Wykstra, "Humean Obstacle," p. 86.

unrecognizable about a table; the difficulty in the example lies entirely in the
fact that our field of vision is seriously obstructed. This parallel would lead
us to think that we can't discern the reason for Bambi's sufferings because of
our inability to find the outweighing good in a complex situation or to recognize the connection between that good and the suffering. Fairly soon,
however, the discussion shifted to a heavy emphasis on goods whose intrinsic
nature is unknown to us. A good example of this move is found in William
Alston's article, "The Inductive Argument from Evil and the Human Cognitive Condition."[13] Alston reviews a number of possible outweighing
goods, derived from various strands of traditional theodicy, and argues that
in a great many cases we are unable to exclude these goods as possible reasons
for God's permitting particular evils. (Examples include suffering as a punishment for sins, suffering as a means of soul-making, suffering as God's way
of bringing us to repentance and salvation, suffering as a test of one's loyalty
toward God [as in martyrdom], and suffering as a vision of the inner life of
God, among others.) In the end, however, he is forced to admit that none of
the goods he has identified can be plausibly supposed to be God's reasons in
the cases of Bambi and Sue. "And hence showing that no one can be justified
in supposing that reasons of the sort considered are not at least part of God's
reasons for one or another case of suffering does not suffice to show that no
one can be justified in supposing that God could have no sufficient reason
for permitting the Bambi and Sue cases." Alston goes on to say, "This lacuna
in the argument is remedied by the point that we cannot be justified in supposing that there are no other reasons, thus far unenvisaged, that would fully
justify God in permitting Rowe's cases. . . . Even if we were fully entitled to
dismiss all the alleged reasons for permitting suffering that have been suggested, we would still have to consider whether there are further possibilities
that are undreamt of in our theodicies."[14] And with this, what has become
known as the "beyond our ken" defense takes center stage; if the good for the
sake of which God might permit some evil is one of which we have no understanding whatever, it is obvious that we don't have evidence that would
enable us to rule it out.

---

[13]William Alston, "The Inductive Argument from Evil and the Human Cognitive Condition," *Philosophical Perspectives* 5 (1991), reprinted in Howard-Snyder, *Evidential Argument from Evil.*
[14]Ibid., p. 119.

In evaluating the skeptical theist defense, I want to begin by acknowledging the value of the reminder about our cognitive limitations in dealing with these matters. This reminder is especially helpful as presented by Alston, as he reviews a number of suggestions for theodicy and points out that in a great many cases we are really in no position to rule them out as justifications for particular evils. The reminder is perhaps especially in order as directed against philosophers; we do sometimes tend to think that, given a pad of paper, a ball-point pen and a couple of hours free of interruption, we can figure out just about anything. We can't, and it is important to be reminded of that. But while epistemic modesty is a good thing, it is important to be modest about the right things and not about the wrong things. (We would not be too impressed by a mathematician who "modestly" disclaimed all knowledge as to whether or not the values given in the multiplication table are correct.) So here is the question we need to ask about skeptical theists: Are they perhaps inappropriately modest about some cases in which we can draw well-supported conclusions? And on the other hand, do they fail to exercise due skepticism on some important matters where skepticism is called for? Let's see.

We need to examine more closely the cognitive limitations that are stressed by skeptical theism. Consider, then, some particular instance of evil that occurs. It may very well be that there is some good that is made possible by that instance of evil that we have simply failed to notice. Or we may be aware of the existence of the good in question but are unaware of the connection between that good and the evil we are investigating. Or we may know of the good state of affairs and recognize that it is a consequence of the instance of evil, but we may fail to estimate properly its importance. Or, finally, the instance of evil may be a necessary condition for some good state of affairs of whose nature we have no conception whatsoever. All of this seems entirely possible—that is, we know of nothing that conclusively rules it out—and so far the skeptical theist case seems to be on solid ground.

But the account of our cognitive limitations is not yet complete. It is also possible that the evil we are considering has led to yet further evils, evils of which we are unaware because we have failed to notice them. Or we may know of the existence of these further evils but are unaware of the connection between them and the original evil. Or we may know of the additional evils and recognize that they are consequence of the original evil, yet fail to estimate properly their importance. Or, finally, the instance of evil may be a necessary condition for some further evil state of affairs of whose nature we have no conception whatsoever. Just as with the elements in the previous list, all of this seems entirely possible; we know of nothing that rules it out.

Now, the point we need to see clearly is this: *Nothing in our evidence gives any reason to think that the possibilities in the first list are more likely to occur than those in the second.* If the possibilities in the first list are realized, the world may be morally a good deal better than we had supposed—that is, many evils that seem to us to be gratuitous may in fact be justified— while if those on the second list are realized, it may be a good deal worse. *The evidence tells us nothing that makes one of these more likely than the other.* But lacking a reason to prefer the possibilities on the first list, the claim that Rowe's Requirement is satisfied *gets no support whatever* from the enumeration of our cognitive limitations. Richard Swinburne asks, "Why should our inadequacies of moral belief lead us to suppose that the world is worse rather than better than it really is?" He contends that "unless we have reason to suppose that our error is more likely to lie in one direction than the other," the appeal to our cognitive imperfections is "worthless."[15]

Swinburne may, however, be a bit too quick in dismissing the skeptical theist defense. Even if, as he rightly says, the recognition of our "inadequacies of moral belief" gives us no reason to think that the world is morally better than it seems to us to be, this recognition might still be advantageous in another respect. Recognizing these limitations may lead us to understand that we really are in no position to judge whether a particular evil is or is not gratuitous in the sense under discussion. And once we understand this, the evidential argument from evil collapses, since its first premise is without evidential support.

This rejoinder to Swinburne seems partly correct in that a consideration of our epistemic limitations may well make us less confident about in-

---

[15]Swinburne, *Providence and the Problem of Evil*, pp. 27, 28. To the best of my knowledge, Swinburne was the first to point out this problem with the skeptical theist defense.

stances of apparently gratuitous evil than we might otherwise be inclined to be. But *how much* less confident should it make us? In order for our awareness of our limitations to remove *all* of our confidence that some of the evils we encounter are gratuitous, we should have to come to believe that we have *no ability whatsoever* to ascertain whether the overall consequences of a particular action or event are, on the whole, good or bad. This, however, is implausible in the extreme—and if we really were convinced of this, it would have a devastating effect on our moral lives. (At this point, the skepticism of skeptical theism really begins to bite.) A more reasonable assessment is that awareness of our cognitive limitations may reduce to some extent our confidence that a given instance of evil is gratuitous but will not and should not eliminate entirely the evidential force of apparently gratuitous evil. And if we keep in mind that, given Rowe's Requirement, God's existence is excluded if there is *even one* instance of genuinely gratuitous evil, I submit that the force of the evidence will be only slightly weakened, for most of us, by consideration of our cognitive limitations.

At this point another possibility suggests itself: can the skeptical theist defense be *combined with* the "G. E. Moore shift"?[16] The idea would be that the skeptical theist strategy reduces the weight of the prima facie evidence for the existence of gratuitous evil to the point where this evidence can readily be outweighed by the believer's positive reasons for believing in God. In principle, this strategy may be feasible. However, it does not comport well with the original intention of the skeptical theist stance, as seen in Wykstra's article. In that article he claimed not merely to reduce the weight of the evidence for gratuitous evil but to eliminate it entirely, insisting that "the adduced situation [i.e., the Bambi case] does not even have ...*prima facie* evidential import." And William Alston undertakes to show that "*no one can be justified in supposing* that God could have no sufficient reason for permitting the Bambi and Sue cases."[17] The present proposal evidently makes a much weaker claim than this. I believe, furthermore, that for the reasons already given the skeptical theist strategy can bring about only a rather modest reduction in the force of the evidence for gratuitous

---

[16]My thanks to an anonymous reader of the manuscript for suggesting this possibility.

[17]Alston, "Inductive Argument from Evil," p. 119 (emphasis added).

evil; the main burden of the argument then must still be borne by the believer's preexisting faith in God.

But are we unable to conclude with confidence that some particular instance of evil is gratuitous? I believe we can do this, and I submit that Rowe's Bambi case is an excellent candidate. I do not suppose that examples of this sort constitute the most serious instances of gratuitous evil. But there are certain reasons why it is easier in this case than in others to construct a strong argument to rule out the possibility of a greater good resulting from the evil. Even so, the case will not be airtight—but I believe most of us, theists and nontheists alike, will find the remaining possibilities highly implausible and unattractive.

Some preliminaries are needed. I begin by articulating the following principle, which I claim applies to goods and evils across the board:

(A) Any good (evil) state of affairs must consist of some actual or possible benefit (harm) to some rational or sentient being.

To see the plausibility of this, consider William James's thought experiment in, "The Moral Philosopher and the Moral Life," of a world entirely devoid of life.[18] Considered just in itself, and not with regard to possible future inhabitants, can anything about such a world be said to be either good or bad? James thinks not, and surely he is right; there is just nothing there for our value judgments to get a grip on. (Of course we must exclude also the possibility of a divine Observer, which is what James does at this stage of his argument.)

Supposing principle (A) to be secured, we next ask: In the Christian view of things, what "rational or sentient beings" might there be to be benefited or harmed by Bambi's suffering? A short but arguably complete list would go as follows:

- God
- human beings
- nonhuman animals
- nonhuman created intelligences (either angelic or extraterrestrial)

Now, consider just one aspect of the Bambi case, namely, the fawn's con-

---

[18]William James, *Essays in Pragmatism* (New York: Hafner, 1969), p. 69.

tinued suffering over several days as it waits for death to come. This suffering could be averted, it would seem, with no perceptible change in the physical situation by the fawn's either dying sooner or going into a coma until death arrives. And now we ask, what greater good could result from this prolonged suffering?

To begin with, we can stipulate that no human being observes or even becomes aware later on of the fawn's tragic death. So no human being learns valuable lessons from contemplating the event. If we think animals learn from each other's sufferings, we can further stipulate that no other animals are left alive in the vicinity. The supposition that God is somehow benefited by his own contemplation of the fawn's suffering, and this is the reason he allows it to suffer, would pose a problem worse than the one it is called upon to solve. We are left, then, with nonhuman created intelligences—angels or extraterrestrials. We can't exclude their awareness of the situation by stipulation, for they may have ways of being aware of it that we could not detect. But what sort of possibilities does this leave us? What kind of benefit can they be supposed to gain from the fawn's suffering that outweighs the suffering itself? If there is an answer to this, it must indeed be a good "beyond our ken." But where else is the skeptical theist to go? At this point, I think, the skepticism that this is a real case of gratuitous evil begins to seem forced and extremely implausible.

Finally, I want to point out one respect in which it seems that skeptical theists are less skeptical than they ought to be and need to be. The skeptical theist has apparently failed to direct his or her skeptical questioning at the key point on which he or she agrees with the evidential argument from evil—namely, Rowe's Requirement. If this requirement can be undermined, then there will be no further need for the (sometimes forced and implausible) skepticism about the existence of gratuitous evil or for the unwarranted assumption that the world is morally a great deal better than it seems to us to be. But can Rowe's Requirement reasonably be doubted? I believe that it can, and I will presently explain why.

CHALLENGING ROWE'S REQUIREMENT

So far, our attempts to find an effective answer to the evidential argument from evil have not been particularly successful. Most philosophers have not been willing to specify in any detail the sorts of goods they think come about as a result of apparently gratuitous evils. (We shall, however, be looking at one theodicy that does just that.) The strategy based on the G. E. Moore shift is a possibility, but it is effective only if the evidence for gratuitous evil is weak, which I have argued is not the case. The skeptical theist defense seemed initially promising, but on closer examination it encounters serious objections. So far, then, the perplexity that arises from the evidential argument remains largely unresolved.

Central to the argument, of course, is Rowe's Requirement, which all the approaches considered so far agree in accepting. Can this principle be challenged? I believe that it can, but the challenge needs to be carefully developed, because the principle seems quite compelling to a good many thinkers, theists and atheists alike.[19] To begin with, we need to have before us a formal statement of the principle, with the amendments noted previously.

> Rowe's Requirement: An omnipotent, omniscient, wholly good being (that is, God) would prevent the occurrence of any serious evil unless he could not do so without thereby losing (without equivalent compensation) some greater good or permitting some evil equally bad or worse.

Rowe's Requirement, as I have noted, has been seen as axiomatic, even self-evident, by a good many philosophers. Yet a closer consideration reveals that there may well be reason to doubt it. It is clear that this principle finds its natural home in a utilitarian or consequentialist scheme of ethics, one in which moral goodness is a matter of bringing about as much good as one possibly can. Now consequentialism in ethics has considerable appeal, but there have also been numerous objections raised against it, and most Christian ethical theories are not consequentialist, at least not entirely so. So we may wonder: If consequentialism is rejected as a theory of ethics for human beings, why is it seen as being extremely plausible where God's moral goodness is concerned? One feature of consequentialism that is apparent in the principle is the assumption that there is a single, universal scale of value on which all particular values can be compared, probably

---

[19]For more extensive development of the line of argument presented here, see my "The Necessity of Gratuitous Evil" and "Can God Permit 'Just Enough' Evil?" chaps. 4 and 5 respectively of *Providence, Evil and the Openness of God*. (The first of these appeared in the January 1992 *Faith and Philosophy*.)

in a quasi-mathematical fashion. (Otherwise the questions as to what is a "greater good" or an "evil equally bad or worse" would have no determinate answers.) It was argued in chapter four that this assumption is false, and if that is correct Rowe's Requirement is undermined as a fundamental principle of moral obligation. I do not claim that these considerations by themselves suffice to refute the principle, but they do show that it is more open to question than has often been supposed.

My claim will be that Rowe's Requirement should be rejected because it comes into conflict with an important principle that is deeply entrenched in the Christian and theistic worldview. I will introduce this argument by citing a theodicy that sets even more stringent conditions for the permission of evils than are established by Rowe's Requirement. The theodicy is one proposed by Eleonore Stump, who claims that

> a perfectly good entity who was also omniscient must govern the evil resulting from the misuse of . . . significant freedom in such a way that the sufferings of any particular person are outweighed by the good which the suffering produces *for that person:* otherwise, we might justifiably expect a good God somehow to prevent *that particular suffering,* either by intervening (in one way or another) to protect the victim, while still allowing the perpetrator his freedom, or by curtailing freedom in some select cases.[20]

Our initial reaction may well be that this claim is simply incredible if put forward as an account of what actually goes on in the world. How can it possibly be, we may wonder, that all of the most terrible evils that happen to people really benefit them rather than doing them harm? Stump, however, has a response that may go some way toward alleviating this reaction. She lays a great deal of stress (as is appropriate in a Christian account of evil) on the "defect in the will" that exists in human beings and forms a barrier between them and God. In order for this defect to be overcome, we must freely will to accept God's help. According to Stump, "Things that contribute to a person's humbling, to his awareness of his own evil, and to his unhappiness with his present state contribute to his willing God's help. I think that both moral and natural evils make such a contribution."[21] She

---

[20]Eleonore Stump, "The Problem of Evil," *Faith and Philosophy* 2 (1985): 411.
[21]Ibid., p. 400.

has a great deal more to say about this, but the upshot is that the primary benefit sufferers receive from their suffering is that it makes them more likely to turn to God in faith and repentance, and to draw closer to God, and this result is of such surpassingly great value that it outweighs all the pain and suffering they have to endure. To be sure, it cannot be guaranteed in an individual case that the suffering of a particular person will be outweighed by the good it produces for that person, for the good in question consists primarily in the person's freely chosen response to God and as such cannot be guaranteed. What is the case, however, is that the suffering is the *best possible means* to that person's salvation and spiritual growth, so that the person without that suffering would be *less likely* to turn to God in repentance and faith than he or she is with it. Furthermore, the suffering never exceeds, either in duration or in intensity, the maximum amount that contributes in a positive way to the sufferer's likelihood of finding salvation and spiritual fulfillment, otherwise the surplus suffering would be gratuitous, and a good God would not permit it.

Now the reader may be inclined to think (as I do) that Stump seriously overestimates the beneficial tendencies of suffering and unjustifiably ignores the multitude of cases where it seems that severe suffering has no such salutary effects as the ones she describes. This, however, is not our primary concern at present. The question I do want to pose is this: If we really believed these claims of Stump's and thoroughly internalized them, what effect would this have on our attitude toward those who suffer serious harms? If we were to do this, we would understand that *no person can ever be ultimately harmed* by anything that happens or is done to her. True, she may endure physical and mental suffering, torture, degradation and death, but all of this will be more than compensated for by the spiritual benefits that will come to the person as a result of that suffering, provided only that she responds to the suffering by allowing her own will to be more fully conformed to God and to his will. Furthermore, if we were to act to relieve the sufferings of another person we would not, on balance, be benefiting her but might actually be doing harm. For the sufferings that come to the person will never in any case exceed the amount needed to give her the best possible opportunity for coming closer to God; if we reduce the total amount of suffering below what it would otherwise be, we may be interfering with precisely what is needed in order for the person to be drawn to God. Our intervention, then, offers a dubious benefit and the real possibility of serious harm.

I doubt that many readers will disagree with me when I say that the attitude toward suffering described here is absolutely appalling; certainly it has little in common with the compassion exhibited by, for instance, Mother Teresa of Calcutta. Fortunately, serious Christians will normally have undergone a process of moral formation that will inhibit them from taking up an attitude toward the suffering of others such as the one described. (I know of no one less likely to be dissuaded from works of mercy by the implications of this theodicy than Eleonore Stump!) Nevertheless, the disturbing implications of the theodicy remain. This, I think, is a prime example of the sort of theodicy we were warned about by D. Z. Phillips in chapter two—a theodicy which, if taken with full seriousness, would tend to undermine our own moral attitude toward life, and in particular toward the sufferings of others.

Now, Rowe's Requirement is not as stringent as Stump's theodicy in the conditions it sets for God's permission of evils; it allows for evils that lead to *some greater good or other* but does not require that the greater good should benefit specifically the person who is suffering. Nevertheless, it will become apparent that Rowe's Requirement also, if taken with full seriousness as an account of God's way of running the world, would have a deleterious effect on our moral lives and on our attitudes toward the suffering of other people. The principle that, I will argue, conflicts with Rowe's Requirement is the *principle of divine moral intention:*

> It is an extremely important part of God's intention for human persons that they should place a high priority on fulfilling moral obligations and should assume major responsibility for the welfare of their fellow human beings.

It is evident that this principle is implicit in the biblical picture of God and God's relationship to the world; this is apparent in the giving of the Ten Commandments, in the instructions of the Sermon on the Mount and in a thousand other places in Scripture. It is also a characteristic emphasis of the other major theistic religions. But why do I say this principle is in conflict with Rowe's Requirement? If we believe God is running the world in compliance with that requirement, it follows that the *offsetting good principle* is true:

Any harm resulting from a morally wrong action will be offset by a "greater good" that God could not have obtained without permitting the evil in question.

This is a straightforward consequence of Rowe's Requirement: If a morally wrong action would result in some harm or other serious evil that would not lead to a greater good, then God would not permit it. So I do not need to worry, as I consider some action that may be morally dubious, whether this action will have a harmful effect on anyone other than myself. If it does have such an effect, this will be because the harm in question is necessary in order for God to be able to bring about some greater good—something that even God could not achieve without permitting that harm. If the harm that might result from my action won't have such a beneficial result, then God simply won't allow it to happen.[22]

Now, I maintain that if it were generally believed that things are really like that, this would have a very serious effect on our incentive to live morally good lives and to take responsibility for the welfare of those around us.[23] (They are being taken care of already by God, so what is there to worry about?) And this is especially likely to be the case when it is a matter of our going out of our way and engaging in difficult and costly endeavors in order to prevent or alleviate harm that may come to other people. This claim of mine has, however, been challenged. Daniel Howard-Snyder comments:

Most of us, I dare say, would be far less affected by the abstract knowledge that our choices will not make things better or worse overall than by the con-

---

[22]There is a complication that needs to be mentioned here. Many people would hold that the mere fact of a person's exercising the power to make a free choice has some intrinsic value, regardless of whether the choice is made well or badly. If so, then some of the evil resulting from a morally wrong choice might be offset by the intrinsic good of the person's making the choice. *How much* evil could be offset in this way depends on how great a value we attribute to a single instance of making a free choice. I believe that the value in question is relatively small and that in the case of severely evil consequences only a small part of the resulting evil could be offset by the intrinsic value of the choice. (Rowe, as it happens, agrees with this assessment.) If so, this consideration does not have a major effect on the argument overall.

[23]I do not say that under these circumstances we would have no obligation to care for others. It might be, as a reader suggested, that God has commanded that the other's suffering be helped through our intervention. If we fail to intervene, then even if God relieves the suffering in another way we are guilty of sin and have harmed our own relationship with God and our neighbor. Nevertheless, I do believe that our *motivation* would be significantly affected in many cases if we genuinely accepted and internalized the view being discussed.

crete reality that our choices will make things better or worse for ourselves, for our loved ones, and for our friends and acquaintances.[24]

There is certainly some point to this. It seems likely that our motivation to benefit and protect ourselves, or persons about whom we care greatly, will be little affected by our beliefs about the overall effect of our actions on the world in general. One wonders about the effect on our actions toward those to whom we are indifferent or antagonistic: given that someone has to suffer, why shouldn't they be the ones? But finally, consider those instances where we need to take responsibility for the welfare of persons far removed and unknown to us personally. What possible reason could there be to relieve the victims of natural disasters or disease epidemics in remote parts of the world—individuals who are not and never will be known to us personally—if we know that whatever harm and suffering we thus prevent will simply show up somewhere else? And the very thought of an obligation to provide for the needs of future generations—say, by not despoiling the planet of its resources—becomes completely vacuous on this view. God, we may rightly say, has all that in hand, and nothing we can do about it will make any difference. These results, however, come sharply into conflict with God's purpose for us, that we should become morally mature and responsible individuals and should take responsibility for caring and providing for one another. I will describe a situation of this kind, in which our moral motivations are undercut by the assurance that God will prevent any action of ours from having a harmful effect on other persons, as one in which *morality is undermined.*

I believe, furthermore, that the detrimental effects of the belief that "it is all for the best" do show up in practice. I suspect that many readers are not unaware of a strain of passivity and fatalism that manifests itself at times among Christians. Worthwhile plans are abandoned prematurely in the face of supposedly "providential" obstacles that could be overcome by persistent effort, and grave illnesses are accepted as "God's will" when there are still promising treatment options available. A more momentous

---

[24]Daniel Howard-Snyder, "Response to Hasker's New and Improved Argument for the Compatibility of God and Gratuitous Evil," unpublished comment on an early version of my "Can God Permit 'Just Enough' Evil?"

example can be found in the civil rights struggle in the American South. In his *Letter from Birmingham Jail* Martin Luther King spoke movingly of the moral failure of white Christians:

> We will have to repent in this generation not merely for the hateful words and actions of the bad people but for the appalling silence of the good people. . . . I have been so greatly disappointed with the white church and its leadership. . . . So often it is an arch-defender of the status quo. Far from being disturbed by the presence of the Church, the power structure of the average community is consoled by the Church's silent—and often vocal— sanction of things as they are.[25]

Additional light is thrown on the situation by considering the mentality of Douglas Hudgins, segregationist pastor of the First Baptist Church of Jackson, Mississippi. In the wake of the bombing of a black church and the disappearance of three civil rights leaders (later found to have been murdered), Hudgins was challenged by a fellow minister with the question,

> "How can it be, Doug, that you are here in this town preaching the Gospel and there's all this hatred and violence?" Hudgins was momentarily silent. Then he said, "You simply don't understand. You know Baptists have no business tinkering in political matters." Hudgins invoked the familiar claim that civil rights for blacks has nothing to do with the gospel.[26]

Later on, when he was forced to respond to a bomb attack on the home of a local Jewish rabbi, Hudgins contented himself with a weak statement couched in generalities and concluded, "The Lord works in mysterious ways."[27] Hudgins was not endorsing the bombing as a righteous act. But a proper faith in providence requires us to acknowledge that "The Lord is working" even in such a happening—and if the Lord is working, it behooves us his servants to keep out of the way. Such passivity in the face of terrible evil is, I am claiming, a natural consequence of

---

[25]Martin Luther King Jr., *The Autobiography of Martin Luther King, Jr.*, ed. Clayborne Carson (New York: Warner Books, 1998), pp. 196, 199, 201. My thanks to Del Doughty for suggesting this example.

[26]Charles Marsh, *God's Long Summer: Stories of Faith and Civil Rights* (Princeton: Princeton University Press, 1997), p. 104.

[27]Ibid., p. 105.

the doctrine that in the providence of God "all is for the best."[28]

These considerations, I believe, constitute strong evidence that Rowe's Requirement should not be accepted by theists as a valid requirement for God's permission of evils. But if this requirement is rejected, the evidential problem of evil goes along with it. There is, however, a perplexity that arises from all this that the reader may already have noticed. I have been claiming that in order for us to have the proper moral motivation God must be willing to allow some gratuitous evil—that is, some evil which is such that *God could prevent it without losing any greater good or bringing about any equal or greater evil*. But how can this be? We are assuming that from God's point of view our becoming morally mature and responsible men and women is a very great good indeed. If God's permitting these evils is necessary for that great good, how can the evils be gratuitous?

To answer this, consider an illustration.[29] Suppose an excellent musical performance is being rewarded with sustained and enthusiastic applause. Each member of the audience who is applauding is contributing to the enthusiastic reception of the performance. But it is certainly not the case that had one member of the audience been prevented from applauding, the performance would not have been enthusiastically received. In the same way, any single instance of gratuitous evil is such that God could have prevented *that particular instance* without thereby undermining morality. If on the other hand God prevented *all* such instances, morality would indeed be undermined. William Rowe nicely summarizes the point by stating that, on this view, "the class of gratuitous evils is not gratuitous," in that *God could not have prevented that class from having any members at all without losing a greater good.*[30]

Rowe, however, is not satisfied with this answer. In response, he develops a line of argument whose objective is to restore Rowe's Requirement and also to reinstate the evidential argument from evil. He asks us to

---

[28]Is it necessary for me to say that I am not *justifying* this pastor's passivity and inaction? What I am suggesting, however, is that a mistaken view of providence was part of what enabled him to justify it to himself—to convince himself that it was consistent with his calling as a minister of the gospel.

[29]Note that the illustration is meant merely to show the coherence of the supposition that God permits gratuitous evil. It is not meant to show that God *must* operate in this way.

[30]William Rowe, "Response to Hasker's 'The Necessity of Gratuitous Evil,'" presented at the Central Division of the American Philosophical Association in Chicago in April of 1988.

consider E, a particular instance of Hasker's class of gratuitous evils. . . .
Now if Hasker is right, a perfect being cannot prevent *every evil like E*, for
then it would lose the greater good of significant morality. But could this being have obtained the greater good of significant morality without permitting E? As we've seen, Hasker's answer is *yes*. For E could be deleted from
the class without in any way undermining morality, so long as the rest of the
class is left intact. How far could the class of gratuitous evils be depleted
without undermining significant morality? I would think a great deal.[31]

To be sure, Rowe admits, a point would eventually be reached where no
further evils could be eliminated without undermining morality. But at
that point none of the remaining evils would be *gratuitous*, since if any of
them were eliminated God would lose the greater good of significant
morality.

And what this means, I'm afraid, is that Hasker's argument contains the
seeds of its own destruction. A world suitable for significant morality would
not require an omnipotent, omniscient, perfectly good being to permit any
gratuitous evil at all.[32]

On the contrary, if Rowe's Requirement is retained, it is Rowe's own position that self-destructs. For consider the situation of an agent who is contemplating the commission of a serious moral fault and is aware of the state
of affairs as described by Rowe. That is to say, *all* of the evil that exists is
nongratuitous; all of it is evil that God must permit if he is to obtain some
greater good. Some of this good, we now know, will consist in the good of
preserving the significance of morality, and some of it will be of other
kinds. But these details need not concern our agent. What is important, is
that it is still true that *whatever harm and suffering may result from a serious
moral offense she might commit, the greater part of this evil (and perhaps all of
it) is compensated by good results that could not have been obtained had she chosen a morally acceptable course of action instead.*[33] So, contrary to Rowe's assertion, morality is undermined for that person after all!

---

[31]Ibid.
[32]Ibid.
[33]The qualification in parentheses is required because of the point noted earlier: some part of the evil—
probably a rather small part—may be compensated by the mere fact of the agent's exercising the
power to make a free choice.

At this point a tempting move seems to be available to the advocate of the evidential argument from evil. What would lead to the undermining of morality is not the mere *fact* that God permits only those evils that are justified according to Rowe's Requirement. Rather, it is the *knowledge* of this by the agent that would weaken our motivation to act morally. What is called for then is that God should indeed act as prescribed by that requirement, but he should systematically conceal from us the fact that he is doing so.

This move is useless for at least two reasons. First, in order to reinstate the evidential argument, its advocate must argue thus: A good God would act in such a way as to prevent unjustified evils but would conceal from us the fact that he is doing this; but in fact God does *not* prevent unjustified evils from occurring, so there is no God. This is patently absurd. If God were to conceal from us the fact that he is acting in the way specified, we may be sure that he would be effective in doing so! On this supposition, then, the evidence available to us would be precisely the same as what we now have; the assertion that God is not acting in this way is completely unsupported by the evidence! But the supposition is incoherent in any case. The claim that God must act according to Rowe's Requirement is supposed to be an *inference from the essential nature of God*—in particular, from his perfect moral goodness. But on any plausible theistic view (and certainly on any Christian view), one of God's most important purposes in his relationship with us is to *bring us to an understanding of his own goodness*. If God's goodness requires that he permit only justified evils, it follows that God, by bringing us to understand his own goodness, would immediately put us in a position to recognize what, on the hypothesis we are now considering, he is at pains to keep us from realizing. There is no hope for the evidential argument from evil in pursuing this line.

It is time to summarize. What has been presented in this section is not a theodicy; it does not claim to give God's reasons for permitting evils to occur. (It would be quite inappropriate to answer the question, Why did God permit the Holocaust? by saying, In order to keep from undermining morality.) What it does accomplish, if the arguments are successful, is to block the evidential argument from evil by showing that its key premise, Rowe's Requirement, should not be accepted. This then is a defense; if a convenient label for it is desired, I suggest that it be called the necessity-of-gratuitous-evil defense—or for brevity, the NGE defense. Given this defense, the evidential argument from evil need not trouble us.[34]

But the NGE defense, like the free-will defense before it, leaves many questions unanswered and will leave many inquirers unsatisfied. If the goodness of God and God's love for particular human beings are not to be spelled out in the way assumed by the evidential argument from evil, then how are these matters to be understood? These questions will be the topic of our final chapter.

---

[34]Can the skeptical theist defense be *combined with* the NGE defense? One reader of the manuscript proposes that the skeptical theist strategy should be understood conditionally: "If one thinks that there must be a reason why God allows evil, then we still have no good grounds for claiming that there are no such reasons" (i.e., that some evil really is gratuitous). In principle, this strategy is a possible one. But if skeptical theists have intended their arguments to be taken in this way, they have been remarkably quiet about it! On the whole, their writings give the impression that they are accepting Rowe's Requirement as an unchallenged principle. In any case, the arguments given here suggest that the skeptical theist defense can make only a minor contribution to the solution of the overall problem.

8

Can God Triumph over Evil?

God's justice is a saving, healing restorative justice, because the God to whom justice belongs is the Creator God who has yet to complete his original plan for creation and whose justice is designed not simply to restore balance to a world out of kilter but to bring to glorious completion and fruition the creation, teeming with life and possibility, that he made in the first place.

N. T. WRIGHT, *EVIL AND THE JUSTICE OF GOD*

Not much has been said thus far in the book about the triumph of God over evil. We have presented theodicies that argue for the goodness of God's plan of creation, both in the world of nature and in the human realm.[1] I have presented defenses intended to show that there is no contradiction in the coexistence of evil with a God who is perfectly good, and that it is unreasonable to expect that a perfectly good God would permit instances of evil only when those instances are a necessary means to some greater good.[2] But little in all this speaks to the *triumph* of God over evil; rather, these arguments are efforts to understand and account for a world in which it is evident that a great deal of evil goes on and has not yet been

---

[1]The natural-order theodicy and the free-will theodicy.
[2]The free-will defense and the NGE defense.

overcome. The strategy of the argument thus far, comprising both defenses and theodicies, has been primarily defensive; my purpose has been to turn back the arguments that urge the evil in the world as a compelling objection against belief in God. Surely this is not unexpected; the philosophical problem of evil, after all, is precisely an attack on theistic belief in the name of philosophical rationality, and if the attack is not to be allowed to succeed, defensive measures are called for.

A purely defensive strategy, however, is not enough; the claim of Christianity is not merely that God can *coexist* with the evil in the world. The claim rather is that in the end God will *not* coexist with evil but will be gloriously triumphant over it. But what would this mean? What would such a triumph of God over evil look like? Is such a belief at all credible in the light of the actual state of the world? These are the questions that must be addressed in this final chapter. In order to address them, however, we need to draw more deeply on the resources of Christian theology than has been done up to this point. In doing this, I am exposed to a twofold complaint. On the one hand, there may be those who would prefer me to stick to a more purely philosophical orientation; I sacrifice too much credibility, it will be said, by appealing to the sectarian (and in the eyes of some, wildly implausible) doctrines of Christianity. In response I can only point out that the Christian story in its essentials simply *is* the story of the battle of God with sin and evil, and his ultimate victory over both; to suppose that anything approximating a Christian account of evil can be given without attending to that story is entirely unreasonable. It is not to be expected that secular critics will find the Christian story easy to believe; faith, after all, is a gift from God. But those who find themselves unable at this juncture to believe the story may at least gain a better understanding of what is at stake in either believing or rejecting it.

The other complaint to be expected at this point comes from those who do believe the Christian story but will think that a better job should be done of presenting it than will be done in the following pages. With this I heartily agree—but with this proviso: Since nearly the entirety of the Christian faith is concerned with God's victory over sin and evil, it is hardly to be expected that a full and adequate account of it should be found in the final chapter of a book on the problem of evil written by a mere philosopher! Nevertheless, these matters do need to be addressed here, however inadequately. May those who could do it better, indeed who have done it better, step forward in a friendly spirit to correct my inadequacies![3] At this point I shall proceed by first giving a brief summary of the account of God, the creation and God's relationship to the created world that emerges from the preceding discussions. This will lead into a brief discussion of competing accounts of divine providence in their bearing on the problem of evil. Then I will attempt to give some account of what God does to overcome evil, and of what the results might be of such an overcoming.

GOD, THE WORLD AND EVIL

God, a being unimaginably great in power, wisdom and goodness, was in no way constrained or necessitated to create our world, or indeed to create any world at all. He did, however, choose to create a world distinct from himself yet upheld from moment to moment by his sustaining power. This was to be a complex, multileveled natural world, one containing vast potentialities for good, and it was allowed (at least for the most part) to develop and to function according to its inherent powers and potentialities.[4] It has come about in the purposes of God that this world contains sentient creatures, some of which (humans on this planet and perhaps others elsewhere) are endowed with reason and with the capacity for moral and spiritual awareness. These creatures possess the power of choice and are responsible both for their personal conduct and for their life together in society. It has been argued that it is *good* that there be such a creation, en-

---

[3]Among those who have done this better than I will be able to I include N. T. Wright, whose book *Evil and the Justice of God* (Downers Grove, Ill.: InterVarsity Press, 2006), will be utilized as a resource in what follows. It should be said, however, that Wright does not address the philosophical problem of evil that has been discussed in this book. His response to that problem is in effect to declare it insoluble and then change the subject. (Wright's own use of the phrase "the problem of evil" refers ambiguously to a variety of other issues.) Nevertheless, Wright's contributions to the matters discussed in this chapter are considerable.

[4]No decision need be made here concerning whether the world's development, and especially the appearance and evolution of living creatures, occurred entirely through the operation of natural forces or whether special divine interventions were required in order for the desired goal to be reached. The first alternative has an undeniable aesthetic appeal, but aesthetic considerations need not be decisive here, and arguably it has not been shown that a purely autonomous development is possible.

dowed as it is with enormous potentialities for the enrichment of life and existence. The relative autonomy allowed both to human beings and to nature means, however, that the good endowments of the creation are open also to the possibility of the events and actions we identify as evil. (As the kabbalist doctrine of *Tzimzum* has it, God "steps back" in order to allow the creation room for an existence of its own.) A world in which this was not so—a world in which creatures either lack powers of their own or in which God constantly intervenes to prevent those powers from acting in ways that are less than optimal—would be a world without internal integrity; the existence of such a world would add little of worth over and above the value of God's simply imagining it. God, however, has instead chosen a creation that is *really there*—that has a genuine integrity and autonomy of its own. And it is good that this is so.

That having been said, it is important to acknowledge the existence of evil in the world as a pervasive reality. This evil mars and obscures but cannot entirely hide or obliterate the goodness inherent in the creation. Nature is inhuman—and how could it be otherwise?—but the most grievous evils stem from "the inhumanity of man to man." Beyond this, there is the undeniable reality of the alienation of human beings from God: having been made for fellowship with God, we instead turn our backs on God and make ourselves the center of "our" universe, and no real repair of the situation is possible so long as this obstacle remains. This pervasive fact of human estrangement from God provides yet another reason why we should not expect God to function as the cosmic "policeman on the beat," ready at any time to intervene in order to prevent acts of cruelty and inhumanity. In view of the underlying state of spiritual alienation, the prevention of individual acts of injustice would be comparable to attempting to clear a swamp of mosquitoes using a fly swatter. Only a far more fundamental remedy has any prospect of success.

We may naturally wonder what human life would have been like without sin, moral wrongdoing and injustice. Just as I said earlier that we lack epistemic access to the heavenly state, I want to say now that we are not in a position to say with any confidence what a truly ideal—that is, sin free—human society would be like. We can, to be sure, form some conception of what human life might be without some of the negative motivations—

pride, envy, greed, hatred—that so corrupt our interactions with each other. But what of natural evils under these circumstances? I have argued that it is a mistake to see the natural world as altered in a fundamental way by sin; to say that is in effect to say that the world of nature we know is not God's good creation, and that is too high a price to pay. We may speculate, if we choose, about ways that natural harms could have been averted. Peter van Inwagen, for instance, puts forward the conjecture that humans living in an original, sin free state

> possessed what theologians used to call preternatural powers—something like what people who believe in them today call paranormal abilities.... Because of their preternatural powers, they were able somehow to protect themselves from wild beasts (which they were able to tame with a word), from disease (which they were able to cure with a touch) and from random, destructive natural events (like earthquakes), which they knew about in advance and were able to avoid.[5]

There is no harm in our imagining such scenarios provided we do not convince ourselves (as van Inwagen does not) that we have compelling reason to think them true.[6]

OPEN THEISM AND ITS ALTERNATIVES

Before we consider God's actions to overcome evil, something more needs to be said about the specific implications of open theism for the matters under consideration. As was explained in chapter four, open theism holds that God's creative plan and choice was for a "broad world type" rather than for a specific world scenario (or "possible world"); the details of the actual future were not available to God logically prior to his creative choice. Among the other implications of this stance, it throws a different light on God's relationship to particular instances of evil in comparison with the way they are viewed by deterministic and Molinist views of providence, according to which God exerts meticulous control

---

[5]Peter van Inwagen, "The Argument from Evil," in *Christian Faith and the Problem of Evil*, ed. Peter van Inwagen (Grand Rapids: Eerdmans, 2004), p. 69.
[6]Van Inwagen puts this forward as part of a story about our earliest human ancestors that is "consistent with what we know of human pre-history." But he does not claim the story is true; in particular, he states "I am not at all sure about 'preternatural powers'" (ibid., pp. 68, 72).

over everything that takes place.[7] According to open theism, God did *not* "freely and knowingly plan, order, and provide for"[8] every event of cruelty, betrayal and agonizing suffering contained in our world's history, as is the case on both of the other views. God initiated the world's existence, sustains it in being and governs its operations by general strategies; he does not, however, endorse and insure the operation of a detailed plan that includes all those tragically evil events. The importance of this comes home to us when we consider such cases as that of Zosia, a young Jewish girl in the Warsaw ghetto, whose eyes were literally ripped from their sockets by Nazi soldiers for their own amusement.[9] Isn't it deeply troubling to assume that God has specifically planned for this abomination to occur in the interest of some "greater good" that it makes possible?[10] Open theism asserts, on the contrary, that God has taken real risks in creating this world, and that God's heart is deeply grieved at the grave misuse many of us make of our freedom.

Determinists and Molinists often claim that the problem of evil is exactly the same for all three views, since in each of them God is said to permit evils that it is in his power to prevent. These claims, however, are mistaken. For determinism, the use of the word *permit* is seriously misleading: God has *deliberately chosen and insured* that these evils shall occur in preference to any logically possible alternative. Molinists may have a better claim to the language of permission insofar as the evils result from free human choices that God would have preferred to have been made differently. Still, *permits* is an inadequate expression of God's relationship to instances of evil, given that God has *specifically planned* for each such instance and has *acted in a way that guarantees* that the evil should take place. In general, we recognize a vast dif-

---

[7]As was explained in chap. 4, the significant alternatives here are limited to theological determinism, middle knowledge (Molinism) and open theism. Views that affirm "simple foreknowledge" (foreknowledge without middle knowledge) and divine timeless knowledge have exactly the same implications as open theism concerning God's providential governance of the world, though proponents of these views often fail to recognize this fact.

[8]See the quotation from Freddoso on p. 175.

[9]See Gregory A. Boyd, *God at War: The Bible and Spiritual Conflict* (Downers Grove, Ill.: InterVarsity Press, 1997), pp. 33-34.

[10]Note that the famous question of Ivan Karamazov, quoted as the epigraph to chap. 1 of this book, rests entirely on the assumption that God has specifically planned the torture and death of the child in order to bring about the "peace and rest" of humankind.

ference between a person's *establishing conditions* under which it is possible for something bad to happen, and someone's *specifically planning* for a tragic evil to occur. A highway engineer planning a new high-speed road will realize that it is likely that lives will be lost in traffic accidents on the new highway, but he is not blamed for this. It would be an entirely different matter if the engineer were to plan in advance the deaths of specific persons and construct the road so as to insure this outcome. The direct and intentional connection between the planner and the tragic outcome in the latter case would amount to criminality on the engineer's part.

There remains, to be sure, the fact that for open theism as for the other views, God does have it in his power to prevent any specific instance of evil. For open theism, however, such prevention would have to take the form of direct divine intervention in the situation leading to the evil, either by a physical miracle or by stripping the human agent of the power to choose evil on that occasion. It is evident, furthermore, that in order to materially affect the overall balance of good and evil in the world such interventions would have to be carried out on a truly massive scale and would seriously undermine the regular operation of nature and the capacity of human beings to act and take responsibility for their own actions. The reasons why God might not wish to intervene on such a scale have already been discussed; once again, God is not the "policeman on the beat."

Yet another important facet of this issue lies in what may be termed the divine pathos.[11] According to the Bible, God responds emotionally to events; he is deeply affected by what transpires in his creation. In the book of Hosea, for example, we hear God saying,

Plead with your mother, plead—
> for she is not my wife,
> and I am not her husband—
that she put away her whoring from her face,
> and her adultery from between her breasts,

---

[11]This term is taken from Abraham Heschel, who writes, "God does not simply command and expect obedience; He is also moved and affected by what happens in the world and he reacts accordingly. Events and human actions arouse in Him joy or sorrow, pleasure or wrath. He is not conceived as judging facts, so to speak, 'objectively,' in detached impassibility. He reacts in an intimate and subjective manner, and thus determines the value of events" (Abraham J. Heschel, *Between God and Man: An Interpretation of Judaism*, ed. Fritz A. Rothschild [New York: Free Press, 1959], p. 116).

or I will strip her naked,
>   and expose her as in the day she was born,
and make her like a wilderness,
>   and turn her into a parched land,
>   and kill her with thirst. (Hosea 2:2-3)

But we hear this as well:

Therefore, I will now allure her,
>   and bring her into the wilderness,
>   and speak tenderly to her.
From there I will give her her vineyards,
>   and make the Valley of Achor a door of hope.
There she shall respond as in the days of her youth,
>   as at the time when she came up out of the land of Egypt. (Hosea 2:14-15)

There is a strong contrast here between the rightful anger of Yahweh as the ill-used husband, and the tender yearning in which he purposes to restore Israel as his beloved bride. Similar dramatic portrayals of divine emotion are common on the pages of Scripture, and open theists take them as presenting an essentially truthful picture, allowing of course for figurative language and anthropomorphism, of God's emotive responses to the various things that occur in the world and in the lives of his people. Determinists and Molinists, however, are unable to accept these passages as being anything even close to the truth about God. If indeed God has a detailed plan for everything that occurs in the world, and everything that takes place is strictly in accord with that plan, then how is it possible to accept at anything like face value the ascription to God of intense emotional responses to the events as they occur? In particular, how are we to understand the adverse responses—the anger against sin, the pain of the spurned lover, the indignation at the harms inflicted by the enemies of Israel? Aren't we forced to discount such reactions—to regard them as part of the dramatic narrative but by no means as accurate depictions of God's state of mind?[12] The difficulty is particularly acute for divine determinism, for on

---

[12]One reader of the manuscript remarks, in defense of the exegesis of the church fathers, that "it quickly becomes clear that the principal hermeneutical tool they are using is *coherence with the orthodox view of God*. Whenever a text says things about God which, taken literally, do not fit with the view of God in the Great Tradition, it must not be taken literally" (private communication). The point is well taken. But when what is in question is precisely the adequacy and correctness of certain aspects of the traditional view of God, such an approach is of limited usefulness.

this view *everything that takes place is exactly as God wishes it to be; there is no possible world God would prefer to the actual world in any respect.* If we are told, then, that God has a deep and abiding anger at the unrighteousness that takes place on the earth, our only possible response is that this simply cannot be: to represent God as angry and hostile to situations that are exactly as he wishes them to be is simply incoherent. And the situation is only a little better for Molinism. As Thomas Flint states the Molinist view, "if Judas sins, it is because God knowingly put him in a set of circumstances in which he would sin, and knowingly refrained from putting him in a set of circumstances in which he would act virtuously."[13] Viewing the situation in a broader context, it remains true that whatever wrongs and harms the world's history may contain, God has specifically chosen the enactment of *that particular history* in preference to any other history that is feasible, given the counterfactuals of freedom that are actually true. At most God's bliss in contemplating this world might be tinged with regret that, in certain respects, things are not even better. There is little room here for the biblical portrayals of God's anger over sin and his agonized compassion for his suffering children.[14]

WHAT GOD DOES ABOUT EVIL

God, then, confronts a world in a state of extreme disorder. This is not merely a failure of implementation of the plan selected by God for his creation; it is also a personal affront that grieves and offends the holy and loving Creator. The good news is that God did not choose to abandon the disordered creation to its own resources; rather, he set about to redeem it. We are in no position to know everything God has done and is doing to restore his erring children, but the central story, according to both Jews and Christians, is the one told in the Bible. In a disordered world, God sought to establish a zone of restored order; in a world under occupation by forces of evil, he planted a beachhead from which it could be liberated. The starting point for this effort, according to Scripture, was God's call to Abraham. Abraham was uprooted from his home in Mesopotamia and told to be-

---

[13]Thomas P. Flint, *Divine Providence* (Ithaca, N.Y.: Cornell University Press, 1998), p. 118.
[14]For a more extensive discussion of the topics of this section, see William Hasker, "Antinomies of Divine Providence," *Philosophia Christi* 4 (2002): 365-79; also included as chap. 10 of *Providence, Evil, and the Openness of God.*

come a wanderer, to go "to the land that I will show you." Abraham's family
will become a great nation, one that will worship the true God rather than
idols and in which human lives will be lived in a way that corresponds to
God's good intentions for them. But the creation of the nation is not an
end in itself, at least not the final end; rather, "in you all the families of the
earth shall be blessed" (Genesis 12:3). The Abrahamic family/nation is to
be the entering wedge for God's work of blessing and restoration for all of
humankind.

And so the rescue effort was begun—but to say that it did not proceed
smoothly is a huge understatement. The problem was not merely that
other human families, and other nations, resisted and, at times, endan-
gered the very survival of the "chosen people." That happened often
enough, to be sure. But the larger problem was closer to home. God's plan
was "daring and risky,"[15] utilizing as the solution to the world's evil people
who were themselves very much enmeshed in that evil and not all that ea-
ger to put it finally behind them. And so

> Israel, the children of Abraham, may be the carriers of the promise, but they
> turn out to be part of the problem themselves. This unwinds through a mas-
> sive and epic narrative, from the patriarchs to the exodus, from Moses to
> David, through the twists and turns of the Israelite monarchy, ending finally
> with Israel in exile.[16]

To summarize that narrative even briefly lies beyond the scope of this
book; suffice it for now to say that the story of the Hebrew Bible ends in
deep ambiguity. The chosen people still exists, and to that extent it can be
said that God's promises to Abraham have not failed. But the promises
seem at best to be in abeyance; the Davidic monarchy, of which so much
was expected, has apparently disappeared for good. The contrast between
the grand future Israel was promised and its present sorry state is matter
for much anguished reflection, not to speak of complaints directed at God
in the later biblical writings. For example, Psalm 89:49-51:

---

[15]Wright, *Evil and the Justice of God*, p. 76. In speaking of God's plan as risky, and also later on in abandoning divine impassibility, Wright strikes notes that are very much in harmony with open theism
and in conflict with opposing views such as determinism and Molinism. I do not, however, know
what his official position is on the various models of providence.

[16]Ibid., p. 46.

Lord, where is your steadfast love of old,
  which by your faithfulness you swore to David?
Remember, O Lord, how your servant is taunted,
  how I bear in my bosom the insults of the peoples,
with which your enemies taunt, O LORD,
  with which they taunted the footsteps of your anointed.

The upshot of the matter is that Israel's history poses a question it cannot answer—that can be answered, both Jews and Christians agree, only by the coming of God's anointed king and servant, the Messiah.

The great disagreement, of course, concerns whether the Messiah is still to be awaited, or whether he was actually born in Palestine sometime around 4 B.C. At this point I must continue with the version of the story I believe to be true and leave it to our Jewish friends to elaborate their own, quite different version. We skip over the early years, of which not much is known anyway, and begin with the inception of Jesus' public ministry. Early on, things seemed to be going well. Jesus gathered a hand-picked inner circle of disciples, but was also successful at times in attracting a much larger following. His teaching commanded widespread attention from the people. His deeds of healing and exorcism were not merely acts of mercy toward individuals (though they were that) but they were an integral part of his announcement of the coming of the rule of God, which would involve an inward transformation of God's true worshipers and also their deliverance from oppression by evil of all kinds. He sent out his disciples to perform similar deeds, and they returned flushed and exhilarated with success.

Before long, however, the tide began to turn against him. For some of his hearers the spectacular "performance" of miracles was the main focus of their interest in him, and when he refused to put on a show for them, they turned away. More ominously, some of the religious leaders of the Jewish people became increasingly suspicious and hostile; these attitudes were in part a response to Jesus' vigorous criticisms directed at them. These were men whose prestige and leadership roles depended on the public perception of their exemplary piety, and they did not readily tolerate criticism that threatened to undermine their position in society. The Roman authorities were to some extent dependent on those same religious leaders to keep

the populace from growing rebellious, so they were open to being manipulated, and they also had their own interest in suppressing a movement
that might lead to popular unrest.

It ended, of course, on the cross. In Jesus' crucifixion numerous forces
can be seen at work. There was the dullness (at best) and resistance of the
people (sometimes including even his close followers), once the novelty
had worn off. There was the deep hostility of the religious authorities, bent
above all else on protecting their own position and privileges. There was
the long arm of Roman authority, indifferent to considerations of guilt and
innocence so long as power could be maintained and popular unrest kept
in check. (Local unrest was little threat to Rome itself, but it was a most
definite threat to a Roman governor who might be judged incompetent if
he failed to maintain order.) Finally, the Gospels more than hint that behind all this there stood deeper powers of evil, powers we can only describe
as demonic, that were intent on defeating Jesus and everything he stood
for. The result, to all appearances, was the final, irrevocable failure of God's
daring and risky plan for rescuing a world gone wrong. It is hard for us today to measure the sadness in the words of one dispirited follower: "We
had hoped that he was the one to redeem Israel" (Luke 24:21).

And then came the resurrection. The one who had died was alive again;
the tomb that held his remains was empty. He showed himself first of all
to some women—improbable witnesses, by the standards of the day, but
deserving of the honor because of their faithful love for him. Then he was
seen by the inner circle of disciples and later on by still others—and suddenly the Jesus movement itself was not dead but very much alive, and was
spreading rapidly throughout Palestine and, a bit later, across the entire
Roman world. The defeat of Jesus and his message was no defeat but the
prelude to a victory more stunning than could ever have been imagined.
The rule of God he announced had truly begun to take hold in the world;
he was indeed a King who won victories by the power of love and not with
force of arms.

An important early development was the opening of the Jesus movement to participation by non-Jews. In order for the door of the kingdom
to be fully open to them, they had to be accepted without the requirement
that they adopt the Jewish lifestyle with its myriad regulations and cere-

monies. There was a lot of controversy about this in the early church, with many Jewish Christians arguing for a stricter approach, but it was the open-door policy that won the day. Gentiles who believed in Jesus became by faith adopted children of Abraham, and so were included in those great promises given to him and his descendants. In a way earlier generations could never have imagined, the promise that through Abraham all the families of the earth would be blessed came true.

Building on hints given by Jesus himself, though not fully understood at the time, the church soon recognized that his death was not merely a terrible miscarriage of justice but also a sacrifice offered to God. Jesus at the Last Supper invited his disciples to partake of his body and blood in the bread and wine, just as Jewish worshipers partook of the sacrifices in the tabernacle and the temple. In some mysterious way Jesus in his death had taken upon himself the sins of all humankind, and in so doing opened a new and more direct way of access to God. Theories about how this worked—about the nature of the atonement—have occupied thoughtful Christians ever since, and we won't go into them here. But that "Christ died for our sins" has been an integral part of the faith right from the beginning.

Another crucial early development was the recognition that Jesus himself was somehow more than merely human. His humanity, to be sure, was on full display for all those who saw and heard him, touched him and ate with him. But there seemed to be something more. He claimed a mysterious authority, of a wholly different kind than that of the priests and scholars who argued about the proper interpretation of the Jewish law. He was convicted of blasphemy by the Jewish council for claiming to be the Son of Man, referred to in the prophecy of Daniel, who would "come with the clouds of heaven." Immediately after his death and resurrection he was recognized as "Lord"—a divine title and an expression of worship. He was celebrated in an early hymn as the one

who, though he was in the form of God,
  did not regard equality with God
  as something to be exploited,
but emptied himself,
  taking the form of a slave,

being born in human likeness.
And being found in human form,
   he humbled himself
   and became obedient to the point of death—
   even death on a cross. (Philippians 2:6-8)

He was the divine Word, or Logos, who somehow both was God and yet was "with God," and was the one through whom "all things came into being" (John 1:1-3). After many years and much discussion these ideas took shape in the doctrine of the Trinity—of God as the complex unity of Father, Son and Holy Spirit. All that took time to work out, but the exalted status of Jesus was there right from the beginning of the church. (Please understand that I am not trying to *prove* these doctrines or even to explain them at all fully. That can be done on another occasion, but they have to be mentioned here because they are a necessary part of the Christian answer to the problem of evil. They are part of the explanation of how God will triumph over evil, and that in turn is crucial to our understanding of why God, in order to carry out his plan, puts up with so much evil in the world today.)

So the rule of God exists in the world today, largely embodied in the Christian church. It goes without saying that now as with ancient Israel things have not run smoothly. (Will God never learn? Shouldn't he know by now that entrusting his plan to sinful human beings will lead to trouble? But then the plan is precisely a plan for the redemption and restoration of those same sinful humans.) So there have been many low points as well as high points, but the church is very much a going concern in the world today. The claimed triumph of secularism is proving to be an illusion. Europe, indeed, shows signs of religious exhaustion after too many centuries of unchristian behavior by professing Christians, but in other parts of the world Christianity moves forward. (Christianity is growing rapidly in Africa, and there are almost certainly more Christians in China today than members of the Communist Party.) All over the world, the followers of Christ pray, "Thy kingdom come, thy will be done . . ."

Is this then the triumph of God over evil? It doesn't look that way. The examples of egregious evil scattered throughout this book come from the Christian era; if such evils had suddenly ceased with the coming of Christ, we would be confronted with a whole different situation. The answer to this given by Christians is that the decisive battle in the war against evil has in fact been won in Jesus' death and resurrection, but God is patient in allowing time for as many as possible to turn toward him in repentance and faith (see 2 Peter 3:9). The New Testament, however, offers little encouragement to the often-expressed hope that the church will so permeate the world and its structures with the spirit of Jesus that the full presence of God's rule will exist on earth through its efforts. On the contrary, it looks forward to a further, decisive intervention by God, in which the kingship of Christ will be fully established (*de facto* as well as *de jure*, one might say)—the eschaton, the end of the age, the Last Judgment.

Here, as on earlier occasions, I am going to decline to say anything about the details of this final, decisive intervention—and I will express some skepticism about the claims of some others to supply those details. Obviously my skepticism is not universally shared; the manufacture of eschatological charts, the convening of prophetic conferences and the writing and reading of scary novels about the "end times" are all going concerns. I can't forget, though, how very wrong the Jews of Jesus' time, even the most devout and thoughtful of them, were about the nature of the coming messianic kingdom. Those who were attuned to God's Spirit recognized the Messiah when he appeared, but it seems that nobody had it right beforehand. It could be that the purveyors of prophetic wisdom in our own time are better placed to tell us all about it—but then again, maybe not. For now, I put those questions to the side.

But apart from the details of the process, what would a triumph of God over evil look like? Is such a thing even conceivable given the evil that has occurred and continues to occur in God's creation? That is the question for the final section of this chapter.

THE SHAPE OF TRIUMPH

What would it be like for evil to be finally overcome? Can we even imagine such a thing? In one sense we certainly can imagine it; the rich imagery found in writings from the Apocalypse to Dante to C. S. Lewis and many others between and since is important for all of us in sustaining and nourishing faith in the coming of God's kingdom. I fully agree with Carol

Zaleski, who asserts that "we have every right to fit ourselves in advance for a pair of wings as long as we recognize that such expectations are no proper measure of the surprise that awaits us."[17] Nevertheless, in this section I will leave the wings to one side, and will try to see what can be said about the life to come in sober (or nearly sober) prose.

What can be said with confidence about the biblical depiction of the world to come can be stated fairly briefly. This will be a bodily existence, though with bodies dramatically changed and improved from those we presently inhabit (see 1 Corinthians 15). It will be a social existence, with redeemed persons existing in an unimaginably rich state of mutual love and communion. It will be an existence fully in the presence of God, saturated with the praise of God and with the experience of God's love. All the forces of evil will have been finally banished, unable to do any more harm (see Revelation 20). Beyond this, it becomes difficult to say more with any confidence. Concerning what might be termed the physical aspect of the life to come, questions multiply quickly. Will the resurrection bodies be made of the same stuff or matter as composes the world today? What laws of nature will obtain in the resurrection world? Will the world to come contain nonhuman animals as well as rational persons? If it does, will they be of the same species as those that have formerly lived on earth? Of all of the same species or only of some? (Could the world to come contain a real-life Jurassic Park—one better managed, it goes without saying, than the fictional one?) Will some, or many, or all of the same individual animals partake in that life? (The majority Christian view has denied a future life for the beasts, but there are eminent dissenting voices.) I doubt that anyone has more than the most purely speculative answers to these questions. Carol Zaleski is right: we should feel free to imagine, but should not suppose that our imaginings are the measure of God's good purposes for us.

Concerning what may be termed the moral side of the life to come, there are questions that may require more sustained attention. It may not be too hard to imagine an idyllic future existence, but there are real difficulties in

---

[17]Carol Zaleski, *The Life of the World to Come: Near-Death Experience and Christian Hope* (New York: Oxford University Press, 1996), p. 3.

understanding how that existence will deal with the enormous evils that the world has contained up until now. To begin with, it is clear that redeemed persons will need to undergo a process of moral and spiritual purification so as to fit them for such a life. (If I could go there in my present state, would heaven really be heaven?) Conceivably this could occur instantaneously, or nearly so, but analogy with the kinds of personal development that occur in the present life suggests a more gradual process, one in which the subject is an active participant. Because of this, some quite orthodox Protestant thinkers have urged the need to reintroduce into Protestant theology something like a doctrine of purgatory.[18] This, however, is only the beginning of the problems. The larger issue is one that was suggested in the protest lodged by John Roth (see pp. 31-35 in chap. 2). Roth, it will be recalled, insists that some evils are simply too terrible to be fully redeemed; he regards as "religious hyperbole" the assertion of the apostle Paul that "the sufferings of this present time are not worth comparing with the glory about to be revealed to us." Stephen Davis, on the other hand, believes that "in the light of the eschaton a perfectly good God morally can allow the waste that we see in human history"; he points out that Roth has emphatically denied that this is so, but has given no argument in support of his denial.[19] I agree that Roth has not supported his objection with a compelling argument; he points to examples of terrible evil but relies on intuition to support his conclusion that a wholly good God could not allow the evils and would not be able fully to redeem them. So Davis is entitled to his faith stance on the issue. Yet it would be more satisfying (and here I am sure Davis would agree) to have something more to offer in response to Roth's protest than a hopeful appeal to ignorance. A number of writers have tried to provide this "something more."

An initial question is, just what would it mean for an evil to be overcome? Considerable attention has been given in this connection to philosopher Roderick Chisholm's notion of the "defeat" of evil.[20] Put simply, this

---

[18]See Jerry Walls, *Heaven: The Logic of Eternal Joy* (New York: Oxford University Press, 2002); and Justin T. Barnard, "Purgatory and the Dilemma of Sanctification," *Faith and Philosophy* 24, no. 3 (2007).

[19]Stephen T. Davis, quoted in John K. Roth, "A Theodicy of Protest," in *Encountering Evil: Live Options in Theology*, ed. Stephen T. Davis, 2nd ed. (Louisville: Westminster John Knox Press, 2001), p. 104.

[20]See Roderick M. Chisholm, "The Defeat of Good and Evil," in *The Problem of Evil*, ed. Marilyn McCord Adams and Robert Merrihew Adams (New York: Oxford University Press, 1990), pp. 53-68.

is the idea that a state of affairs that is intrinsically bad may contribute to
a state of affairs that is good, in such a way that the goodness of the good
state depends on the badness of the bad. An example given by Chisholm
concerns courage: courage is certainly a good thing, but one cannot be courageous unless there is something that one fears, and fear is something that
is bad. So we can say that when a person is courageous the badness of the
fear he or she experiences is *defeated* by the goodness of his or her courage.
We cannot coherently say, in such a case, "I am glad she showed courage
but I wish she had the courage without the fear." The goodness of a person's courage depends precisely on the fear he or she had to overcome; it
even seems to be true that the greater the fear that is overcome, the greater
and better is the courage that is shown. The defeat of evil is contrasted with
the "balancing off" of evil. To take a simple example of the latter, suppose
a young boy skins his knee, and to cheer him up his mother buys him an
ice cream cone. The enjoyment of the ice cream may *balance off* the pain of
the skinned knee, so that overall the child is as happy as he would be had
neither event occurred. But the pain of the knee is not defeated by the
pleasure of the ice cream, because the badness of the pain is not necessary
for the goodness of the enjoyment of the ice cream. We might very well say
(and the child would certainly agree), Well, it's nice that he enjoyed the ice
cream, but I wish he had not skinned his knee.

Defeat in Chisholm's sense is certainly an important and impressive way
in which evil can be overcome. And this has led to the idea that, in a proper
conception of divine providence, all evils whatsoever should be defeated
and not merely balanced off. (Already in chapter three we saw Marilyn
Adams's insistence that horrendous evils must be defeated for those who
participate in them or suffer them [see p. 71].) There is, furthermore, an
important biblical text that seems to support this view: "We know that all
things work together for good for those who love God, who are called according to his purpose" (Romans 8:28). Is this, then, what should be
meant by the triumph of good over evil?

I believe this line of thought is seriously mistaken. An important point
here is made explicitly by Chisholm: "When evil is merely balanced off,
and not defeated, by a whole that is good, then one may regret or resent its
presence in that whole. But if evil is ever defeated by a whole that is good,

then, as I have suggested, we may well be thankful for the very part that is bad."[21] Now, my objection is not to the idea that, in God's good providence, evils may sometimes be defeated and not merely balanced off. No Christian could possibly object to that! The crucifixion of Jesus is surely an example of terrible evil but also a means to the salvation of the world; Christians may grieve for his sufferings and at the same time give thanks to God that they occurred. What is objectionable, however, is the claim that if God is good then *necessarily* all evils will be defeated. This is precisely the same claim that was discussed and rejected in chapter seven: that God would permit no evil unless it is a necessary condition for a greater good that God could obtain in no other way. If we knew in advance that any evil that might occur would be defeated, then it would be quite inappropriate, as Chisholm correctly saw, to "regret or resent" its presence in the world. But if we really, seriously, took this attitude toward evils (and thank God, we usually don't, even those of us who are persuaded of it theoretically), this would inevitably have the effect of undermining our own motivation to prevent the evils from occurring. If Romans 8:28, as translated by the NRSV, is given a fully literal interpretation, then even *one's own sins* "work together" for one's good; we are always better off when we have committed a sinful action than we would be if we had not done so—and that is completely unacceptable. As it happens, there is an alternative textual reading that is preferred by several recent translations: "And we know that *in all things* God works for the good of those who love him, who have been called according to his purpose" (Romans 8:28 NIV, emphasis added; see also RSV and text note in NRSV). This retains the idea that God works to bring good out of evil, but does not have the untenable implication that every sin that is committed leads to a good result.[22]

But if the triumph of God over evil does not mean that all evil is de-

---

[21]Ibid., p. 62.

[22]When work on this chapter was nearly complete I encountered a quotation that wonderfully illustrates the point at issue here. It is from a letter written to Peter van Inwagen by a pastor, Dr. Stephen Bilynskyj: "A grieving person needs to be able to trust in God's direction in her life and the world, without having to make God directly responsible for every event that occurs. The message of the Gospel is not, I believe, that everything that occurs has some purpose. Rather, it is that God's power is able to use and transform any event through the grace of Jesus Christ. Thus a person may cease a fruitless search for reasons for what happens, and seek the strength that God offers to live with what happens" (quoted in Peter van Inwagen, *The Problem of Evil* [Oxford: Clarendon, 2006], p. 11).

feated in Chisholm's sense,[23] what does it mean? It does not seem adequate that evil is "balanced off" by a preponderance of good. Arguably this is the case in the creation overall even today, but evil is still very much alive and active; it certainly has not been fully overcome. An important clue, I suggest, is that it is the nature of evil to *actively oppose* that which is good—it seeks to damage or destroy or corrupt the good. It seems to me that the triumph of good over evil must mean at a minimum that *evil is no longer able to oppose the good.* When "death and Hades [are] thrown into the lake of fire" (Revelation 20:14), they need no longer be reckoned with as the enemies of God and of his people; their power to harm has become a cipher. I do not claim, at this point, that this is obviously a sufficient condition of God's triumphing over evil, but it does seem to be a necessary condition.

What more can be said about the ways that evils may be overcome and not merely balanced off? Attempts to answer this question have usually been directed at the problem of human suffering, especially undeserved suffering. We have seen one important suggestion in chapter seven: as Eleonore Stump rightly affirms, suffering can be the means to bring a person to see the need for faith in God, or to draw a person closer to God. A great many people can testify to the truth of this from their own experience. (The problem with her view lies not in the idea itself but in the attempt to generalize it to apply to all cases of suffering.) A related idea is the notion that the sufferings of Christians can somehow be experienced as a participation in the redemptive suffering of Christ. We have seen this already in chapter four in the thought of Simone Weil, and it is an important theme in the encyclical of Pope John Paul II, *Salvifici Doloris.*[24] The pope refers to the apostle Paul's words, "I am now rejoicing in my suffering for your sake, and in my flesh I am completing what is lacking in Christ's afflictions for the sake of his body, that is, the church" (Colossians 1:24). The words

---

[23]I am inclined to think that Chisholm's choice of terminology here has proved to be unfortunate. If the "defeat" of evil is what Chisholm says it is, then evil that is not overcome in this particular way is "undefeated," and it seems unfitting that a proper view of providence should allow for undefeated evil. Surely the right conclusion is that there are other ways in which evil can be overcome besides "defeat" in this specific sense.

[24]English translation, *On the Christian Meaning of Human Suffering* (Boston: Daughters of St. Paul, 1984).

should not be taken, he emphasizes, to imply that Christ's suffering are *insufficient* for the purpose of the world's redemption. "But at the same time, in the mystery of the Church as His Body, Christ has in a sense opened His redemptive suffering to all human suffering."[25] Now, the sense of this may be fairly clear when, as in the case of Paul, the suffering is endured as part of a Christian mission or as part of one's testimony and faithfulness to the gospel. The pope, however, seems to want to extend this to include all sufferings of Christians, and at least in principle all the sufferings of all human beings. I must confess that it is unclear to me how Paul's words can be extended so broadly as this—yet these thoughts are the product of profound reflection backed by a great deal of personal and pastoral experience with suffering.

Another important suggestion comes from Marilyn Adams. As we saw in chapter three, her main concern is with "horrendous evils," which she defines as "evils the participation in (the doing or suffering) of which gives one prima facie reason to doubt whether one's life could (given their inclusion in it) be a great good to one on the whole."[26] She supposes that God's reasons for permitting such evils in anyone's life are "reasons that we are cognitively, emotionally, and/or spiritually too immature to fathom (the way a two-year-old child is incapable of understanding its mother's reasons for permitting the surgery)."[27] So the search for the "reason why" in such cases is unlikely to be successful, though it may all the same prove to be spiritually rewarding ("after all, it won Job a face-to-face encounter with the Maker of all things").[28] Still, "the two-year-old heart patient is convinced of its mother's love, not by her cognitively inaccessible reasons, but by her intimate care and presence through its painful experience."[29] Even so God, unable to explain his reasons to us, can still reassure us of his goodness by relating sufferers appropriately to "relevant and great goods." But

---

[25]Ibid., p. 38.

[26]Marilyn McCord Adams, "Horrendous Evils and the Goodness of God," in *The Problem of Evil,* ed. Adams and Adams, pp. 209-21. This essay provides a concise summary of the view she develops at greater length in her book, *Horrendous Evils and the Goodness of God* (Ithaca, N.Y.: Cornell University Press, 1999).

[27]Adams, "'Horrendous Evils," p. 216-17.

[28]Adams, "Afterword," in Davis, *Encountering Evil,* p. 196.

[29]Adams, "Horrendous Evils," p. 217.

"the depth of horrific evil cannot be accurately estimated without recognizing it to be incommensurate with any package of merely non-transcendent goods and so unable to be balanced off, much less defeated, thereby."[30]

What is needed, then, is a transcendent good, such as would be provided by "beatific, face-to-face intimacy with God." Such intimacy "would *engulf* (in a sense analogous to Chisholmian balancing off) even the horrendous evils humans experience in this present life here below, and overcome any prima-facie reasons the individual had to doubt whether his/her life would or could be worth living." Such an engulfing, she thinks, "would guarantee that immeasurable divine goodness to any person thus benefited. She goes on:

> But there is good theological reason for Christians to believe that God would go further, beyond engulfment to defeat. For it is the nature of persons to look for meaning, both in their lives and in the world. Divine respect for and commitment to created personhood would drive God to make all those sufferings which threaten to destroy the positive meaning of a person's life meaningful through positive defeat.[31]

How could God bring this off? Only, Adams thinks, "by integrating participation in horrendous evils into a person's relationship with God."[32] She suggests three ways in which this could be done.[33] First, through identification with the sufferings of Christ. (We have already seen this idea in Simone Weil and John Paul II.) Second,

> Julian of Norwich's description of heavenly welcome suggests the possible defeat of horrendous evil through divine gratitude. According to Julian, before the elect have a chance to thank God for all He has done for them, God will say, "Thank you for all your suffering, the suffering of your youth." She says that the creature's experience of divine gratitude will bring such full and unending joy as could not be merited by the whole sea of human pain and suffering throughout the ages.[34]

---

[30]Ibid.

[31]Ibid., p. 218.

[32]Ibid.

[33]See pp. 155-80 of "Horrendous Evils" for fuller discussion as well as the consideration of additional possibilities.

[34]Ibid., p. 219.

And finally, "A third idea identifies temporal suffering itself with a vision into the inner life of God." She admits that "For the most part, horrors are not recognized as experiences of God. . . . But Christian mysticism might claim, at least from the post-mortem perspective of the beatific vision, such sufferings will be seen for what they were, and retrospectively no one will wish away any intimate encounters with God from his/her life-history in this world."[35]

At this point I must beg the reader's forgiveness, as well as that of Adams herself, for this all-too-brief sketch of ideas that are much more richly developed than can be done justice to in such a summary. What then should be said by way of evaluation? First, I believe that these ideas about the defeat of evil can well be separated from Adams's commitment to universalism. After all, if there are persons who resolutely refuse to come face-to-face with God's loving presence (and whether there are such persons is precisely the point at issue in universalism), it would be absurd to suggest that horrendous evils in their lives are defeated by intimacy with God. But even for those who do open themselves to the divine presence, there are problems. It needs to be recalled that the category of horrendous evils includes the *doing* of such evils and not merely the suffering of them—that is, it includes the commission of atrocities by prison-camp guards and officials, and not merely the suffering of the victims. But to say that these evils are defeated is to say that the entire package—atrocities committed plus the defeating greater good—is a *benefit overall* to the person who committed them in such a way that it would no longer be appropriate for that person to "regret or resent its presence" in his or her life. It seems to me that this is simply an unacceptable attitude to have, whether in the present or in the life to come, toward one's own commission of terrible evil. If that is so, then to say that evils such as this are defeated—at least to say that they are *fully* defeated—is not an option.[36]

---

[35]Ibid.

[36]Adams may be right that God would choose to defeat horrendous evil rather than merely balance it off, *when such defeat is possible*. But what goods are logically possible in a particular situation is presumably not a matter of God's decision, though assuredly God is able to bring about goods that would be beyond reach for any finite agent. Nor is it a matter of God's decision whether the available goods are related to the instances of horrendous evil in the special way that is required for the latter to be defeated.

These objections are, however, (like my objections to Stump's theodicy) not so much objections to the ideas themselves as to their being applied in too general and indiscriminate a fashion. I see no conclusive objection to the idea that horrendous evils may be defeated in the ways Adams suggests, so long as it is not extended so broadly that it implies that one should not regret the sins one has committed. As to the merits of her suggestions, I don't find it easy to reach a definite conclusion (and I don't think she finds this easy either). For the present, I am content to leave them on the table as important suggestions, without arriving at any final verdict about them.

The final proposal to be considered comes from N. T. Wright, who poses the question we have already seen asked, in a different way, by John Roth: "How can it be possible, let alone right, for God to bring about a situation where all is genuinely well, and all manner of thing is truly well, granted all that has happened and, God help us, continues to happen?"[37] In answering this question, Wright lays great stress on the importance of forgiveness in the overcoming of evil. This is the more welcome because it offers a promising approach to evils for which a person is at fault—something we have seen causes difficulties when viewed in the light of Adams's proposals concerning defeat. The idea that evils one has committed need to be forgiven in order to be overcome may seem obvious, but Wright develops this theme in some important but less familiar ways. He emphasizes that forgiveness is not the same as tolerance, and does not minimize or condone evil; only when evil and the evildoer have been identified as what they are can forgiveness begin. An important insight, however, is that

> when we forgive someone we not only release *them* from the burden of our anger and its possible consequences; we release *ourselves* from the burden of whatever it was they had done to us, and from the crippled emotional state in which we shall go on living if we don't forgive them and instead cling to our anger and bitterness.[38]

In some cases, to be sure, forgiving others who have done great wrongs may seem virtually impossible. However, "Just as in God's new world all his people will have passed beyond death, disease, decay and so forth, so

---

[37]Wright, *Evil and the Justice of God*, p. 138.
[38]Ibid., p. 135.

that their new resurrection bodies will be incapable of any such thing, so their moral, thinking, cognitive, affective selves will also be renewed. And in that renewal, they will be enabled fully and finally to forgive all the evil done to them so that they, too, will no longer be affected or infected by it."[39] Wright boldly applies this insight not only to us but also to God himself: "God will forgive; and with that forgiveness God will not only release the world from its burden of guilt but will also, so to speak, release himself from the burden of always having to be angry with a world gone wrong."[40] And finally, if we truly receive and accept God's forgiveness, we must also learn to *forgive ourselves*—not denying or minimizing or condoning the wrong we have done but "drawing down from God's ultimate future, in which I will know myself to be completely loved and accepted because of the work of Jesus and the Spirit."[41]

The insight that by offering forgiveness God frees himself of the burden of past evils has important implications for the problem of universal salvation. Wright, drawing upon insights found in C. S. Lewis's *The Great Divorce*, points out that our instinctive sympathy for "someone who's left out of the party" contributes to a common argument for universalism: "it cannot be right, we are told, for the redeemed to enjoy their heaven as long as one soul is left in hell." He points out, however, that "by thus appealing to our sense of feeling sorry for the one left outside the party, we put that person in a position of peculiar power, able to exercise in perpetuity a veto on the triumph of grace."[42] But this can't be right:

> The continuing power of evil in the present world cannot blackmail the new world and veto its creation because the power of forgiveness, organically linked to the power of Jesus' resurrection, is precisely that it enables both God and God's people to avoid the imposition of other people's evil.
>
> This does not require that all human beings will come to repent and share the joy of God's new world, wonderful though that would be. . . . [W]e do not have the choice to sulk in such a way as to prevent God's party going ahead without us. We have the right, like the older brother, to sit it out; God

---

[39]Ibid., p. 143.
[40]Ibid., p. 136.
[41]Ibid., p. 162.
[42]Ibid., p. 140.

has the right to come and reason with us; but the fatted calf is going to be eaten whether we join in or not. Those who accept God's invitation to God's party on God's terms will indeed celebrate the feast of deliverance from evil.[43]

This answer to the problem of universalism works, however, only if, as Lewis says, "All that are in Hell, choose it. Without that self-choice there could be no Hell."[44] But this in turn requires that God's forgiveness is genuinely available to all people, and its acceptance is a genuine possibility for every one. Frankly, it is difficult to see how this is the case in the present life, when many grow up and live their lives in conditions that seem virtually to preclude their coming to understand and accept this offer. It may well be, then, that at least in some cases a postmortem opportunity for repentance and faith is required. (In Lewis's book some of the inhabitants of hell take a day trip to heaven and are invited to remain there; at least one of them takes up the offer. Lewis, however, wisely disclaims any attempt to give an actual description of conditions in the afterlife.) I leave this question to be worked out by the theologians.

And now, finally, we are in a position to answer the question, What could be meant by a triumph of God over evil? The broad outlines of the Christian hope are clear, though the details remain unknown to us. The world to come is to be a world of fulfilled human lives, free from suffering, death and evil, and permeated with the knowledge and love of God. The evils God's people have suffered, horrendous evils included, will be, as Adams suggests, engulfed in the experience of intimacy with God. God will work, indeed is working, in many ways to bring good out of evil, though we should not generalize and make it out to be a necessary truth that all evil will be "defeated" in Chisholm's technical sense. God's amazing forgiveness, made possible through the cross of Christ, not only obviates punishment for sins but removes the emotional burden of sin and evil, both for those sinned against and the forgiven sinners themselves. If there continue to be persons who resolutely reject God's love and forgiveness, that will be because the very best God can do for them, in such a state, is to leave them

---

[43]Ibid., pp. 146-47.
[44]C. S. Lewis, *The Great Divorce* (New York: Macmillan, 1946), p. 72.

alone in their forlorn and empty rebellion—empty, because they no longer have any power to disrupt or detract from the greatness of God's creation and his purposes for it. Evil may still exist in the sense of "privation of the good," in that there are persons made to love and enjoy God but who fail to do so. But these persons will have no active power against the good, whether physical or moral or emotional. (In *The Great Divorce* the occupants of hell who take the day-long bus trip to heaven are seen to be so insubstantial, in comparison with the reality of heaven, as to be in effect ghosts; their weight is not sufficient to bend a blade of grass, their strength is severely tested to lift a fallen leaf. In this way Lewis represents the nothingness and vacuity of hell in comparison with heaven.)

Throughout this chapter, I have avoided the rich imagery of depictions of heaven in the interest of as much conceptual clarity as it is possible to achieve in these matters. I conclude, however, with a marvelous passage of hope from Isaiah, one that I think is unduly neglected (though a friend told me he had it read at his wedding):

> On this mountain the LORD of hosts will make for all peoples
>   a feast of rich food, a feast of well-aged wines,
>   of rich food filled with marrow, of well-aged wines strained clear.
> And he will destroy on this mountain
>   the shroud that is cast over all peoples,
>   the sheet that is spread over all nations;
> he will swallow up death for ever.
> Then the Lord GOD will wipe away the tears from all faces,
>   and the disgrace of his people he will take away from all the earth,
>   for the LORD has spoken. (Isaiah 25:6-8)

Index